The Kent Downs

The Kent Downs

Dan Tuson

Dedicated to my parents and brother

Front cover: Warren Banks near Lydden

Back cover: Stour Valley near Chilham; cowslip; winter sunset; pyramidal orchid

First published in 2007 by Tempus Publishing

Reprinted in 2010 by
The History Press
The Mill, Brimscombe Port,
Stroud, Gloucestershire, GL5 2QG
www.thehistorypress.co.uk

British Library Cataloguing in Publication Data.
A catalogue record for this book is available from the British Library.

ISBN 978 0 7524 4405 5

Typesetting and origination by Tempus Publishing
Printed and bound in Great Britain by
Marston Book Services Limited, Didcot

CONTENTS

ACKNOWLEDGEMENTS

The author is very grateful to the following institutions and people for permission to reproduce items in their collections:

The National Archives, Kew, (colour plate 14); Landmark Information Group Ltd, Exeter, owners of the Old Maps Website (43), acknowledged as © Crown copyright and Landmark Information Group Ltd (All rights reserved June 2007);The Museum of English Rural Life, The University of Reading (colour plate 13), and for (46) from an original sketch by Thomas Hennell for which the author also gratefully acknowledges the permission of Michael MacLeod, author of Thomas Hennell: Countryman, Artist and Writer (1989 1st edn), to use this image; (colour plates 15 and 16) and (63) reproduced courtesy of The Tate Gallery © Tate, London 2007; Film Still image (64) from A Canterbury Tale (1944) reproduced courtesy of ITV PLC (GRANADA INT'L)/LFI; Image (84) supplied courtesy of Dr John van Whye, University of Cambridge and reproduced with permission from The Complete Work of Charles Darwin Online; Steve Bartrick of Antique Prints and Maps (colour plate 28); Kent Downs Area of Outstanding Natural Beauty Unit (50).

The author gratefully acknowledges permission to quote copyright and other written material from: The Bubblegate Co. Ltd, Stowting and John Hammon for extracts from *Before it's all Forgotten, Recollections of Stowting*; extracts from *The Wild Orchids of Britain* by Jocelyn Brooke, published by The Bodley Head, reprinted by permission of The Random House Group Ltd; extracts from *A Mine of Serpents* (Copyright © Jocelyn Brooke 1949), *December Spring* (Copyright © Jocelyn Brooke 1946) *The Dog at Clambercrown* (Copyright © Jocelyn Brooke 1955), *The Military Orchid* (Copyright © Jocelyn Brooke 1948), published by The Bodley Head and reprinted by permission of A.M. Heath & Co. Ltd Author's Agents; extracts from *Kent* by Richard Church reproduced by permission of Pollinger Ltd and the proprietor; extracts from *The Country Heart* by H.E. Bates reproduced by permission of Pollinger Ltd and the proprietor; for extracts from *The Old Road* by Hilaire Belloc, permission has been granted by Peters Fraser and Dunlop on behalf of the Estate of Hilaire Belloc; for extracts from *The Kentish Stour* by R.H. Goodsall the author acknowledges Cassel Plc, a division of the Orion Publishing Group (London) as the Publishers. Please note that all attempts at tracing the copyright holder proved unsuccessful; for extracts from *In Black and White*, by R. Cutbush, and *English Downland* by H.J. Massingham please note that all attempts at tracing the copyright holders proved unsuccessful.

All photographs were taken by the author. Illustrations 3, 11, 15, 21, 22, 24, 27, 31, 49, 65, 67, 68, 72, colour plates 1 and 22 were produced by Angel Design, Lydd (copyright reserved). Illustrations 26, 52 and 57 were designed by the author for The Orchid newspaper and kindly permitted for use by the Kent Downs Area of Outstanding Natural Beauty (AONB) Unit, Brabourne. I would like to extend particular thanks to the many landowners who have granted permission to access their land and take photography, in particular: Joe and Helen Stuart-Smith, John Leigh Pemberton, Greg Ellis, Gerry Minister, Ian and Claire Smith, John Bovington, John Seath, Anthony Martin, Rod Christie, Ian Potts and staff at Brook Agricultural Museum.

I am especially grateful to Mark Tuson, Christina Dandison and Frances Clayton for their help and support, to Claire and Bob at Angel Design for their beautiful illustrations and to the following people who have assisted me in various ways: Tristan Lavender, Ken and Gill Wiggins, Emma Griffiths, staff at the Kent Downs AONB unit, John McAllister and John Badmin.

PREFACE

Kent has long been appreciated for its diversity of landscapes. From the wind-swept open grazing marshes of the north Kent coast to the shrouded woodlands of the Weald, 'Kent,' wrote H.E. Bates, 'has a little of everything … the charm of this country lies simply not in its richness, which is remarkable, but in its rich variations within a comparatively small space'. Over the centuries these various districts have at one time or another played their part in bringing the county economic prosperity and prestige. Its densely wooded Weald revelled in the limelight in the sixteenth and seventeenth centuries as the centre of a bustling iron industry. The fertile grasslands of the Romney Marsh provided the foundation for the English woollen industry in medieval times, while the orchards and hop gardens of the well-drained brickearth and sandy soils have long been associated with the county's fame as the Garden of England.

Yet nestled within the heart of this county lies a range of hills that have largely remained untouched and remote from the changing fortunes of farming, forestry and industry. Bereft of fertile soils, sparsely settled and distanced from the bustling centres of trade and commerce, there has been little here to attract the material wealth that has been afforded to its more prosperous neighbours. For generations this tract of country, popularly known as the North, or Kent Downs, has instead come to be cherished as an asset far more highly prized than that bestowed by economic or commercial gain. The coombe-fretted heights of its escarpment or the enveloping hollows of its wood-shrouded hinterland may have offered little to the enterprising farmer or ambitious merchant, but for many these features symbolise the immense natural beauty and hidden charm that is found within these hills.

Through tracing the origins and evolution of this landscape, the aim of this book is simply to unravel the story of the Downs, the history of its settlement and colonisation and the legacy of its rich and varied natural treasures that define its special characteristics; the rare and the commonplace; the peculiar and the unique; the mysterious and the haunting.

In many ways this book is a celebration of the Kent Downs and of the rich culture, traditions and customs that have shaped man's relationship with this landscape throughout the centuries. It is very much a tribute to the many who have found solace and inspiration here, expressed in verse, poem and painting.

Having spent most of my life living and working in the East Kent Downs, I am naturally inclined to draw inspiration from this area which, for me, symbolises the spirit and heart of this landscape. This spirit is very much a personal and individual interpretation yet I hope that the writing of this book will go some small way in conveying the beauty of this unique part of Kent to the reader and in so doing may encourage others to embrace, cherish and safeguard the Kent Downs for future generations.

Fig. 1 The East Kent Downs near Dover.

INTRODUCTION

THE CHALK COUNTRY

> Picturesque is the epithet, par excellence, applicable to this landscape as a whole. Its graceful and tender beauty wins upon you as well by its variety as by its permanence. The aspect is incessantly changing, but depends upon no seasonal fluctuation or elemental conjunction for its attractiveness. Under the dullest of grey skies and in those mid-winter days when nature seems actually dead, the outlines keep their charm ... Their broad sweeping curves of crest, hollow and slope, here absolutely smooth, or ridged only in the lines which mark where the sheep have browsed, there studded with bushes or clothed with trees from the summit downward, so bold and spacious in their effects on light and shade ...
>
> Henry Gay Hewlett, *Studies in Kentish Chalk* (1880)

The chalk downlands of lowland England have long been treasured for their immense aesthetic appeal and, for many, epitomise the quintessential beauty of the English landscape. Forming a reassuring and familiar horizon, the characteristic ranges of broad buttressed hills, coombes and ridges that course through the southern counties have occupied a special place in the heart of traveller and native alike since the days of early settlers. Indeed, there are few counties in southern England that lie untouched by the great seams of chalk whose swelling masses and ridge-edged scarps puncture and rise above the fabric of the lowlands. Sprawling from the central chalk masses of the Hampshire and Wiltshire uplands, fingers of downland radiate to the east, south and west to form the South and North Downs, Chilterns and the chalk ranges of Dorset.

Embossed and scored by the hand of man in earth-cast mound, ridge, ditch and bank, the chalk country bears testament to a deeply rooted association between man and the land which stretches back to the early days of the first Neolithic farmers and beyond. Early man found security and protection on these elevated uplands. Over the centuries, the light workable soils and open aspect have favoured crops and livestock, while in more recent times their open ridges and sheltered coombes have been cherished by generations as a place for recreation and leisure.

The aesthetic appeal of downland scenery, so poetically expressed within the writings of Gilbert White, Richard Jefferies and Harold John Massingham has long been recognised. Of all the exponents of the chalk country, it was Gilbert White, author of *The Natural History and Antiquities of Selbourne* (1789), whose impressions of the South Downs first captured their serene and captivating beauty:

> For my own part, I think there is something peculiarly sweet and amusing in the shapely-figured aspect of the chalk hills in preference to those of stone … something analogous to growth in their gentle swellings and smooth fungus-like protuberances, their fluted sides and regular hollows and slopes … as they swell and heave their broad backs into the sky, so much above the less animated clay of the wild below.

One of a group of 'ruralist' British writers of the early twentieth century, Harold John Massingham (1888–1952), was equally touched by the grace and majesty of this scenery and devoted several of his works to the chalk country including *English Downland* (1936) in which he described the compelling attraction of this landscape:

> Every detail of the unenclosed chalk landscape – the protruded spur, the fluted hollow, the giant but unrestrained buttress, the flowing lateral ribbing, the sinuous curve, the blunted promontory, the unbroken passage of ridge, the dipping and soaring of the range-bespeak a calm, a remoteness from the tumult of our mortal days …

Such poetic insights will undoubtedly strike a chord with many who know and love the Kent Downs. Those who have wandered the coombe-riddled folds of the hills above the historic village of Wye or experienced the solitude of the gorse-clad crests of the cliff tops above Folkestone and Dover will have found empathy with the writings of Gilbert White's South Downs. The nineteenth-century essayist Henry Gay Hewlett, who lived at Shaw Hall at the foot of the Kent Downs near Addington, was one of the early exponents of the romance of this landscape, inspired by the prose of White and touched to find the characteristic broad sweeping curves of crest, hollow and slope. Noting in his *Studies in Kentish Chalk* (1880), he remarked, '… these hills partake of the "sweetness" if not of the "majesty", of the South Downs:

> At whatever season of the year you may take your first view of this landscape, the feature which will thrust itself upon your notice before all others is the uniform roundness of the outlines. The hills bear upon them the stamp of their aqueous origin. Gradually narrowing upwards from the base with a gentle acclivity, their slopes and crests are smooth; the former often vertically scored by the flow of water into deep central depressions, on either side of which the ground swells softly like the curves of a bosom …

Henry Gay Hewlett, *Studies in Kentish Chalk* (1880)

Fig. 2 Downland scenery at Lydden and Temple Ewell Downs National Nature Reserve.

For the unacquainted traveller of the Kent Downs, however, the drawing of such hasty generalisations is perhaps a dangerous affair. True enough, the soft rounded contours of hill and bank are, in places, reassuringly reminiscent of the 'skywedded' downland of the southern counties, yet within the hinterland country of these hills, they are everywhere cloaked by a curious impostor rarely encountered on the other southern chalk ranges. For this is a country where woodland and trees have long occupied centre stage, a landscape shrouded in dusky impenetrable thickets, riddled with tree-muffled holloways, and laden with the lacework of hedgerow, spinney and copse.

It is this enduring presence of woodland and hedgerow that imparts the strong sense of seclusion and remoteness so deeply ingrained within the Kent Downs landscape. The exposed chalk of the southern chalklands of Sussex, Hampshire and Wiltshire may have succumbed to early woodland clearance for farming, settlement and occupation, yet for the Kent Downs, such activities have been persistently thwarted by the layers of clays, flints and gravels that mantle the valleys and plateaus of this country. Unlike the thinner chalky soils encountered on the steeper banks and slopes the heavy, sticky and impoverished clays have remained stubbornly unyielding to the toils and efforts of early farmers and settlers, fit for little else other than wood and forest. Inevitably, with the mechanisation and advances of farming in recent history, the inroads of clearance and cultivation have made their mark, yet in many places this process has been piecemeal and small scale. It is for this reason that the centuries-old landscape of the Kent Downs has remained largely intact.

Native and traveller alike were no stranger to the adversities of heavy 'wheel-cloying' clays and it is no surprise that for centuries, this has remained a remote landscape, secluded and intimate and retaining a modest and humble feel. Early topographical accounts and perambulations of the county naturally associated this remoteness with a poverty-stricken landscape, difficult to traverse, and of little agricultural value. The eminent county topographer and historian, Edward Hasted, described much of this downland country in a similar vein, his parochial accounts of the late eighteenth century littered with dismissive and disparaging remarks on the 'dreary', 'wild' and 'forlorn' country, burdened by 'poor' and 'barren' soils.[1]

It was not until the nineteenth century, when public perception of landscapes began to change, that the romance and hidden charm of the Downs became fully appreciated. For the Victorian natural historians, walkers, geologists, artists and poets, the North Downs of Kent became a veritable honeypot of inspiration. Many such as Adam and Charles Black, whose well-known series of guides remained in the forefront of the rapidly developing tourist industry from the 1850s to the turn of the twentieth century, extolled the virtues of this hidden charm in journey accounts and perambulations:

> To look down from the Canterbury road upon the lowlands beneath is to gaze upon a truly English picture, one of those fair leafy landscapes familiar to us in the canvas of Inskipp and Creswich. Even the Downs have lost their ruggedness, and rear above us, their verduous sides all dappled with flocks of sheep, like ships upon a distant sea.[2]

THE KENT DOWNS

The Kent Downs refer to the eastern end of the ridge of chalk hills, familiarly known as the North Downs, that extend from Farnham in Surrey to the Kent coast at Dover (Fig. 3). Designated as an Area of Outstanding Natural Beauty (AONB) in 1968 the Kent Downs cover an area of some 878 square kilometres (339 square miles), from the county border in the west to the coast in the east, accounting for some 23 per cent of the land area of the county of Kent. The designated AONB area also encompasses the higher parts of the hills and escarpment associated with the greensand geology, notably around Lympne in the east of the county, and Sevenoaks in the west.

The westerly ranges of the Kent Downs occupy a relatively narrow band of the county, pinched in by the sands and clays of the Weald to the south and the gravels of the Kent plain to the north. East of the Medway valley, the chalk geology embraces a gradually widening tract of countryside, at its most impressive in the hinterland of downland to the south of Canterbury. Whilst the exposed chalk bedrock continues in the undulating open farmland east of the modern day A2 towards the east Kent coast, the designated AONB area confines itself to the more characteristic deep-furrowed valleys and plateau-lands south west of the A2, defined, in 'landscape character' terms, as the East Kent Downs.

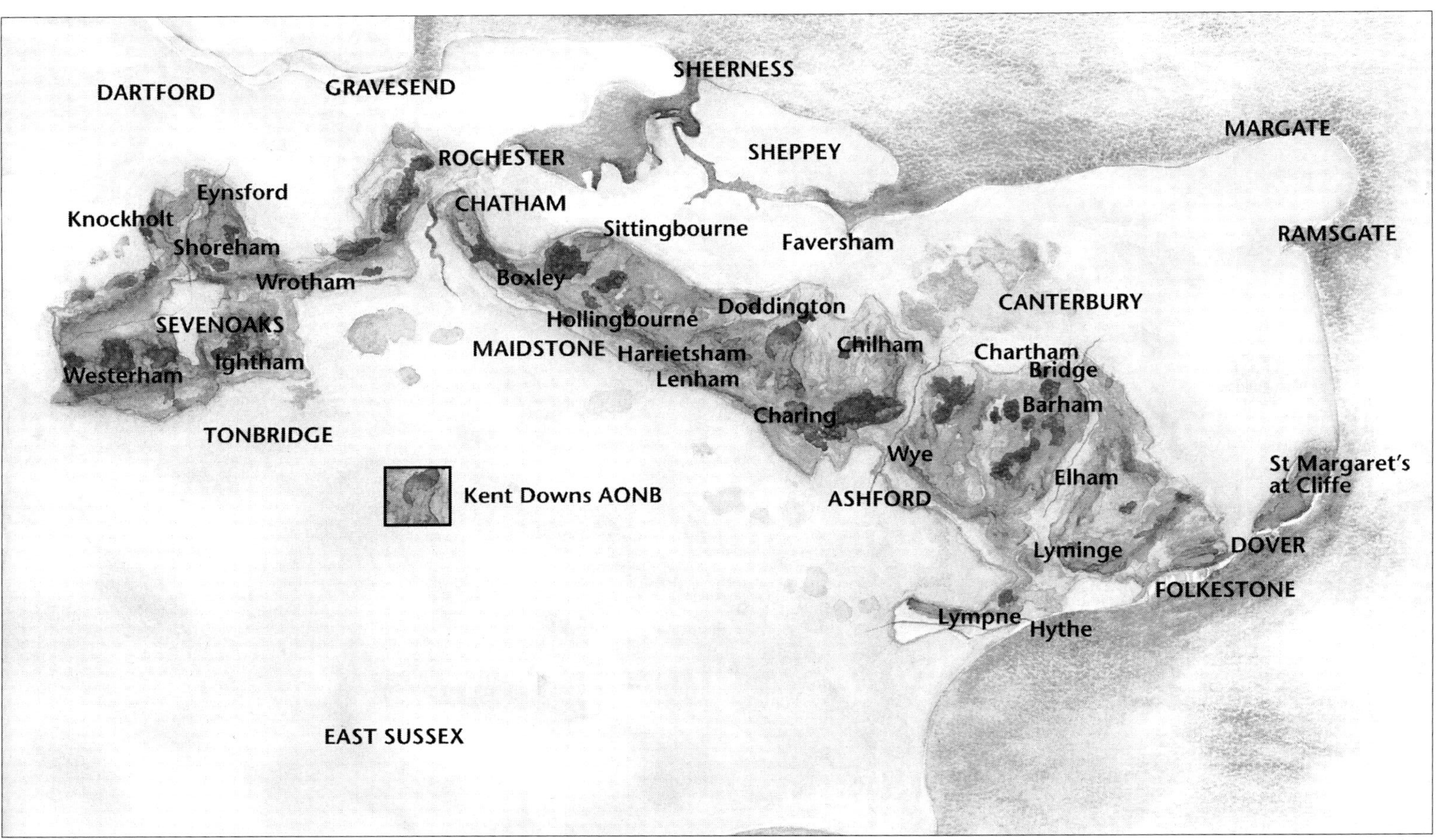

Fig. 3 The Kent Downs Area of Outstanding Natural Beauty.

Throughout their length, the Kent Downs encompass twelve of these 'landscape character' areas in which the underlying fabric of chalkland geology is delicately interwoven with variations in soils, drainage, landform and vegetation to allow characterisation of the downland scenery at a more local scale. While these local divisions provide a convenient means of reference for planners and landscape professionals, for many, the essence of the Downs is no better expressed than within the more familiar distinction of the 'chalk escarpment' and the 'dry valley' country.

THE CHALK ESCARPMENT

Overlooking a vast expanse of countryside and attaining a height of over 250m (760ft) at Westerham, the escarpment of the Downs has long been its keystone feature, forming a natural division between the uplands of the county to the north and the lower lying clay vales and flat lands to the south. This imposing landform is, in itself, a diversity of form and feature, its character as strong in its steep, coombe-ridden folds as in its gentle and rounded cultivated slopes.

The high vantage points of the scarp and its familiarity as a reassuring backdrop to the Wealden country to the south, have long afforded it an attraction to settler and traveller. The popular author H.E. Bates, who resided in the beautiful village of Little Chart in the lowlands to the south of the Downs, had a great empathy for this range of hills whose slopes formed a natural horizon and comforting reference point:

> … however you get lost on these roads there is always an unfailing compass-point; it can be seen from almost everywhere in this flatter land-the straight back of the North Downs and the great bearskin of woodland, almost black in winter and summer, fiery-bronze in autumn, that lies above the sun-bleached loins of chalk. As the sea attracts you to the south, so this line of hills has some sort of magnetism as you turn north.[3]

For the traveller seeking directness and ease of passage, uncompromising to natural obstacle and hindrance, the continuous elevated ridge of the Downs has long been a popular thoroughfare. A sweeping arc leading from the Channel coast to the heartland of southern England, its natural accessibility has bestowed upon it an attraction and appeal as a journey and trade route for centuries. Hilaire Belloc, the prolific writer of the early twentieth century, who was inspired by the romance of the old pilgrimage route of the Downs, penned of this range of hills in *The Old Road* (1904):

> I am led to describe the natural causeway which seems to call for a traveller landing in Kent to use it if he would go westward … A man who should leave the Straits with the object of reaching the Hampshire centres would find a moderately steep, dry, chalky slope, always looking full towards the southern sun, bare of trees, cut by three river valleys. This conspicuous range would lead him by the mere view of it straight on to his destination.

Along its length, the subtle variation in aspect, gradient and vegetation provide an ever-changing kaleidoscope of light and shade throughout the seasons. From its most easterly point, where the huge mass of the North Downs is exposed in cross section as the majestic White Cliffs of Dover and Folkestone, the escarpment begins its journey.

The cliffs occupy a special place in the national psyche and have long formed one of our most cherished and iconic landmarks, described and epitomised by the county historian Edward Hasted as the 'lock and key' of the homeland.[4] The salt-laden winds that whip both shoreline and cliff make for a fascinating and diverse array of specialist plants that perch and nestle on the crumbling ledges, or jostle for space in the luxuriant microclimate of the area of undercliff known as 'The Warren'. This area, in particular, has long been appreciated for its wealth of plant life that abounds in the warm and damp conditions beneath the mighty cliffs. London-born author, Richard Church, affectionally described this area in his book *Kent* (1948) as a place of:

> savage outbreaks of subsoil, trees thrown into extravagant gestures, small ponds formed in cracks, luxuriant undergrowth of grasses, creepers and wild flowers. The place abounds in orchids and butterflies, which flourish here under sub-tropical conditions. Not only the intimacy, but also the general view is delightful, for to look along the Warren from the town entrance observing its trees, broken ravines and patches of velvet turf, and to see behind it the sea and the get a curve of the cliffs sheltering Dover – , well that is a picture that comes back in later years upon the heart.

The contrast with the coombe-fretted buttresses of open grassland that rise up behind the town of Folkestone could not be more complete. Upon the lofty ridges of the scarp lie the traces of some of man's earliest comings and goings of a dim and distant age. Burial mounds and earthworks from a range of historical periods bear testament to a rich legacy of human occupation and activity on these hills. Centuries of agricultural advancement and change may have taken their toll on the cultivated landscape below, yet the terraced slopes on which these barrows perch have largely escaped these changes and the same open-prospected, sheep-grazed, 'tumbled area of bare, grassy chalk downs'[5] that was familiar to the nineteenth-century travel writers are still very much an enduring landmark of this area today.

The warmth afforded to these south-facing slopes in summer months is such to endow a distinctly continental flavour to the plant communities of these grasslands. Among these plants are the more common characteristic downland 'specialists' such as dwarf thistle (*Cirsium acaule*), horseshoe vetch (*Hippocrepis comosa*) and squinancywort (*Asperula cynanchica*). For other more localised plants such as the scarce late spider orchid (*Ophrys fuciflora*), more at home on the calcareous rocks of southern Europe, these hills provide the ideal climatic and physical conditions that allow them to harbour their stronghold and sole UK populations here. Ever since the heyday ofVictorian botanising these Downs have naturally become rich hunting grounds for plant lovers and naturalists. At the foot of the scarp lies Holywell Coombe, an important site for the geological record of fossil remains that lie buried here. The clear springs that emerge here are fascinating features of these escarpment coombes, often situated in lush leafy hollows, beneath the main floor of the coombe and marking the point where the chalk rock meets the underlying Gault Clay.

Prominent within this area of the scarp lie the hills of 'Belvedere' and 'Summerhouse' (Fig. 4), lying detached from the escarpment of the Downs and 'rising up into bold sugarloaf peaks and cones'.[6] Standing in front of the main chalk outcrop, these hills bear witness to a fault line which has shifted the chalk so that it forms a tongue extending southward. Erosion of the surrounding rocks of Gault Clay and sandstone, combined with spring-water erosion on the northern side has led to this chalk tongue becoming isolated to leave the hills which stand today. This stretch of the escarpment was deeply enshrined within the childhood memories of local author Jocelyn Brooke, their steep chalky flanks representing 'impregnable bastions' and forming, 'an effectual barrier between the semi-urban world which I inhabited and "The Country" ... a wild mysterious kingdom'.[7]

Further west, between the villages of Newington and Etchinghill, the scarp turns inland slightly as a striking series of spurs and coombes, best viewed when the slanting rays of a setting sun accentuate their ridges and hollows in golden and shadowed outlines. This tract of plant-rich downland overlooks the southerly point of the picturesque Elham valley, one of a number of valleys within the East Kent Downs that are characterised by the appearance of intermittent seasonal streams known locally as 'nailbournes'.

Continuing westwards and furrowing its way behind the pretty villages of Postling, Stowting and East Brabourne the steep banks of the scarp provide some of the most stunning viewpoints in Kent. It was these hills, overlooking the lands of the Pent, the Stour valley and, on a clear day, the Channel and French coast, that became one of the most treasured haunts for the celebrated author Joseph Conrad.

From the footslope villages of Brook and Wye, the spectacular 'V'-shaped coombe of the Devil's Kneading Trough forms an arresting backdrop. The banks and spurs of this stretch of downland have been grazed for centuries and support some of the most flower-rich tracts of grassland within the county. Designated as a National Nature Reserve, it provides a popular place for walking and recreation, affording stunning panoramic views over the coast and Weald of Kent and Sussex. The valley of the Stour, near Wye, forms the first of three main breaks in the scarp. These river valleys have a long history of occupation and settlement providing early man with fertile soils and relatively easy access into the heartland of the county (Fig. 5). The stretch of the Stour north of Wye, as it meanders its way past Chilham and Chartham, has long been appreciated for its beauty. It was here that the nineteenth-century poet W.H. Prideaux penned in 1841 his poem 'The Banks of Stour'.[8] The seventeenth-century English writer Izaak Walton also found inspiration within these reaches of the river whose 'flowery meads' and 'crystal streams' formed the subject of the poem 'The Angler's Wish' in his widely celebrated *The Compleat Angler* published in 1653.

Right: Fig. 4 The escarpment at Folkestone overlooking Summerhouse Hill and the English Channel beyond.

'Against the hot blue sky, the terraced knoll loomed enormous, its summit lost in a shimmering heat-haze. The grassy flanks seemed to radiate a reflected heat, enfolding us in a weighted, thyme-scented silence, enhanced rather than disturbed by the monotone of a thousand insects.'
Jocelyn Brooke, *A Mine of Serpents* (1949)

Below: Fig. 5 The River Stour at Godmersham.

On the opposite side of the valley, the slopes are fringed by King's Wood, an extensive tract of ancient woodland which once formed part of a royal hunting estate, now owned and managed by the Forestry Commission and a popular area for walking. Pockets of woodland dominate the scarp moving west above the spring-line villages of Westwell and Charing. Some, such as Charing Beech Hangers, a 'Site of Special Scientific Interest' (SSSI), are amongst the best examples of beech woodlands within the county which thrive on the thin chalky soils of the Downs. Historically forming part of an area known as Westwell Downs, it is evident that tree cover here was not so extensive in times past and the slopes were of a much more open nature, supporting swathes of open downland grazed by sheep or cattle. A clue to the former appearance of these banks is evident within the seventeenth-century poet William Strode's (1600-1645) poem 'On Westwell Downes' written at a time when the idea of 'landscape' was first becoming appreciated for its aesthetic qualities:

... where cleanly wynds the greene did sweepe,
Methought a landskipp there was spread,
Here a bush and there a sheepe ...

The slender food upon the downe
Is allwayes even, allwayes bare,
Which neither spring nor winter's frowne
Can ought improve or ought impayre ...

Winding its way along the foot of the scarp here can be found some of the most peaceful sections of the 'Old Road' of the Downs. Throughout its length the long-trodden trackways of the scarp bear witness to millennia of human traffic and hark of an age when the dry, firm-footed flanks offered some relief from the heavy-going clays of the wooded vales and flat-lands beneath. From the passage of prehistoric ancestor to the pilgrimage of medieval traveller, the 'Old Road' is steeped in tradition and timeless antiquity and has provided a rich source of inspiration for writers and artists:

> The effect of this common vista, combined with the elation due to the atmosphere and light always accompanying a chalk sub-soil, puts the traveller into a state of mind which must be described as rapture. Everybody who takes that road remarks on the heightening of his emotional response to the scene; the smell of the chalk flowers such as thyme ... and all the miniature herbs dwarfed through long ages of cropping by sheep on the thin soil.

Richard Church, *Kent* (1948).

Beyond the charming village of Charing the scarp gives way to a more open aspect and gentler gradient, supporting large rolling and gently rising fields of tilled farmland. Here for the first time along its length, the slopes have succumbed to the earthy hues of cultivation, the few remnant pockets of ancient chalk grassland and

Fig. 6 The sunken trackways and holloways of the Kent Downs bear witness to the antiquity of the landscape.

woodland clinging on precariously within a more intensively farmed landscape. Yet such diversion from gradient and incline is but a short-lived distraction, as the tightening contours of scarp and ridge regain their more familiar composure in the steep banks above the spring-line settlements of Hollingbourne, Thurnham and Boxley. The village of Boxley nestles below a long sweep of woodland, scrub and chalk grassland, designated as a Site of Special Scientific Interest for its diverse assortment of chalk-loving plants and shrubs. These banks support a range of the more common chalk grassland flowers as well as scarce plants such as stinking hellebore (*Helleborus foetidus*) and the rare box tree (*Buxus sempervirens*) to which the village owes its name. The box tree here was first documented by the herbalist John Ray (1627-1705) who noted its presence here in the seventeenth century.[9] Today, only a few trees remain at Boxley, although it has also naturalised further west along the scarp slope at Trosley Country Park. It was these slopes too that provided one of the last known refuges of the secretive woodland mammal, the pine marten, in Kent, a Maidstone Journal of 1802 recording a rare sighting of a 'marten cat' at Upper Blue Bell by the local woodmen of Boxley Hill.[10]

Where the scarp turns northward into the Medway valley, the remnant stones of the Kit's Coty long barrow (colour plate 6), situated on the rolling footslopes of the escarpment, are testament to this area's long association with human activity and occupation. The presence of other massive stones here, lying half-forgotten in hedgerows and field corners, bear witness to other scatters of megalithic remains. The chalk pits that pock-mark the lower slopes of the valley include Upper and Lower Culand pits which form an important part of the industrial heritage of the area, once providing chalk for the lime industry and, more recently, cement manufacture. Today they are protected for their geological interest, yielding rich and diverse collections of fossil fishes and one of the best Lower and Middle Chalk fossilised reptile faunas.

West of the Medway valley, the scarp reaffirms its presence in a long and unbroken sweep of wood-fringed flanks, occasionally punctuated by pockets of grassland and forming a strong visual backdrop to the modern day M20 motorway. Beech (*Fagus sylvatica*) and the dark foliage of yew (*Taxus baccata*) are especially noticeable on this stretch of the scarp which thrive on the thin chalk soils, typically complemented by a ground flora of plants such as dog's mercury (*Mercurialis perennis*), stinking iris (*Iris foetidissima*) and the scarce lady orchid (*Orchis purpurea*) (colour plate 29).

On the gently rising slopes above the villages of Wrotham and Trottiscliffe, larger fields supporting productive farmland are characteristic of the footslope soils along the entire length of the Kent Downs escarpment. Here, the continual downwash of soil from the steep scarp has produced a sheltered strip of fertile land, watered by small springs that emerge at the base. The row of spring-line settlements found along the length of the Downs, such as at Kemsing and Otford, originated to take advantage of the productive farmland and the ready supply of water.

At the village of Otford, on the outskirts of Sevenoaks, the Darenth valley marks the third break of the scarp. The rich fertile soils of the floodplain have been valued by farmers and settlers for centuries and the area is endowed with a rich history of habitation and passage, recognised as 'one of the cradles of English settlement in Kent'.[11] The more visible Roman remains such as those at Lullingstone Villa represent just a small part of the wealth of archaeology that lies buried here. For centuries these river valleys supported large tracts of seasonally flooded water meadows and were valued for the high quality pastures. While agricultural mechanisation and improvement has taken its toll on this traditional landscape, traces of this old way of farming can still be found within the riverside pollard trees and relic drainage ditches which would have once fed these seasonally flooded pastures. The nineteenth-century 'Romantic' artist Samuel Palmer cherished this area of the Downs calling this stretch of the Darenth, 'The Valley of Vision.' He lived in Shoreham in the 1820s and drew much inspiration from the idyllic rural scenes that formed the subject for much of his work.

THE DRY VALLEYS

Just as the scarp affords a prominent landmark to the lowlands to the south of the county, so its steep and imposing flanks define a natural watershed for the extensive tract of the county to the north; a hinterland of country that cannot be so marked in contrast. For here lies a country of wood-cloaked tablelands, furrowed by a network of narrow secluded valleys which carve their way down to the flatter land of the North Kent Plain. These valleys are traversed by a lattice-work and tangle of tree-muffled sunken lanes hemmed in by steep banks which every now and then rise and fall affording tantalising glimpses into the countryside beyond.

In many places the chalk substrate is mantled by 'drift' deposits of clays and sands which makes for a diverse array of land uses and wildlife-rich habitats. Fields and banks of arable, grassland, hay meadows, orchards and hops jostle for space in a patchwork field pattern, framed by a template of woodland, copse and hedgerow.

Where chalk lies near the surface, the steeper valley sides support pockets of flower-rich chalk grassland, at their best in early summer when the rich purple and blue drifts of field scabious (*Knautia arvensis*), orchids and black knapweed (*Centaurea nigra*) intermingle with the subtle yellow shades of common rock-rose (*Helianthemum chamaecistus*), yellow-wort (*Blackstonia perfoliata*) and lady's bedstraw (*Galium verum*) (colour plate 26). Many of these valley sides are furnished with woodlands and 'shaves' (strips of woodland also known as 'shaws') of beech (*Fagus sylvatica*), hazel (*Corylus avellana*), ash (*Fraxinus excelsior*), field maple (*Acer campestre*) and whitebeam (*Sorbus aria*).

Yew (*Taxus baccata*) may have formerly covered more extensive areas on the chalk, as is still evident in a few locations such as the woodlands of the Medway valley area, yet, elsewhere it often appears as scattered individuals within a woodland. Where the tree is more abundant it can often form spectacular yew 'groves', perhaps best experienced from the shady depths of a sunken woodland lane or holloway.

Much of this broadleaved woodland was formerly coppiced and, whilst the tradition has declined in recent years, many downland woods are still carpeted with a rich ground and shrub flora, indicative of the antiquity of these centuries-old habitats. Plants and shrubs such as yellow archangel (*Galeobdolon luteum*), dog's mercury (*Mercurialis perennis*), moschatel (*Adoxa moschatellina*), honeysuckle (*Lonicera periclymenum*) and spindle (*Euonymus europaeus*) abound on the chalkier soils, often grading into drifts of wood anemone (*Anemone nemorosa*), bluebell (*Endymion non-scriptus*) and ramsons (wild garlic) (*Allium ursinum*) on the damper clay soils of the summit plateau country.

The dry valley woodlands support some of our best-loved members of the orchid family. The early purple orchid (*Orchis mascula*), with its conspicuous black-blotched leaves, is a particular denizen of these woodlands, dotted amongst a sea of bluebells in spring. The elegant lady orchid (*Orchis purpurea*) has a particular stronghold in the woodlands of east Kent, occasionally found in the company of the much more slender fly orchid (*Ophrys insectifera*) which favours the chalky soils and sun-lit dappled edges of woodland rides and scrubland.

Fig. 7 The Alkham valley between Folkestone and Dover is typical of the picturesque dry valley country of the East Kent Downs.

'For the most part it is a quiet land of wood and coombes, of sudden winding valleys, lonely farms and solitary churches, everywhere laced with an intricate network of narrow lanes, steep hills and shady holloways, peaceful, silent and in many parts remote.'

Alan Everitt, *Continuity and Colonization* (1986)

Fig. 8 Ramsons, also known as wild garlic, under a hazel coppice.

On the shallower, cultivated chalky slopes of the valley sides arable farming predominates, yet, even here, fragments of another rich botanical resource persist in field edges and corners. Here the chalky soils provide the conditions for a range of 'cornfield plants' that rely on the annual disturbance wrought by plough and harrow. Once the bane of farmers country-wide, these 'annual' cornfield flowers readily grew on tilled land, jostling for space and light within the crops of wheat, barley and oats. In the days before agricultural chemicals they were naturally difficult to suppress and many a time would a crop be ruined by the weed that overtook it. Some, such as members of the fumitory and poppy family are still widespread and can be seen adorning cornfield edges in the summer months. Others, such as the once familiar corncockle (*Agrostemma githago*) and cornflower (*Centaurea cyanus*) have borne the brunt of agricultural intensification and are now confined to just a few localities. The rolling chalk fields of the upper slopes of the Medway valley have long been associated with a rich and diverse arable flora and, today, through sympathetic management, form a stronghold for populations of some of the rarer arable plants such as ground-pine (*Ajuga chamaepitys*), broad-leaved cudweed (*Filago spathulata*), and rough mallow (*Althaea hirsuta*).

Where the chalk is capped by drifts of clay, sand and gravel, plants and trees characteristic of more neutral and acidic soils can be found. Ancient, mixed broadleaved woodlands support oak (*Quercus robur*), hornbeam (*Carpinus betulus*) and sweet chestnut

(*Castanea sativa*). Elsewhere the acidic conditions found on some of these plateau soils give rise to a range of plants more commonly associated with heaths and commons. Plants such as heath bedstraw (*Galium saxatile*) and sheep's sorrel (*Rumex acetosella*) can still be found in traditionally managed grasslands and bear testimony to the large tracts of heath and common land that once occupied much of this plateau country. Cleared of woodland, many of these unproductive grassland heaths, sometimes referred to as 'minnises' or 'lees', would have once provided areas of common rough pasture. Enclosure, followed by cultivation and abandonment of grazing, led to their demise and today their former presence is only marked in place names. Stelling Minnis, between Hythe and Canterbury, near to the old Roman thoroughfare of Stone Street, is the largest remnant area of common within the Downs and still supports heathland 'specialists' such as western gorse (*Ulex gallii*).

Historically, the farmers of the Downs have long struggled with this wooded 'cledgy' country. The sticky, wieldy and impoverished soils won little praise from the agricultural commentators of the eighteenth and nineteenth centuries, who were apt to pour scorn on the foolhardy souls who tried to eke a living from this land. Reclamation of woodland for cultivation and cropping has always been a piecemeal affair here and for that reason the landscape today is still dominated by the presence of woodland, shave and copse. While the steady incursion of development, agriculture and roads have taken their toll on many of our lowland landscapes, the wooded country of the Downs has always proved stubbornly resistant to such advances and thus has been able to preserve the details of a landscape of great antiquity. No more so is this apparent than in the East Kent Downs where the chalk hinterland encompasses a swathe of untouched and secluded countryside that extends north and east to the Chartham, Barham and Lydden Downs from where it gradually ripples out across the rolling open farmlands of east Kent. This tract of wood-shrouded plateau country is furrowed by a series of long, parallel and branching valley systems which wind their way northwards. The Petham, Elham and Alkham valleys, host to the curious intermittent streams known as 'nailbournes', are familiar to many, but between these lie a succession of remote and beautiful miniature valleys and ranges, where, 'once caught', in the words of the writer Richard Church, 'the wanderer becomes a latter-day Ulysses on the island of Circe'.[12] The nineteenth-century writer Henry Gay Hewlett was one of the many to extol the virtues of these hidden areas of the Downs, that could only be truly appreciated by getting off the beaten track:

> A condition prevenient for the true enjoyment of a country such as this is that one should be an active walker. 'The proud ones who in their coaches roll along the turnpike-road' can form but the most meagre idea of its variety and beauty. Even the horseman will be unable to penetrate many a recess specially haunted by its charm.[13]

Times may have changed since the days of Victorian travel itineraries yet the sense of seclusion and remoteness that so enthralled the nineteenth-century journeymen and travel writers is still very much a defining hallmark of the Kent Downs today.

ONE

Chalk and Flints

THE GEOLOGY OF THE DOWNS

The solid chalk bedrock of the Kent Downs is the result of a long succession of geological deposition and erosion spanning millions of years within a region that has become commonly known in geological terms as the 'Wealden' district. The long arc of the North Downs which runs through Kent and Surrey forms the northern rim of this 'lozenge'-shaped area, bounded to the south by the South Downs, to the west by the Butser hills in Hampshire and, to the east by the Bas Boullanais region of northern France. The formation of the rocks came about through the gradual accumulation of sands, clays and microscopic organisms mostly from marine and freshwater deposits and laid down under varying depths of deep and shallow water.

The story starts some 120 million years ago when a series of earth movements led to the formation of an extensive lake over the area of present day south-east England, into which flowed many rivers. Successive layers of river-borne muds and clays settled to form clay and sandstone formations, exposed today in the central Wealden areas of the Hastings Beds and Tunbridge Wells Sands. Continued subsidence of the area led to the development of the lake into a shallow salt-water bay. Over time, the deposition of sands and clays on the sea floor led to the formation of layers of material that we now know as the Lower Greensand (Fig. 9) and Gault Clay rock layers of the Weald.

As the land mass continued to subside, this shallow sea evolved into a deeper ocean. The tropical climate that prevailed at this time provided ideal conditions for a diverse oceanic 'soup' of microscopic organisms, rich in calcium carbonate, which, on their death, rained down onto the sea-bed to form a thick white calcareous ooze. Over millions of years the accumulation of these fossilised organisms solidified to form the thick deposits of the rock we now know as chalk.

This soft white limestone is commonly divided into three distinct beds which relate to different periods of deposition of calcareous and siliceous material. The 'Upper Chalk' is the thickest bed and forms the greater part of the chalk outcrop.

The White Cliffs of Dover stand testament to the depth of this layer which measures up to 165m (550ft) deep. Consisting of over 95 per cent calcium carbonate it is a well-bedded soft chalk layer and contains a large numbers of rocks known as flints.

The 'Middle Chalk' layer has relatively few flints. Being composed of a much harder and brittle chalk, it is evident in many places as the steep escarpment of the Downs. The deeper layers of the 'Lower Chalk' beds are greyish in colour and lack flints but contain much clay. This bottom layer is only exposed on some of the steeper slopes, most notably at locations along the foot of the escarpment.

– FLINTS –

The characteristic grey and black nodules that litter the soils of the Downs, and that can be found at depth as seams of stone within the chalk bedrock, are known as flints. They are known to be composed of almost pure silica and mainly lie within the 'Upper Chalk' layers usually occurring in thin layers and bands. Their formation is thought to originate from the infiltration of silica-rich water into the chalk bedrock which became trapped in pores and was then redistributed in the form of nodules during several stages of crystallisation.

Found in abundance throughout the Kent Downs, this hard-wearing stone has been used over the centuries for a variety of purposes. Early man shaped the stone, through striking it (a practice known as flint 'knapping'), into tools such as hand axes, scrapers and spear heads. Its 'easy to work' size have also made it a valuable building material. Evident today in churches, walls and houses throughout the Downs, it forms a distinctive part of the vernacular architecture of the area. In earlier times the crude flint was bonded into walls using lime and mortar as can be seen within the remaining walls at Richborough Roman Fort near Sandwich. The use of irregular-sized flint as a 'fill' or 'rubble' embedded in mortar was also characteristic of the Norman period, exemplified by the flint walls that date to this period at Godmersham church.

The fourteenth century marked a period when the art and beauty of flint 'knapping' for building work reached a very high standard and meticulous detail was paid to the shaping and facing of each flint, a practice requiring great skill and labour. A good example of this work can be seen in the chancel of Crundale church (Fig. 10). After the Black Death it appears that the use of flint in buildings declined, although the craftsmanship in building work appears to have been maintained, with care being taken to ensure that flints were laid in regular courses.

A resurgence of the use of flint occurred in the Gothic revival period of the nineteenth century and flints were characteristically laid in tightly packed even courses. Often these flints were laid as unchipped nodular flints but occasionally they were knapped to give a flat surface to the finished wall as can be seen at the eastern end of St Margaret's church in Canterbury.[1]

Its durability also made it a highly prized stone for the gun flint industry of the nineteenth century and in the days before tarmacadam it was commonly used to surface the tracks and lanes of the Downs.

Fig. 9 Outcrop of Lower Greensand at The Roughs near Hythe.

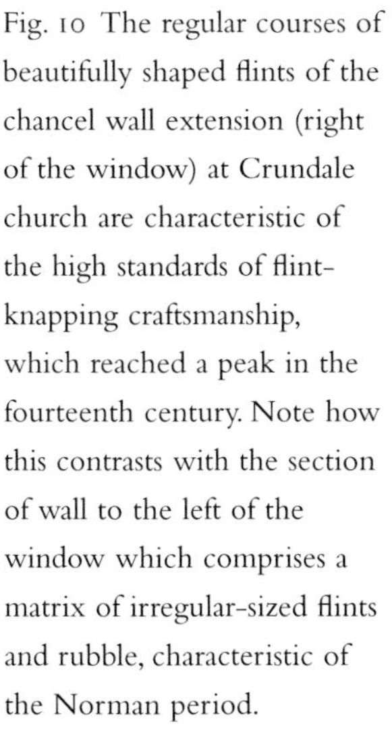

Fig. 10 The regular courses of beautifully shaped flints of the chancel wall extension (right of the window) at Crundale church are characteristic of the high standards of flint-knapping craftsmanship, which reached a peak in the fourteenth century. Note how this contrasts with the section of wall to the left of the window which comprises a matrix of irregular-sized flints and rubble, characteristic of the Norman period.

Towards the end of the Cretaceous Period some 65 million years ago, the land mass of the Wealden region began to rise. The initial period of uplift led to the formation of a low island of chalk between shallower seas. The centre of the present day Weald probably remained exposed as a high tableland of chalk and was subjected to the wear and tear of weathering by rain, frost, ice and snow. Towards the edges of this land mass, muds, clays, sands and pebbles were laid down in the shallow seas and estuaries to become the rocks of the present day London and Hampshire basins.

The Tertiary Period marked the start of a sustained and dramatic period of greater uplift following a period of intense 'earth storms' when large tracts of the earth's surface were affected by intense pressures from within the crust. Mountain ranges, notably the Alps, were formed as the crust buckled into great folds, rippling outwards to push the Wealden district into a long elongated dome (known as an 'anticline'). As this dome-shaped land mass developed, the continued buckling of the underlying strata formed folds and faults, producing the troughs of the Thames valley and English Channel. Over millions of years of exposure to the natural elements, the layers of rock of the anticline were eroded down (Fig. 11), with material being transported away by an extensive drainage network of streams and rivers.

The original streams of the dome probably followed a natural pattern flowing to the north and south, cutting valleys in the overlying chalk. Gradually, the underlying older sands and clays would have become exposed and, being less resistant to weathering, eroded at a greater rate than the harder chalk. Over time the drainage network eventually began to undermine the more resistant chalk, forming the familiar steep inward-facing escarpment slope of the Downs that we see today.

Intervening phases of uplift brought about changes to the drainage network with streams and rivers gradually adjusting themselves to the changing gradient and conditions, and laying down deposits of gravels and muds along their courses. As the land surface gradually rose, the streams cut deeper into the rocks leaving their former beds of mud and gravel as flatter terraces. Where this process involved a more sudden adjustment, features known as 'benches' were formed, marking the point where the river increased its power and began to cut down through the rock at a greater rate. These features are visible in some of the dry valleys today. On a spur east of Wickham Bushes near Lydden in the East Kent Downs, a bench is present some 23m (75ft) above the valley floor while in the nearby Alkham valley, benches can be seen 12-15m (40-50ft) above the present valley bottom.[2]

Around 2.5 million years ago the global temperatures began to cool and ice sheets began to extend across much of our northerly latitudes. Evidence suggests that these ice sheets extended as far south as an area just to the north of the Thames, advancing and retreating in alternating phases of colder and warmer climates. Lying further south, the Wealden district escaped the grip of ice sheets and glaciers, yet even so, the harsh tundra-like (periglacial) conditions rendered this part of the world a hostile landscape, at the mercy of bitterly cold temperatures in the winter and rubble-laden torrents of meltwater in summer months. The network of streams and rivers that had already developed rapidly acquired greater force, scoring the landscape with

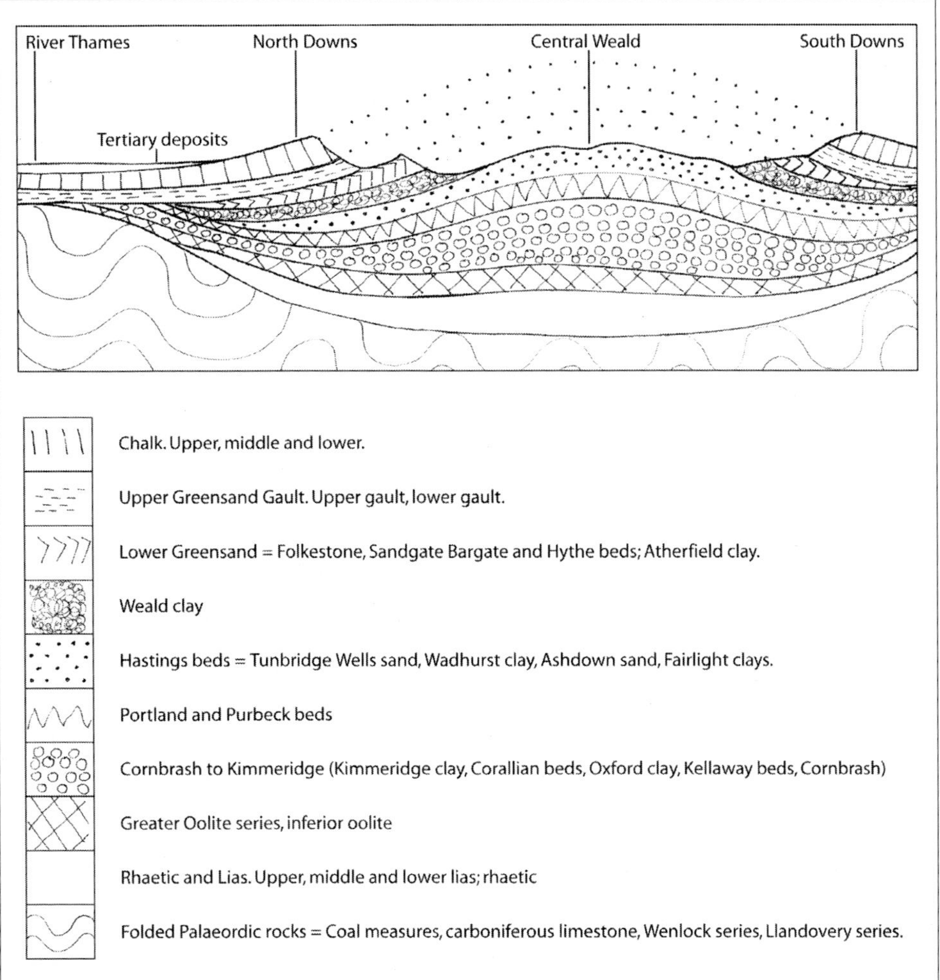

Fig. 11 The geology of the Weald.

steep sided valleys and transporting the rock-shattered debris away in torrents of floodwater. These powerful streams exploited areas of weakness within the beds of chalk to form the coombes and dry valleys of the modern day landscape.

The end of the last phase of colder climate (the Last Glaciation) some 12,000 years ago heralded the beginning of the warm Atlantic Period and with it the colonisation of trees. The first were trees such as birch (*Betula sp.*) and aspen (*Populus tremula*), followed in turn by species suited to warmer conditions as the climate gradually changed. Over time, hazel (*Corylus avellana*), oak (*Quercus sp.*), lime (*Tilia sp.*), elm (*Ulmus sp.*), ash (*Fraxinus excelsior*) and holly (*Ilex aguifolium*) were able to colonise. Traditionally it was believed that this early Atlantic Period also witnessed the breaking of the land bridge with the continent. Recent archaeological research however suggests that the separation from the continent may have occurred at least some 250,000 years ago.

– SEA URCHINS AND SEA CLIFFS –
THE EARLY DAYS OF GEOLOGICAL STUDY

Ever since the days of early nineteenth-century interest in natural history, the chalk bedrock of the Kent Downs has been the focus of much geological study and interest. Early antiquarians remarked upon the similarities between the cliffs of Dover and France and speculated:

> that Britain was at some remote period joined to Gaul by an isthmus or neck of land ... which by the incessant rush of waters on either side, was at length worn away, and a chasm made, whereby that which had originally been an isthmus was, by friction, changed to a narrow sea.[3]

The majestic white cliffs that have long stood as a symbolic landmark to the nation, have been recognised as one of the most accessible and complete records of the story of chalk formation. The description of the cliffs between Folkestone and Walmer by William Phillips in 1822 was one of the earliest attempts to divide the English chalk into layers.[4] The lowest division recognised by him was the 'grey chalk', at least 200ft (60m) thick and distinguished from the layers above by its darker colour and softer consistency. Geologists of the later nineteenth century developed this classification system further using the slight differences in the composition of the chalk to identify additional layers such as the marl-rich 'Lower Chalk' and the flint-laden harder bands of the 'Upper Chalk'. It soon became apparent however that such characteristics were not necessarily always reliable indicators of bed division. By a close study of chalk fossils, the highly gifted geologist Arthur Walter Rowe, was able to develop a more reliable means of dividing chalk into zones.[5] Fossils such as sea urchins were found to be particularly useful in identifying chalk layers and his work has formed the basis for the tripartite division of 'Lower', 'Middle' and 'Upper' chalk that is still used today.

The quality and diversity of the fossils found in the chalk of the Kent Downs has been recognised for centuries. The 'golden age' for fossil collecting was the eighteenth and nineteenth centuries, when numerous large, hand-worked quarries produced many beautiful specimens. Though the turnover for such high quality material is much reduced today, rare and well-preserved specimens can still be found by the persistent collector.

– THE WEALDEN CONTROVERSY –

The Kent Downs sparked one of the most controversial debates of early Wealden geological study. Prior to the mid-nineteenth century, the widely accepted school of thought amongst the foremost geologists of the time was that the escarpments of the North and South Downs were ancient sea cliffs, with the intervening lower lying parts of the Weald 'resembling the flat sands and laid bare by the receding tide' of a long-forgotten sea.[6] Later geologists of the nineteenth century began to challenge this view and it was realised that the escarpments and valleys of the Downs were instead the result of erosion by precipitation (rain and snow) and rivers. The arguments were advanced by William Whittaker whose paper, 'On Subaerial Denudation, and on Cliffs and Escarpments of the Chalk and the Lower Tertiary Beds', was published in full in the *Geological Magazine* in 1867, finally demonstrating that the origins of the present day landscape lay in the resistance of different rocks to the weathering effect of the natural elements.

Throughout the Downs there exist a range of more recent superficial deposits, patchily distributed and comprising clays, sands and gravels. The location of some of these deposits may have been the result of re-sorting and redistribution of materials during periglacial conditions. One of the most familiar and widely distributed on the Downs is the **'clay-with-flints'** layer. Characterised by a reddish-brown or yellow-brown clay and littered with flints of varying sizes, this layer is thought to have been formed by the deposition of clay, filtering from overlying pervious deposits, into voids within the chalk.

The **'plateau drift'**, which mantles many of the higher flatter parts of the Downs, is a mixed body of material, usually comprising brown and red-mottled clays and sands with flints, pebbles and iron-rich material. This layer is though to have been formed when weathering dissolved the chalk to leave a residue of flinty clay which, in flatter areas, impeded the drainage of the sandy soils above, so creating the 'mottled' appearance to the deposits.

Along the crest of the escarpment and higher parts of the Downs appear scattered patches of sand, typically rusty-brown in colour, known as the **Lenham Beds**. It is believed that these sands are the remains of a more extensive sheet of material laid down when an area, that is now east Kent, was submerged under a shallow sea in late Miocene and early Pliocene times. The Lenham Beds layer is evident at the small hamlet of Paddlesworth at almost 180m (600ft) above sea level, where sandstone rocks have been used in the construction of Paddlesworth church (Fig. 12). Elsewhere, on the ridges above the footslope villages of Wye and Westwell, scatterings of small pits are believed to be associated with attempts to mine iron ore from this layer by early man (Fig. 25).

Coombe Deposits are common in the dry valleys of the dipslope and are comprised of chalk material that has been subject to downslope movement during periods of periglacial conditions. In these colder times the frost-shattered rocks and soils turned into a sludgy mass which gradually crept downhill during the summer thaws on an underlying bed of frozen soil (known as 'permafrost'). Remnants of this material are evident in many locations. At Wye, for example, a chalky coombe deposit underlies much of the Wye College area and has been exposed in various localities in the village such as Scotton Street.

At various places in the Kent Downs, loamy soils known as **Brickearths** are present, often of a dark or light reddish-brown colour. Some of these deposits are believed to be wind-blown in origin, while others may have come about through the redistribution of materials during periods of colder climate when periglacial conditions prevailed. In times past these deposits sustained an important local brick-making industry throughout the Downs. At Derringstone near Barham, brickearth was extensively quarried for brick making. Further along the Elham valley at Exted, clay was dug and 'puddled' near Exted Farm and brought to kilns near Elham station where it was made into bricks.

Where chalk is overlain by other deposits, its surface is often characterised by irregular hollows which are termed 'pipes'. These have resulted from the solution of the chalk by slightly acid water to leave pockets or voids into which insoluble material (clays etc) has collapsed. Sometimes these pipes can be exposed in chalk pits and give the appearance of 'red carrots' growing down into the chalk (Fig. 13).

The calcareous stone known as **Tufa** is believed to be a relatively recent geological deposit that has formed from intermittent springs and watercourses in the chalk valleys in times past. It is a rough, rock-like deposit of calcium carbonate. Its durability made it attractive as a building material in Roman times and it appears in villas at Eccles near Maidstone, Folkestone and Dover. The Norman period witnessed a revival of its use and it is evident in a number of churches throughout the Downs, particularly in the Medway area such as at Luddesdown and Dode (Fig. 14).

Above left: Fig. 12 Sandstone rocks from the Lenham Beds used in the construction of Paddlesworth church.

Above centre: Fig. 13 A 'pipe' exposed in a chalk pit near East Brabourne.

Above right: Fig. 14 Blocks of tufa used in the walls of Luddesdown church.

– NAILBOURNES AND WOE-WATERS –

This is the fell season,
Predestined and foreknown-
With the woe-waters rising
In the hollow hills,
Above Ottinge and Lyminge:
The sudden disastrous waters
Flooding the frost-bound valley
And the sullen pastures;
Washing the wood's fringe, lapping
The low-built farm:
Heralds of the spring-fever,
Foretelling harm ...

Jocelyn Brooke, 'Month's Mind'
from *December Spring* (1946)

Fig. 15

For a district largely devoid of running surface water, the intermittent streams that appear in several of the East Kent Downs chalk valleys have always been a source of fascination and interest. It is evident that these streams, known locally as 'nailbournes', have been a familiar feature of this area for hundreds of years and from as early as the sixteenth century they have drawn regular attention from historians, topographers and geographers of the county. The historian Edward Hasted wrote of these curious phenomena in the latter years of the eighteenth century:

> These nailbournes or temporary land springs are not unusual in these parts of this county eastward of Sittingbourne ... I know only of Addington to the west ... Their time of breaking forth is very uncertain ... Sometimes they may break out for one or perhaps two successive years and at others with two, three or more years intervention.[7]

For centuries their irregularity and unpredictable nature defied explanation and attracted a wealth of local superstition and folklore, many believing that their appearance coincided with a seven-year cycle. It was not until the scientific revolution of the Victorian era that people began to study them in more detail and search for a scientific explanation for their origin. The work of the East Kent Scientific Society provided a forum for discussion and research for a number of scientists such as Charles Buckingham who devoted much time to studying these curious phenomena. His research drew on earlier observations of nailbourne 'risings', some of which date back to the eighteenth century. It was noted for example that in 1772 the Petham nailbourne, flowed through to the Stour at Shalmsford Street on 22 February and continued to run until 16 June of the same year.[8]

The notes of the East Kent Scientific Society provided a valuable reference for the dedicated and painstaking work of F.C. Snell in the early twentieth century whose publication, *The Intermittent (or Nailbourne) Streams of East Kent* (1938), remains one of the most detailed and comprehensive accounts of the nailbournes of Kent. Based on anecdotal evidence, memories of villagers and personal observations it appears that in former times these streams flowed on a much more regular basis and for longer durations, indicating that water levels within the chalk were once much higher than the present day:

> Old people tell us, as with other nailbournes, that the flowing periods came much oftener in the past than they do now. Villagers at Barham talk of the time when the Elham nailbourne came through almost every year.[9]

The early part of the twentieth century appears to have been a particularly active period for these streams. Between 1910 and 1919 and again between 1925 and 1931 Snell recorded a nailbourne flowing every winter. Local author Jocelyn Brooke also remarked upon their unusual activity of this time, noting that the Elham nailbourne, 'rose with an unaccustomed frequency immediately before and during the First World War ... and appears to have emerged fairly often during the twenties and thirties'.[10]

Fig. 16 The Elham Nailbourne at Lyminge.

Fig. 17 Road bridge at Kingston constructed in the early twentieth century when the rising of the Elham Nailbourne was a more regular occurrence.

At the end of the nineteenth century, the widely held belief for the origin of the streams lay in the 'Cavity Theory' which argued that rainfall drained into great hollows or cavities within the chalk, gradually filling up until the cavity overflowed to break forth as a surface stream. Acting as a siphon, the cavity eventually emptied and was left to once more fill up with water, the rate at which equated to a seven-year period. Although this view found favour with a number of geologists of the time, closer observation revealed that the streams' appearances did not always adhere to the seven-year cycle and this led scientists to seek alternative theories. The 'Saturation Level Theory' of the early twentieth century contended that the origin of a nailbourne lay in the gradual rise of the underground water table which, after a sustained period of rainfall, emerges above ground level in the form of a temporary stream. This theory then sought to attribute the appearance of the stream as a direct result of the build up of groundwater levels after a long period of rainfall.

This was further developed by other geologists who speculated that the emergence of the nailbournes at particular locations could only be associated with fissures within the bedrock which act as springs when the water table rises above ground level. It is this theory that forms the basis of our understanding of these features today. Nailbournes then are simply the result of groundwater levels responding to the accumulative affects of sustained or heavy rainfall events, materialising on the surface as streams through the complex network of fissures and collection points of the underlying strata.

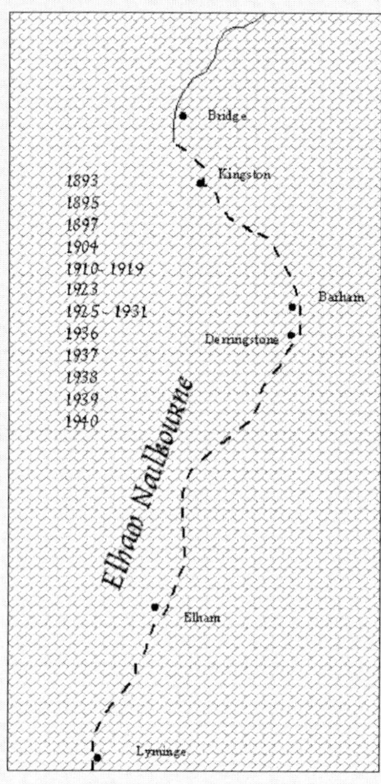

The **Elham nailbourne** is perhaps the most familiar of the Kent Downs, flowing at its peak over some 15 miles from its source near Lyminge to the point where the Lesser Stour rises as permanently flowing springs near the village of Bekesbourne. In many years the spring-fed lakes at Bourne Park near Bishopsbourne provided sufficient supply to make it a familiar sight at its lower reaches. In exceptionally wet years the cumulative effects of seasonally high rainfall allows the stream to appear at progressively higher points up the valley through Derringstone, Barham, Elham, and Lyminge with water, first welling out in pools, and then flowing on into its regular course. Evidence of the former activity of this nailbourne in the early twentieth century can still be seen today at Kingston and Derringstone where the regularity and depth of flow at this time was clearly sufficient to warrant the construction of two road bridges built around 1910 (Fig. 17).

The **Petham nailbourne** has long held a deep-rooted association with the villages and farmsteads along the Petham valley. Its appearance is often heralded by the overtopping of the Marble Pond in the village of Petham. From here the stream follows the valley bottom through to Swarling Manor, Kenfield and Garlinge Green, meeting the River Stour at Shalmsford Street. In wetter years it has been known to rise at Duckpits Farm, and in exceptional years, rises some three miles further up the valley at Dean Farm. Appearances at its highest reaches were noted in the particularly wet winters of 1916, 1928 and 1936. Prior to this time local folklore tells of an exceptional year in the mid-nineteenth century:

> The last time the Nailbourne flowed straight into Chartham River was 1881, that time the water ran out of Marble pond before Christmas 1880 ... The last time water came from Dene Farm is between fifty and sixty years ago: about that time a man named Dilnot rented Ansdore Farm, Waltham and the water came up so rapidly that his men were all one Sunday opening a ditch to let the water through because it should not flood the land. The old men have said that when the water ran into the Chartham river that the eels have found their way into Petham and have been taken out of Marble Pond.[11]

The year 1860 also appears to have been an exceptionally active time for this nailbourne when prolonged rainfall throughout the year led to it flowing throughout the summer and into the following winter and spring.

Locally known as the **'Drellingore'**, the **Alkham nailbourne** derives its name from the small hamlet of Drellingore situated at the Folkestone end of the Alkham valley. Its rising is characteristically marked by the appearance of springs at successive points up the valley to its source where a depression in a field near Drellingore Farm forms a natural basin once known as 'The Pit'. The eighteenth-century topographer Charles Seymour recorded that the depth of flow was sufficient in former times to carry a boat.[12] Another incident tells of the Drellingore flowing twice in one year and even at harvest time when the local farmers, 'on leaving the church had to move the stocks of reaped corn out of the way of the coming stream'.[13]

The **Ospringe nailbourne** was once a familiar occurrence in the Ospringe valley, near Faversham, rising at Westbrook and running through the hamlet of Whitehill and on through Ospringe village. 'Water Lane' at Ospringe and the presence of a water mill at Queen's Court bear witness to the activity of this stream in times past which, according to Edward Hasted, was reliable enough to drive the mill wheel for the manufacture of madder (a crop used to produce dye) and corn:

> It braks out about half a mile southward of Whitehill near Kennways and flows in Faversham creek. In February 1674 it began to run but stopped before Michaelmas. It broke forth in February 1712 and ran with such violence along the high road that trenches were dug to carry the water off. It had continued dry till it broke out afresh in 1753 and continued to run till summer 1778 when it stopped and has continued dry ever since.[14]

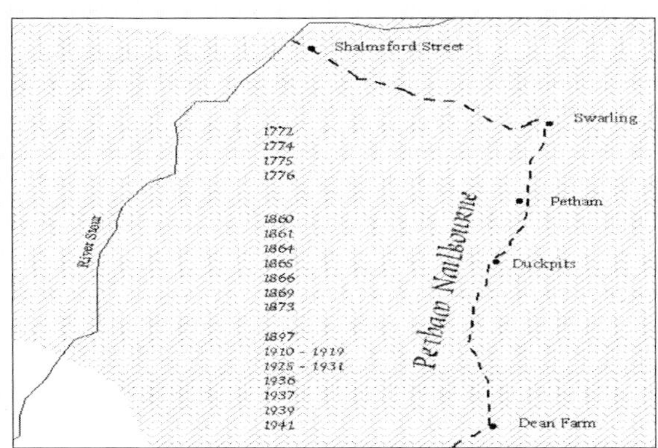

Opposite: Fig. 18 Elham nailbourne.

Right: Fig. 19 Petham nailbourne.

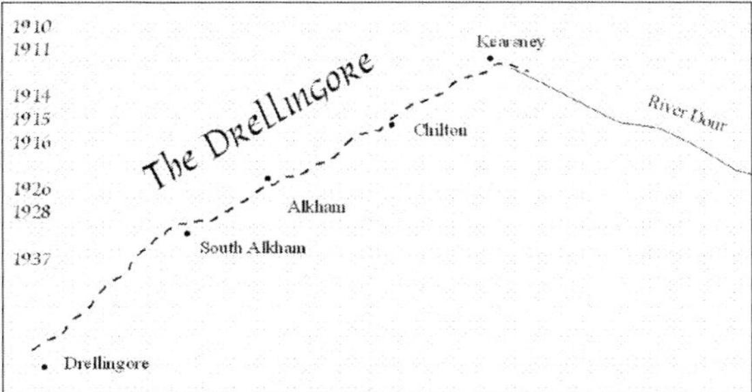

Fig. 20 Alkham nailbourne.

THE WOE-WATER LEGEND

For centuries the nailbournes of east Kent have formed an important part of the legend and local folklore of the villages through which they pass. Their ephemeral and mysterious appearances have historically been associated with misfortune and brought upon them a reputation as harbingers of bad luck. Known locally as 'woe-waters', their appearance was often seen as portent of doom, Edward Hasted (1797-1801) noting in the eighteenth century that their rising, 'is held by the common people as the forerunner of scarcity and dearness of corn and victuals.' The rising of the Drellingore in the Alkham valley was locally regarded as a sign of a poor harvest which gave rise to the local rhyme:

When drellingore stream flows to Dover town
wheat shall be forty shillings and barley a pound.[15]

One possible source of this association with bad luck and misfortune is the legend of St Augustine and the pagan gods. The arrival of St Augustine and the Anglo-Saxons' conversion to Christianity apparently coincided with a period of history noted for its dry summers and winters, leading to poor harvests and thirst-ridden livestock. Locals who had converted to Christianity, forsaking their old pagan gods Woden and Thor, became sceptical of the new religion. When Christian priests prayed for rain it is said that a miracle occurred and a spring gushed forth from the spot where St Augustine had knelt, transforming the parched Elham valley into a green fertile landscape. The old gods however fought back and the stream dried up, whereupon the 'angel' of the bourne descended and the stream returned. It is said that the battle rages to this day, thereby explaining the periodic recurrent appearances of the stream.[16]

Fig. 21

The superstition and local folklore that was associated with these streams continued well into the twentieth century. Local author Jocelyn Brooke wrote that the rising of the Elham nailbourne in the spring of 1935 was widely supposed to have been a portent of the death of King George V.[17]

A local tradition that was still a popular source of fun for local children in Barham in the 1950s was the 'following of the nailbourne' when youngsters would run to Elham and follow the rising of the stream back to Barham. This nailbourne is also believed to have been the inspiration for the 'Magic River' which appears in several of local illustrator Mary Tourtel's Rupert the Bear stories.

Although flowing less frequently than in the past, the nailbournes of the Downs still provide a fascinating spectacle and continue to hold a special identity with the villages and hamlets through which they pass.

TWO

LONG BARROWS AND LYNCHETS

EARLY MAN IN THE DOWNS

The discovery of a human skull at Swanscombe near Rochester provides some of the earliest evidence of prehistoric man within the current day downland region. Dated to around 400,000 years ago, 'Swanscombe Man' is believed to be contemporary with some of the earliest prehistoric cultures that colonised the present day British Isles from the European and African land masses. These early phases of occupation are believed to have coincided with intervals of warmer climate (interglacial periods) which witnessed the ebb and flow of our early ancestors over present day southern England. The passage of hundreds of thousands of years has witnessed the total transformation of these early Palaeolithic landscapes and has erased virtually all signs of these early settlers, yet public interest was greatly stirred when tantalising evidence came to light in the nineteenth century of seemingly worked flints, termed **eoliths**, which were claimed to date from very early prehistoric communities.

– THE EOLITH CONTROVERSY –

Eoliths were first described by Benjamin Harrison from the dipslopes of the North Downs in west Kent where they were found in large numbers over ploughland, embedded in the drift deposits of the plateau country. Harrison and his supporters, including the eminent geologist Professor Joseph Prestwich, maintained that these coarsely worked flints were the product of human manufacture of some ancient prehistoric society. Our present day knowledge of the Pliocene deposits in which they were found suggest a date of some 2-4 million years ago. One of the sites frequented by Harrison was Parsonage Farm near Stansted where, on 22 May 1865, he found a spread of worn gravel deposits. For many years Harrison and his associates visited the site and found many eoliths and other worked flints of the Neolithic period within these deposits.

Harrison's claims inspired a wealth of debate in the nineteenth and early twentieth centuries, with many geologists and antiquarians arguing that the stones were simply the result of the natural flaking of flints as a result of sub-soil pressures. The debate continued for three decades and more and more evidence was discovered that suggested a purely natural origin for eoliths.

Evidence in the form of primitive flint tools and animal bones indicates that early man probably lived a nomadic-hunter existence, following the migration patterns of wild animals such as deer, wild cattle and horse. Archaeological discoveries suggest that these prehistoric cultures concentrated in river valleys and coastal areas where food resources were more abundant.[1] Flint axes, for example, have been found in considerable numbers within the gravel beds of the Dartford and Medway areas where the rivers Medway, Thames and Darenth converge. Similar finds within the gravel beds at Westbere near Canterbury indicate that the present day Stour valley was of attraction to these early societies. During the colder climatic phases early man probably abandoned these hunting grounds and sought refuge in the warmer southerly latitudes of the European continent. The intervening warmer phases perhaps witnessed hunting groups venturing back for longer periods to seek out food and gradually rekindle a year-round existence in the region. Over time these hunting groups became better adapted to the periods of colder climate, utilising rock shelters and caves such as at Oldbury Hill near Ightham, steadily advancing the sophistication of their flint-tool technology to improve hunting efficiency.

The gradual warming of the climate that followed the end of the last Ice Age some 10,000 years ago witnessed a new era of human settlement and activity that has lasted uninterrupted until the present day. Artefact scatters found on the higher ridges of the Downs suggest that these high vantage points offered some attraction to Mesolithic man, perhaps providing summer camping grounds away from the more-frequented river valleys and coastal plains. As hunting techniques became more refined and as flint-tool technology became more sophisticated, it is possible that these early settlers exploited areas of grassland and wood pasture, 'managing' them through periodic tree felling to maintain open areas of grassland attractive to wild herbivores, on which they could hunt.

Over time these hunter-gatherer based societies became increasingly exposed to the ideas and practices associated with the first early farming societies that were beginning to evolve on the continental land mass. The gradual rise in sea levels that had characterised the early Mesolithic period and led to the deepening of the English Channel would have hardly presented any major obstacle to the continual passage and activities of early man, who were able to traverse the much narrower sea that would have formed the Dover Straits. Twenty-first century fast ferries may well be a far cry from the wooden dug-outs of our early ancestors yet it does not take a great leap of the imagination to picture the same enterprising spirit of these earlier cross-channel travellers plying to and fro across a relatively shallow and island dotted channel. It is this proximity to the continental land mass that saw the early Neolithic farmers of northern Europe gradually introducing the new inventions of agriculture and seeking new opportunities on the chalklands of modern day Kent. Evidence seems to suggest that the hunter-gatherer groups of Mesolithic society perhaps existed side by side with Neolithic communities for some time, evolving and adopting the new Neolithic culture and technology.[2]

THE LONG BARROWS

Ashbee (1999) has suggested that the presence of two concentrations of long barrows within the county, both situated within the Kent Downs, may reflect the early embracing of Neolithic culture from north-west Europe. These two clusters centred around the Medway and Stour valleys are typified by a distinctive form of barrow resembling those found in the Netherlands and Germany. When first built, the long barrows had high rectangular chambers, with their entrances blocked by a focal portal stone which was positioned at the eastern end. The Medway long barrows number among the few within the country that are constructed from sarsen stones, huge slabs and boulders of a naturally occurring dense hard rock comprised of silicified sand. These stones once formed the walls and roof of the barrow chambers. Spreads of sarsen stone are found on the Marlborough Downs in Wiltshire and the North Downs in Kent where it is largely confined to the slopes of the Medway valley area. Occasional stones found in other areas of the Kent Downs such as near Charing may provide clues as to the former existence of sarsen barrows in times past.

The Medway long barrow sites comprise Kit's Coty (colour plate 6), Lower Kit's Coty, the Coffin Stone, Warren Farm chamber, Coldrum, The Chestnuts and Addington Long Barrow. The antiquarian William Stukely, an archaeological pioneer of the eighteenth century and noted for his work on the Stonehenge and Avebury monuments, took a strong interest in these stones on his excursions into Kent. During his three tours of the area in 1722, 1724 and 1725 he made informative drawings which have proved invaluable in gaining an impression of the former extent and spread of these stones before the damaging effects of an increasing population and changing countryside had taken their toll on these monuments.

It is evident that the existing stones probably formed part of a much wider scattering of sarsen stones on these footslopes which may have once marked the locations of other 'megalithic' long barrows. Within the area once known as Great Tottington there existed a scattering of many stones, some in groups, others isolated, that littered the fields, hedgerows and woods.[3] The fate of many of these stones remains a mystery. Many were no doubt hauled to the edges of fields, destroyed or buried over the centuries by generations of farmers naturally keen to remove obstacles and impediments to plough and harrow. Reports and accounts of commentators of the nineteenth century suggest that many of these stones were blasted apart into chunks with gunpowder which were then further broken down for use in road mending and building materials. The stones have long formed an important part of the cultural heritage of the area and have become steeped in a rich tradition of folklore and superstition. Writing in the late nineteenth century the naturalist and antiquarian Revd Cecil Henry Fielding recounts:

> Superstition alone saved the relics that are left. The field of the 'countless stones' near Aylesford was said to be impossible to clear, and that several who had taken the farm were ruined because they wickedly attempted to remove the stones.[4]

Fig. 22

The Stour valley cluster of long barrows represent a small group of earthen burial mounds comprising sites at Julliberrie's Grave near Chilham, Jackets Field near Challock and Shrubs Wood near Elmsted. The curiously named Julliberrie's Grave, lying at the foot of Chilmans Downs to the east of Chilham village, has received much attention from historians and archaeologists and has been a familiar land mark to generations within the Stour valley for hundreds of years. Recorded in antiquarian accounts from the sixteenth century, the folklore that perpetuated for many centuries contended that the barrow was the grave of a tribune of Caesar's army, named Quintus Laberius Durus, who was killed by the Britons during Caesar's first campaigns in England. It was not until the 1930s that this legend was put to rest when the careful examination of the barrow by the renowned archaeologist Ronald Jessup verified that it originated as a Neolithic long barrow. Steeped in legend and mystery, the barrow has become an important part of the rich cultural heritage of the area. It is believed to have provided the backdrop to the fictional detective tale *The Penrose Mystery* (1936) by R. Austin Freeman in which Dr Thorndyke solves the mysterious disappearance of Penrose, discovering him buried within a Kentish barrow. The barrow also provides the backdrop to scenes in the film *A Canterbury Tale* (1944) by Michael Powell (Fig. 64).

The other two long barrows in the Stour valley area at Jackets Field near Challock and Shrubs Wood near Elmsted are both situated within the wooded plateau country of the Kent Downs. They provide revealing evidence of occupation in downland areas that traditionally were thought to be unattractive to early man. The appeal of prominent and highly visible sites for burial mounds is believed to be characteristic of Neolithic society and this perhaps suggests that in former times these tablelands of the Downs were of a far more open prospect.

NEOLITHIC SETTLERS

The gradual emergence of Neolithic culture around 3,000 BC heralded the move from the itinerant lifestyle of the Mesolithic hunter-gatherer culture to a much more communal and sedentary society, founded on an agricultural economy and dependent for the first time on the husbandry of livestock and the growing of crops. Its proximity to the European mainland and its resource of well-watered and fertile soils would naturally suggest that the Kent area was of great attraction to Neolithic society, and so it is surprising that, in contrast to other chalk downland areas of southern England, the hills of Kent appear to support a relatively scarce resource of Neolithic round barrows, also known as 'tumuli' (Fig. 23 and colour plate 5), that elsewhere bear witness to an extensively occupied downland domain. The light scattering of Bronze Age round barrows that occasionally punctuate the turf of the Kent Downs pale into insignificance when compared with the rash of burial mounds that riddle many parts of the Dorset and Wiltshire Downs, many of which were excavated and documented during the heydays of Victorian antiquarian interest. The possible reasons for this curious anomaly has attracted much speculation. It is unlikely, as Champion (1982) contends, that Kent was home to Neolithic tribes who adopted alternative customs of burying their dead. A more plausible explanation is the possibility that many barrows may have simply disappeared over time as a result of plough and cultivation damage. Parfitt (2004) suggests that widespread destruction of many monuments had already taken place by the start of the nineteenth century. This suggestion may well be borne out by the wealth of underlying archaeology on ploughland that has now come to light following advances in archaeological detection techniques. The area of the gently undulating chalk dipslope in the east of Kent is a case in point where a growing number of previously unrecorded barrow monuments have become apparent as crop-marks in fields as aerial surveying techniques have advanced in the last twenty-five years.

Perhaps of more significance is the wealth of archaeology that lies unrecorded within the woodlands of the Downs and in particular the lack of attention that this has received in the past. Traditionally dismissed by archaeologists, not least because of the difficulties of surveying and accessing woodland, the enormous untapped resource of preserved woodland archaeology in the form of banks, ditches, pits and field systems is now only fully being realised.[5] Advances in detection techniques are beginning to yield fascinating evidence of historic landscapes in woodlands throughout the country and, given the prevalence of woodland within the Kent Downs landscape it is interesting to speculate on the wealth of prehistoric archaeology that may come to light in the future.

Despite this apparent dearth of evidence, the scattering of artefacts and burial features that do exist within the downland region of Kent afford useful speculation on the nature and extent of Neolithic activity. Evidence in the form of pot sherds, metalwork and domestic artefacts points to a thriving and wealthy society, centred largely in the river valleys and coastal areas where the fertile and free-draining soils offered obvious advantages for these early farmers.

– THE BARROW DIGGERS –

The earliest 'round barrows' such as at Great Watersend, near Dover, date to the Bronze Age although they continued to be used as a means of burial custom through the Roman and Saxon periods. They were normally a simple structure consisting of a large mound of earth surrounded by a ditch and contained grave goods such as pottery jars, buckles and jewellery made of various stones and precious metals.

Many barrows were excavated in Victorian times when interest in antiquities became popular. An account of the excavation of Holborough Knob barrow near Snodland provides an interesting insight into the nature of these early 'excavations' and the form of entertainment that it provided for antiquarians. Believed to date from the Roman period, the barrow was first documented by William Lambarde in 1576, yet it was Thomas Wright who in 1844, accompanied by local clergy, their ladies, an Oxford undergraduate and a dozen labourers first embarked on a more detailed examination:

Fig. 23 Bronze Age barrow at Great Watersend near Dover.

Fig. 24

It was the labour of four long days to cut entirely through the barrow: but we who were not absolute diggers contrived to pass out time to the full satisfaction of all the party. We had hired one of the boats which are used in this part of the country for carrying the amateur toxophilites along the Medway to their archery meetings; and each morning after an early breakfast we were rowed down the river, which is here picturesque and singularly tortuous, to the place of landing.

A plentiful supply of provisions had been procured for picnicing on the hill and we remained by the barrow all day, watching and directing operations ... The method of excavation was to dig a long irregular trench 5-7 feet wide through the centre of the mound down to the natural chalk ... We contrived to pass our time at intervals between digging and picnicing in games of various descriptions and other amusements. The care of the ladies was, of course, an important duty on such an expedition – not exactly such as those which the builders of the mound celebrated when they laid the deceased on his funeral pile. At much the same time during one of Payne's mudlarks to secure Roman pots from Otterham Creek near Sittingbourne, for instance, they were entertained during the business with 'anecdotes of past experiences' and 'songs from one of Planche's extravaganzas' ...[6]

The clearance of woodland for agriculture in Neolithic times has been viewed as one of the most fundamental transformations that our modern day landscapes have witnessed. As the population expanded throughout southern England, the frontier of agriculture advanced gradually into the wooded hinterland regions such as the Downs. Through a combination of selective felling, ring-barking and burning, areas of woodland and wood pasture were cleared for arable crops or left to revert to grassland for stock grazing. Such advances may well have exploited existing woodland clearings and glades created naturally through the browsing and grazing action of wild herbivores such as wild horses, cattle and deer. The abundance of stone and flints axes found throughout the country bear testament to the extent and immense scale of this clearance, and the downland of Kent is no exception with many flint axe finds scattered throughout the valleys and slopes. Hundreds of Neolithic hand axes, scrapers, flakes, and worked flints on the clay plateau above Elham at Dreal's Farm suggest occupation sites existed in a relatively open landscape at this time. How much of this post-glacial landscape succumbed to the axe of Neolithic man is uncertain although the primitive nature of the hand axe technology coupled with the sheer difficulties involved in removing tree stumps suggests an ever-shifting kaleidoscope and cycle of piecemeal clearance for arable land, followed by the partial recolonisation of grassland and scrub whenever grazing pressure was relaxed.

IRON AGE AND ROMAN OCCUPATION

The increasing sophistication of metal-making technologies on the continent witnessed the influx of a new waves of settlers from northern Europe and by around 500 BC Celtic settlers had begun to occupy the region, gradually bringing about a transition from bronze to iron technology. The tradition of trading of goods between communities that characterised the late Neolithic era developed further with the birth of coinage. It is this period that perhaps saw some of the first attempts to mine iron ore within the Downs (Fig. 25).

Fig. 25 Iron pits on the Wye Downs.

Fuelled by the needs of an ever-growing population, it seems likely that inroads were made from the more populated fertile river valleys and coastal plains into marginal areas such as the Downs which may have witnessed a renewed and sustained phase of wood and tree clearance for the growing of crops. It seems probable, for example, that more accessible valley bottom areas of the Downs were exploited for farming and habitation as is evidenced at Luddesdown Court, near Cobham, where discovery of late Iron Age pottery suggests occupation at this time.

~ LYNCHETS ~

Throughout the Kent Downs the imprint of historic cultivation patterns is evident in the form of undulations and banks known as 'lynchets'. Characteristic of downland landscapes, these features are visible as well-defined banks and ridges within fields, often appearing as terraces on steep-sided slopes (colour plate 3).

They are the product of the gradual downslope movement of soil caused by the action of ploughing over long periods of time. Where field boundaries existed, soil would accumulate against them forming 'positive' lynchets on the upper side, while on the lower side, soil was pushed downslope to form 'negative' lynchets (Fig. 26).

Many of these features date from ploughing during medieval times, such as at Petham in a field once known as 'Moonshine' near Court Lodge. This particular lynchet measures about 2ft (0.6m) high and is thought to date from the thirteenth century. A good example of earlier lynchets can be seen on the Godmersham Downs between Canterbury and Ashford. These are thought to date to Roman or possibly Neolithic times.

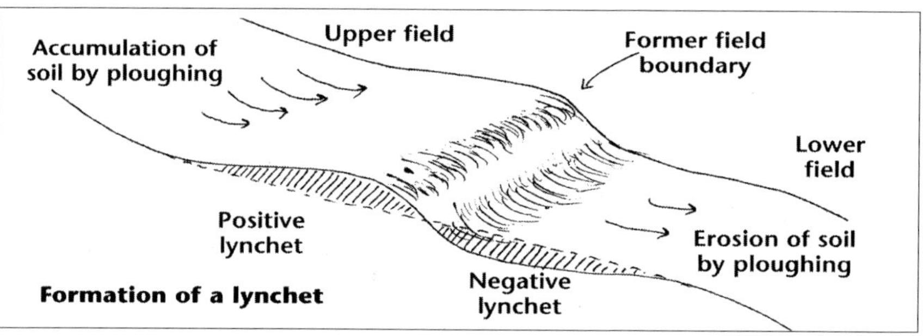

Fig. 26 The formation of a lynchet.

For the relatively advanced Iron Age society of Kent, the coming of the Romans and the integration of their culture may well have entailed little more than a rise in living standards and degree of comfort. In the towns of Roman Kent, life probably continued as normal for the well-established settlements, and the industries, practices and traditions that had evolved over the preceding centuries of Iron Age settlement remained intact.

Archaeological evidence seems to suggest that, by and large, rural settlements were also little-affected, the life of the ordinary farmer continuing unchanged at least for the first few generations. Evidence of Iron Age and Roman field systems at Sittingbourne, for example, uncovered by archaeological excavation in 2002, indicates that the basic Iron Age field system was remodelled but still retained much of the original layout.[7] For the smaller rural farmsteads, typically enclosed by circular or rectilinear ditches, most may not have progressed much beyond their Iron Age condition. These smaller farmsteads probably also existed alongside more prosperous farms where the dwelling house was built on stone foundations. These larger farms appear to have been concentrated in the fertile river valleys and lower footslopes of the Downs such as at Charing, Burham, Cobham, and Otford.

Elsewhere in the more populated areas of the county some Iron Age settlements may have witnessed growth and expansion and evolved to become larger villages and towns, yet the basic template of settlement distribution remained largely the same: the fertile North Kent Plain and river valleys of the Darenth, Medway and Stour continued to support much of the population while the impoverished hinterlands of the Downs and Weald were occupied by a much lower density of farmsteads and smaller settlements concentrated in some of the more accessible smaller valleys and along the corridors of the Roman road network. Areas such as the Elham valley, for example, appear to have been settled with evidence of occupation found throughout the valley but particularly from the villages and environs of Lyminge, Elham and Ottinge. The nearby Stone Street was one of the few Roman roads that traversed the upland area of the Kent Downs. Running in an almost perfectly straight line between Hythe and Canterbury it served to connect the fort at Lympne (Lemanis) with Canterbury.

'Oh, carry me up on the Stone Street Road
And lay me soft on the Down;
There let me stay, looking out on the Bay,
And meadow, and copse, and town.
For I cannot rest as a churchyard guest,
Nor sleep 'neath a sombre yew–
So make me a home on the ancient road
That the stalwart Romans knew...'

'A Song of Stone Street', Alice Davis (1908)

Fig. 27

It is also evident that much of the downland area supported a number of small-scale industries. With the increased demand for building materials, the small-scale lime burning industry witnessed expansion as a result of the growing demand for plaster and building mortar from the expanding towns, and new villas and farmsteads. Evidence from sites at Eccles, near Maidstone and Dover also suggests that hewn chalk blocks were also incorporated into buildings for internal walls. Iron working too appears to have been evident at a number of locations in the Downs such as at Swarling near Petham.

The drain of Roman military power from England in the early fifth century rendered the country increasingly susceptible to the repeated incursions and raids of the north European tribes of Picts, Angles and Saxons. A victim of its own success, the well-integrated heartland of Romano-British society that had characterised the last hundred or so years of Roman rule was ill equipped to deal with this new threat. Although the last vestiges of Roman civic administration had disappeared, the daily life of the Romano-British population changed little and the social practices and culture of the former empire probably persisted for several generations before the over-riding influence of the successive waves of the north European settlers finally made their mark.

– THE 'OLD ROAD' –

> ... It commands a sufficient view of what is below and what lies before: it is well on the chalk, just too high to interfere with cultivation ... it is well dried by an exposure only a little west of the south; it is well drained by the slope and by the porous soil.
>
> Hilaire Belloc, The Old Road (1904)

From prehistoric times the great ridge of the North Downs has provided an important thoroughfare and corridor for the traffic of our early ancestors, connecting the principal habitation sites of lowland southern England with the channel coast and thence to mainland Europe. Unencumbered by the perils and pitfalls of the heavy-going wooded clays to the south, early man took advantage of this naturally well-drained and open-prospected highway. While traces of man's earliest passage may now be lost in the mists of time, evidence suggests that certainly by the late Neolithic and early Iron Age period the escarpment track had become a busy trading route for goods such as tin and ore, forming the easterly segment of the prehistoric Harrow Way route which linked Kent and the continent with the southern and westerly fringes of the British Isles.

Ivan Margary, a leading authority on ancient roads and best known for his works on Roman roads in Britain, was among the first to advocate the dual nature of the trackway, being comprised of a ridgeway route and a parallel terraceway route running below the escarpment.[8] It is this terraceway track that has become immortalised over time as the 'Old Road', a profile which was to be given a new and unprecedented lease of life in the nineteenth century when it became more popularly known as the 'Pilgrim's' Way', an association which probably owes more to the musings of Victorian romantics rather than any genuine connection with the pilgrim tradition. Yet such inaccuracies should not detract from the antiquity of this route as an important and well-used thoroughfare, immediately apparent to anyone who has ever followed its winding and well-trodden course.

Running parallel on the uppermost reaches of the scarp, the ridgeway route is less well-preserved. Broken stretches of track, road, path and field boundary are all that remain of this once important thoroughfare that commanded far-ranging views over the Wealden lowlands to the south. Margary (1951) suggests that both routes may have

Fig. 28 The 'Old Road' at Westwell.

evolved as seasonal conditions underfoot dictated, with the terraceway or 'lower' route favoured in winter months when the exposed and clay-capped ridgeway path offered little comfort to the weary traveller. As settlements evolved on the footslopes of the Downs, the terraceway route naturally developed as the more popular route, affording the closest links to these communities for the weary journeymen and opportunist merchants who travelled its length.

For many, the course of the Old Road, softly writhing between the upland and the lowland woods, has come to symbolise the antiquity of the downland landscape. Along its length, the tunnelled **holloways** and root-riddled banks echo the weary tread of our long distant ancestors. Studded by ancient burial mounds and scored by chalk pits and hollows, the signs of millennia of use along its length are plain to see. It is no surprise that the Old Road journey has captured the imagination of writers and artists over the generations. The surge in antiquarian interest that characterised the Victorian era generated an association with pilgrimage that continued well into the twentieth century. Many, such as the clergyman and antiquarian Francis Watt who published his *Canterbury Pilgrims and their Ways* (1917) followed in the footsteps of Hilaire Belloc. Deeply inspired by his journey along the route, Belloc revived the romance of this ancient thoroughfare in *The Old Road* (1904), where, 'that repeated suggestion of the immense antiquity of the trail we were pursuing came to us from it again'.[9]

The route has also naturally become the focus of much folklore and legend. In the early twentieth century, one local folklore that abounded in the village of Godmersham recounted that a certain 'gully' path on Godmersham Downs remained devoid of vegetation because the passage of pilgrims was so great in former times that the grass growth never recovered.

THREE

STEADS AND SOLES

SETTLEMENT AND THE EVOLUTION OF THE LANDSCAPE

> The appearance of a country, diversified in surface, and amply wooded, as are the hills under view, cannot fail to interest: especially, where the vallies are cleared, and the hills remain capped with woods which bend over their brows and fall with irregular outlines down their sides of the vallies: passages of beautiful scenery, which not unfrequently meet the eye …
>
> William Marshall, *The Rural Economy of the Southern Counties* (1798)

The richness and diversity of the Kent Downs landscape has long been celebrated as one of its most cherished and enduring qualities. The mosaic of woodland, hedgerow and copse, surrounding a patchwork of small fields and open down is a defining characteristic of this area (colour plate 12) and bears testament to a countryside which has remained relatively unchanged for centuries. H.E. Bates captures the essence of this timeless beauty in his work *The Country Heart* (1949):

> This is the sort of country so rich in natural contour and so much more enriched by woods that are like slices of forgotten forest, which we cry out to have preserved, but which in a way successfully preserve itself. For there is little man can do with these steep slopes; the farmsteads here seem small…you sometimes see a small strip of cornland, a few chickens, a little meadow of hay.

DROVERS AND COMMONS

The origins of the modern day downland countryside and the evolution of its villages and hamlets can be traced to the Anglo-Saxon period, and in particular the wave of settlers, commonly referred to as the Jutes, who colonised Kent in the fifth and sixth centuries after the Roman withdrawal.

The Jutish system of civic administration was based on the 'lathe' system in which estates of land were aligned on a broadly north – south fashion across the county. Each tract of land comprised a primary settlement, characteristically centred on the fertile arable lands and river valley areas of North Kent, from which the estate would extend southwards into outlying areas of woodland, marsh and upland that were exploited on a seasonal basis for grazing.

The seasonal movement of stock known as 'transhumance' was integral to the layout of the estate and involved the shepherding and droving of livestock along well-established routes to forage on pastures and clearings in outlying areas of the territory. It was this practice, so readily associated with the establishment of the Wealden 'dens' in the later post-Conquest centuries, that was the driving force behind the much earlier colonisation and development of settlement within the Kent Downs. Many of the lanes and sunken tracks known as **holloways** (Fig. 34) owe their origins to this time.

The story of this gradual colonisation, it has been suggested, began with the annual droving in summer months of sheep, swine and cattle into the heavily wooded downland region, taking advantage of the existing natural and former clearings of earlier generations of drovers, and gradually enlarging them through a process of piecemeal clearance. The browsing and grazing action of livestock helped to ensure that regrowth from cut vegetation was kept in check. As population levels gradually increased in the principal settlements and the associated growing demand for new land, these temporary summer grazing sites in the Downs began to develop into permanent farmsteads as herdsmen returned year after year, perhaps providing an ideal opportunity for the sons and generations of younger colonists keen to strike out from the family homesteads of the main settlements and make a living from the relative security of stock farming.[1] It is this period of gradual piecemeal colonisation perhaps spanning five or six centuries between AD 600 and 1300 and embracing the ebb and flow of Jutish, Anglo-Saxon and post-Conquest society that has set the template of the current day downland settlement pattern, a countryside littered with small hamlets, isolated farmsteads and churches.

Everitt (1986) draws particular attention to the dispersed nature of the settlement pattern in the Downs, characterised by these small hamlets and farmsteads many of which lie on parish boundaries. As the gradual irregular piecemeal clearance of woodland (known as 'assarting') for grazing pasture advanced in the Anglo-Saxon period, the remaining un-appropriated tracts of land would have conveniently acted as both boundary lands and a shared grazing resource (**commons and minnises**) for the neighbouring farmsteads. These areas later became attractive to successive waves of colonisers who, in turn, set up seasonal or 'summer shielings' on these lands, which then gradually evolved into permanent farmsteads and acted as convenient boundary markers. Among the several lines of evidence that Everitt uses to substantiate this theory is the nature of the place names of these boundary farmsteads and hamlets. Many contain elements that reflect an origin in woodland colonisation or pastoral usage. The boundary of Elham parish for example is marked by a number of settlements

Fig. 29 Hamlets such as Wheelbarrow Town lying on the Elham and Stelling Minnis parish boundary may have originated as seasonal grazing lands that later became permanently settled and acted as boundary markers for neighbouring settlements.

and hamlets many of which contain elements in their place names which suggest that they originated from the clearance of woodland. On the Lyminge border to the south lies Rhodes Minnis containing the element 'rod' meaning a 'clearing' or 'assart'. To the north, on the Acrise border, lies Ladwood, containing the element 'wudu' meaning a 'wood', while to the west on the Stelling Minnis border lies the hamlet of Wheelbarrow Town (Fig. 29) containing the element 'wald' meaning a 'wood' or 'forest'.

Importantly, it appears that as these settlements and farmsteads became established their dependency and ecclesiastical attachments to the original principal estate centres were lost, and so led to the development of an independent community made up of a number of relatively small private landowners and tenants. This differed substantially from the more populated lands of the estate centres where land remained largely within the ownership of the church and society relied upon a shared and communal use of resources. Each downland parish thus evolved more as a loose collection of independently functioning farmsteads.

Through this process of colonisation and partitioning of land, the detail and fabric of the downland landscape began to take shape: a fragmented wooded landscape, dotted with a loose collection of farmsteads and minor hamlets, which now form the boundaries and parish centres of the modern day landscape. This supported a stock-based economy of many small-scale farms who operated largely independently although with the benefit of a shared outlying grazing resource of commons and 'minnises' for pigs, sheep and cattle.

– PLACE NAMES –

Fig. 30 Place names of the Downs.

Paddlesworth, Stowting, Acrise, Postling, the odd outlandish names of these inland villages acquired for me each its own special and private magic.

Jocelyn Brooke, *The Dog at Clambercrown* (1955)

Place names provide a valuable insight into the origins and evolution of modern day settlements. While corruption of many place names has occurred over the passage of time, most names can be traced back to their original old English derivation and meaning.

The preponderance of names believed to be associated with stock farming reveals the extent to which the downland area served to support a pastoral farming system. One of the more common elements of place names in the Kent Downs is the suffix 'stead', believed to derive from the Old English for 'stock farm'. The elements 'tye', 'lees', 'minnis', 'sole', 'swan' and 'den' are also indicative of pastoral origins and feature within the names of many downland settlements. Everitt (1986) identifies over 1,000 place names of this type. The element 'swan' and 'den' in the east Kent area, for example, between Lydden, Swingfield and Alkham may reflect the primary use of this area for swine pastures by the Jutish estates of north-east Kent which, owing to their geographical position, were more restricted in their share of the Wealden dens.[2]

Whilst many of these early settlements were of pre-Conquest origin, later centuries witnessed the continued evolution of the settlement pattern as population levels increased and new farmsteads, hamlets and villages sprang up and developed. Some names derived from the owner or occupier of a place such as at Dreal's Place near Elham and Digge's Place near Barham. Others appear to have a French derivation and probably originated in the Anglo-Norman period such as at Grandacre near Waltham and Fredville near Nonington. The numerous place names comprising the element 'lees' or 'minnis' probably originated as squatters' communities that arose on shared common and pastures at a time of rising population pressure.

Fig. 31

Other more fanciful names such as Kettlebender and the now abandoned Filchborough, near Sole Street, are not first recorded until the eighteenth and nineteenth centuries and are clearly indicative of more recent foundations.[3]

GAVELKIND AND ENCLOSURE

An important driving force in the fragmentation and enclosure of the landscape was the ancient Kentish custom of land inheritance known as 'Gavelkind'. This custom was based on the principle of 'partible inheritance' in which, on the death of a landholder, property was divided between all sons or daughters as opposed to being allotted to a single eldest heir. The nature of this system of land tenure inevitably resulted in a partitioned and parcelled landscape and field pattern with each successive sub-division of land producing a multiplicity of small holdings. In the Downs the effect of this partitioning was perhaps more widely felt in those areas of higher population density. Where lighter soils supported more profitable farming and competition for land was more intense, the inevitable result of successive partitioning sometimes led to holdings becoming too small to be an economically viable unit and consequently lands were sometimes 'disgavelled' (re-amalgamated). In 1276 at Cobham, land was disgavelled on the grounds that excessive partitioning had reduced holdings below subsistence size.

Conversely, the generally lower population densities associated with the clay-capped tablelands of the Downs probably limited the extent of partitioning and excessive sub-division of farmsteads in these areas was less commonplace. Documents of the thirteenth and fifteenth centuries indicate that settlement in the Manor of Wrotham, for example, was largely concentrated around the church with relatively few farmsteads on the heavily wooded clay-with-flints above the escarpment.[4]

The partitioning of holdings was also tempered to some extent by the effect of other local customs. The ability of land to be farmed jointly by co-heirs or brothers, coupled with the option for co-heirs to lease, exchange or sell land to a partner or to an outsider allowed the consolidation and expansion of units of land into profitable and workable family holdings.[5]

Another probable factor that encouraged the early enclosure of the downland countryside lay in the more independent nature of the pastoral farming enterprise within the county. Livestock-based farming practices naturally discouraged the adoption of open-field farming, a system which elsewhere in the country was dependent upon a shared, 'unenclosed' communal resource. Normally, open-field farming relied upon a fixed crop rotation so that strips of land belonging to different owners could be grazed during winter months. The abundance of wastes and commons within the downland region, however, may have provided sufficient areas of common grazing land to reduce the need for communal grazing of arable fields in the winter months. Where open-field farming did occur there is little evidence to suggest that fixed crop rotations were adopted and this, it has been suggested, may reflect the much more independent nature of farming in Kent which was based on a system whereby each owner retained full control of his strips and was therefore more able to effect enclosure.[6]

THE MEDIEVAL AND TUDOR PERIODS

To some degree, the rising population levels that marked the twelfth and thirteenth centuries, together with the increasing partitioning of the landscape in the more populated river valley and coastal plains, may have contributed to the continued colonisation of marginal areas of the county such as the Downs. As pressure and space for land continued to grow, the hinterland regions of the Downs continued to provide the opportunity for the young generations of farmers to start afresh in a new abode or outlying part of an estate. The frequency of place names in the Downs with the element 'boi' or 'cild', meaning a 'boy', 'young man' or 'servant', perhaps suggests that the downland provided a foothold for the younger sons to establish themselves as stock farmers, while the elder sons may have remained on the parental farm. Examples include the hamlet of Boyke near Elham, Boyington Court near Swingfield and Chilton near Alkham.[7]

It is this later medieval period, when population levels were increasing dramatically throughout the county, that may have also witnessed a further extension of settlement onto the previously uninhabited areas of common grazing land. Everitt (1986) draws attention to a number of settlements that contain the pastoral elements of 'minnis', 'lees' and 'tye'. It is possible that these settlements originated within the tracts of common and rough pasture utilised by distant settlements, but that became settled as squatters' communities at a time of rising population. Boughton Lees, Olantigh, Ewell Minnis and Stelling Minnis are examples of settlements that grew up on these **commons and minnises**.

For the stock farmers of the Downs, the livestock and timber-based economy provided an increasingly valued resource for an expanding medieval population. The seasonal wood pastures that had formed the mainstay of the early colonisation template became more attractive for the standing timber and underwood resource for building work and woodfuel, while areas of pasture that were considered fit for the plough were given over to cropped land, often greatly improved with a generous and regular dressing of chalk. It was this period that marked considerable activity in the digging and use of **deneholes** throughout the Downs which were used for the extraction of chalk, an important commodity in the downland farmer's armoury of techniques for enhancing the condition and workability of the heavy clay soils. The impact of the growing population and increasing number of mouths to feed was felt not only on the land. Overcrowding in Petham church was such that it was rebuilt in the thirteenth century to accommodate the growing population (Fig. 32).

When the catastrophic Black Death ravaged the country in the mid-fourteenth century, the villages and hamlets of the Downs may have fared better than the

Fig. 32 All Saints church at Petham was rebuilt in the thirteenth century to accommodate a larger congregation associated with population growth in the medieval period.

overcrowded towns and cities of the county, yet when the plague did arrive in these sparsely populated hinterlands the impact of depopulation and abandonment must have been felt for some considerable time. Evidence of the abandonment of villages at this time is often difficult to detect, although traces of former settlements as at Bredhurst near St Peter's church, half a mile or so away from the current day village, may be contemporary with this period. The eighteenth-century historian Edward Hasted refers to this settlement as Bredhurst Town and it is evident from excavations that building foundations and pottery dated to the fourteenth century indicates that the site was in use up until late medieval times, but then appears to have been abandoned. Langridge's study of population levels in the village of Chartham, near Canterbury, during the medieval period suggests that the recovery of population levels here, following the catastrophic outbreaks of the mid-fourteenth century, may well have been hindered by emigration, and perhaps increased mortality among children and young adults in later outbreaks. Of the seventy-three families that survived the Black Death, fifty-nine had disappeared by the early fifteenth century to be replaced with new families, although many of these in turn failed to survive for more than twenty years.[8]

Over the following centuries further sporadic outbreaks of the plague, coupled with the attendant hardships of ekeing a living from the poor marginal soils of the Downs, acted as a continual check on population levels and it is likely that most villages witnessed periods of population loss and recovery. An example of the recurrence of plague events and their impact on village populations in later centuries can be found in the burial records for the parish of Lydden. A note in the margin of the burial register for the year 1543 records, 'In this year 1543 plague was in Lydde(n) and most in the parish died of it'.

The register continues with a long list of the village inhabitants who were the unlucky victims of this virulent outbreak, the protracted effects of which appear to have lasted for a full two years until the year 1547 is reached when the register note records: 'In the year 1547 none buried.'[9]

The impact of these cycles of population change on the land would have been reflected in a continually shifting pattern of abandonment of land to scrub and woodland during hard times and conversely, reclamation of land to arable when times were good (see Chapter 7). Yet against the ever-shifting mosaic of woodland, grass and arable the basic template of field and farmstead remained. The enclosed field pattern had already been in place by Tudor times and as the custom of disposing of land by will became increasingly popular, the further partitioning of holdings through gavelkind became less commonplace.

By the seventeenth century, the only areas of the county that lay 'unenclosed' were situated in east Kent and on the Hoo peninsula, Edward Hasted describing it as 'open champaign' country. The downland region thus continued to provide the natural dividing land between the small-field landscape of the Wealden pastures to the south and the larger, open, arable field pattern of the North Kent Plain. Seventeenth-century estate maps show that fields to the north of the Downs were generally twice as large as those in the Weald.

THE EIGHTEENTH AND NINETEENTH CENTURIES

The legacy of the enclosed and partitioned field pattern of the Downs was still strikingly apparent by the time that the agricultural commentator William Marshall undertook his tour of the region at the end of the eighteenth century. He noted that 'the greater part of the hills, under view, are inclosed', although it is evident that this pattern of enclosure was particularly prevalent on 'the parts which are covered with strong clayey soil'. This template of enclosed land was broken here and there by the remaining areas of unenclosed commons and wastes and, on the steeper slopes, areas of open downland, 'especially on the sides and lower parts of the hills; where the soil is of a loamy, chalky nature'.[10]

At the field scale, changing agricultural patterns and fashions of the successive centuries continued to shape the local landscape of the Downs. 'Disparking' of earlier **medieval parkland** and gradual enclosure of the commons and wastes had allowed further phases of piecemeal enclosure throughout Tudor times, yet by the eighteenth and nineteenth centuries the new fashion of **designed parklands** provided wealthy landowners with the opportunity to do away with hedge boundaries and small fields in order to open up commanding vistas across the landscape. The eighteenth century also witnessed a period of expansion into different crops and land uses as the advances and innovations of the seventeenth-century agricultural revolution filtered through into the farms and small-holdings of the Downs. The area of land devoted to orchards and hops increased particularly in the more sheltered dipslope valleys, while crops such as turnips and sainfoin became increasingly popular within the arable landscape, providing a valuable rest or 'break' crop in the four-course arable rotation.

Towards the end of the eighteenth century the steady advance of arable farming that was making inroads into the grasslands and woodlands of the hinterland of the Downs was soon to be given a new surge of life as the effects of an unprecedented period of population growth and the knock-on economic pressures of the Napoleonic War took their toll. The rapid growth in the population rate that characterised the middle of the eighteenth century continued through to the mid-nineteenth century, perpetuated notably by lower death rates associated with the advances in medical science and practice. The county's town and cities may have borne the brunt of the ever-increasing demand for new housing, yet even in the remote areas of the Downs, villages and farmsteads witnessed a period of settlement expansion as new and rebuilt brick and flint cottages sprang up to accommodate farm workers and labourers and an increasing rural population. Brick cottages often in groups of three and four were built particularly in the east of the county where the growth in hop and fruit farming necessitated a higher labour force.

The economic depression that followed the Napoleonic Wars continued well into the nineteenth century and witnessed a period of great upheaval within the rural communities of the Downs. Depression and poverty formed the background to a series of agricultural revolts, known as the 'Swing Riots' (see Chapter 4), and many were forced to move to the towns and cities or emigrate in order to find work. Villages in east Kent were particularly affected and many experienced population declines that lingered on well into the twentieth century (Fig. 33).

	Waltham	Frinsted	Lydden
1801	383	153	103
1841	544	202	248
1881	506	208	203
1921	313	150	210

Fig. 33 Populations declined in many downland parishes throughout the late nineteenth and early twentieth centuries when the effects of agricultural depression and mechanisation of farm practices forced many to seek employment in towns or emigrate overseas.

THE TWENTIETH CENTURY

The last century has seen unprecedented changes in the scale and pace of development in the English countryside. In many areas the piecemeal expansion of settlements through house-building and infrastructure has witnessed the complete transformation of villages and hamlets that would have perhaps been unimaginable two centuries ago. Added to this has been the widespread changes in the nature of land use and field patterns that have come about from the post-war agricultural drive towards increased yields and efficiency.Yet against this backdrop of change the villages and countryside of the Kent Downs have remained relatively unscathed by the pace of development; many of its villages have undoubtedly grown in size and population, yet most still retain the heart and feel of a small rural community that has persisted for centuries; many of its hamlets remain as they have stood for centuries as simply a cluster of farmsteads and cottages. Much of its countryside too is equally intact. Land use and field boundaries may have altered dramatically in some districts yet by and large such alterations are localised and the character of field pattern, and woodland is remarkably well-preserved, 'the debris of historic times scattered all among the little hollows, everywhere'.[11]

– DROVEWAYS AND HOLLOWAYS –

An hours riding had brought them among the woods of Acryse; and they were about to descend one of those green and leafy lanes, rendered by matted and overarching branches alike impervious to shower or sunbeam ...

Revd R.H. Barham, 'The Leech of Folkestone' from *The Ingoldsby Legends* (1891)

Fig. 34 Holloway near Alkham.

The network of sunken, narrow leafy lanes, sometimes termed 'holloways', that weave and twist through the hinterland areas of the downland countryside, are an enchanting feature of this landscape. Many owe their existence to the centuries-worn passage of man and livestock, serving to connect farmsteads, villages and markets, often running 'cornice-wise' along banks and hill sides or 'thread-like' through valley bottoms and coombes. Those that climb or plunge down through deep and dense woodlands afford scant and rare glimpses of the countryside beyond, enfolding the traveller within their high-banked and shady hollows. Occasionally, on reaching the summit of a hill one is rewarded with an open prospect, yet such opportunities are all too often abruptly curtailed as before long one is once again plunged into another steep tree-shrouded tortuous descent.

Most of these single-track carriageways evolved to accommodate the everyday traffic of carts, horses and oxen yet it is evident that negotiation of these lanes has always been fraught with danger. In a discourse on the agriculture of the district in the late eighteenth century, William Marshall made particular mention of the customs contrived to minimise the hazard of collisions:

> ... the village roads, since I first knew these hills, were mere wagon tracks through woods, narrow lanes and hollow ways; with few places in which even two carts could pass each other ... Hence, the probable origin of 'Bell teams'. A constant alarm was necessary ... where, by loading the horses with bells, the teams in motion provided a continual source of ringing, 'to apprize the respective drivers of each other's approach.'[12]

Everitt's (1986) study of the development of the agrarian landscape of Kent draws particular attention to the origin of these holloways, many of which are believed to date back to the early medieval tradition of the seasonal herding of livestock to and from distant foraging areas. The outlying woodlands and pasture lands located in the Wealden districts of Kent and East Sussex once provided a valuable resource for the summer fattening of pigs as well as for the supply of timber. With most of the primary settlements located in the north Kent plains and river valleys, the routeways and droveways that developed were aligned on a north-east to south-west pattern, running across the North Downs and into the lowlands of the Weald beyond. It is possible that some of these droveways may actually be of a far greater age, particularly those that cut directly across the ancient prehistoric trackway that runs along the foot of the Downs.

The distinctive alignment of these lanes is still strikingly apparent within the modern day road network and often makes travelling east to west across the Downs a troublesome affair. Throughout the districts of Charing and Lenham the pattern of lanes, footpaths and byways bears testament to the importance of these former droveways, many of which can be traced in their entirety from north to south across the broad back of the Downs and into the Wealden countryside.

For many, the quiet lanes and holloways have come to symbolise the sense of intimacy and peacefulness of this landscape. For the early twentieth-century writer Ford Madox Hueffer, these lanes embodied the antiquity of the landscape, poetically expressed by him as an:

> ... index of the ancientness of the forgotten countryside ... Never been altered from their course which they took in times when the dale-dwellers cared nothing for their steepness: have been worn deeper and deeper into the hillsides, will go on deeper and deeper and deeper for ever.[13]

Way-finding amongst this labyrinth of lanes is often naturally plagued with problems. The Kent author Richard Church, who spent much of his childhood exploring the remote downland country around Bromley, recalls the:

> ... desolate stretch of plateau country ... netted over with a reticulation of these small lanes, and we never quite succeeded in mapping them out to our satisfaction. I doubt if we should have been satisfied had we done so, for the savour was in the exciting confusion with which week after week, we explored one or another of them, coming out from time to time suddenly upon a bit which we recognised with a shout.[14]

MOUNTING BLOCKS

Lost amongst the undergrowth of some of these lanes one can occasionally happen upon a roadside structure that would have once been a familiar sight on the tracks and roads of the county. In times past, when horseback provided the popular means of travel, blocks of stone and brick were built at suitable points along highways and byways to assist the packman or traveller to mount and dismount at will. Many of these mounting blocks have long since disappeared from our roadsides yet alongside a few of the quiet lanes and tracks of the Kent Downs one can still stumble upon a long-forgotten block (Fig. 35).

Fig. 35 Mounting block at Torry Hill, Frinsted.

Many were naturally positioned at the foot or top of a steep incline. One of the most familiar of mounting blocks for many years to riders ascending the scarp slope above Boxley was the local landmark known as 'The Jostling Stone'. This mounting block dating to 1609 was provided for riders who faced the long trudge up Boxley Hill. It once carried an inscription which read:

Here was I set
With Labour
Great – Judg as
You please, T'was
For your ease-1609

THE FLORA OF WAYSIDES

Many of the wayside banks and verges that line the lanes and holloways are home to a wealth of plant life. Taller grassland flowers such as greater knapweed (*Centaurea scabiosa*), field scabious (*Knautia arvensis*) and oxeye daisy (*Chrysanthemum leucanthemum*) (Fig. 36) still thrive on many of these banks. Here too can occasionally be found agrimony (*Agrimonia eupatoria*), once valued as an important medicinal plant and also used for dressing leather in former times.

A relative of the cultivated variety, wild marjoram (*Origanum vulgare*) often grows in abundance on these waysides (colour plate 24). Its aromatic sweet-scented flowers provide a nectar source for many of our downland butterflies and in former times they were used to produce a dye and a herb tea infusion.

Today these wayside grassland communities often provide the only surviving relics of extensive areas of flower-rich grassland that once existed in the surrounding pastures and meadows. Untouched by the changes and disturbance in the wider countryside, many of these wayside verges have been afforded special recognition as 'Roadside Nature Reserves' and are specifically managed to protect and benefit the wild flowers that live on them.

Fig. 36 Ox-eye daisies on a Roadside Nature Reserve at Lydden near Dover.

The variety of hedgerow plants and shrubs that line the lanes and byways bear testament to the age and antiquity of some of these lanes (colour plates 7–10). Some shrubs such as the wayfaring tree (*Viburnum lantana*), named the 'wayfarer's tree' by the sixteenth- century herbalist John Gerard because of its familiarity to him on the old roads and tracks of the Downs, are chalk 'specialists' confined to the downland countryside and, being calcareous soil loving plants, are seldom found elsewhere in the county. Its conspicuous umbrella of creamy white flowers is a common sight in early May. Rosehips, once locally known as 'Canker-berrys', are the fruit of the dog rose (*Rosa canina*) and field rose (*Rosa arvensis*) and adorn many of these waysides in autumn months.

Jostling for space in the thick bushy hedgerows that line many of the lanes, the spindle tree (*Euonymus europaeus)* is a spectacular sight in the autumnal months when its clusters of pinkish-red coloured seeds stand in stark contrast to the greens and browns of autumnal foliage. In Kent this plant was also known in former times as the 'Gatteridge Tree'.[16]

Perhaps one of the more familiar hedgerow plants, the hazel (*Corylus avellana*) has long been valued for its versatility for a range of everyday uses. Its strong, yet supple straight growth, that responds well to regular coppicing, has given it an advantage over other woods for hurdle-making, wattle, basket-weaving and thatch pegging. Traditionally the nuts have always been prized as a high source of protein for man and are equally sought after by a host of other creatures such as squirrels, dormice, bank voles and wood mice.

Many of these hedgerows are adorned with climbers such as black bryony (*Tamus communis*), honeysuckle (*Lonicera periclymenum*) and traveller's joy (*Clematis vitalba*). Traveller's Joy or 'woodbine' is a chalk-loving plant and familiar to many with its rope-like stems which festoon hedgerows and copses. The cluster of white flowers appear in May and June and are followed in autumn by the long feathery awns which, unsurprisingly, are responsible for its other familiar name of 'old mans beard'. In times past the tough green stalks were used by farmers to fasten gates and hurdles together.

– COMMONS AND MINNISES –

The hills here on each side very high and mountainous, and the vales between them very deep and hollow; the hills are almost wholly unenclosed, some of them arable and the others covered with greensward, having furzes and broom interspersed on them at different intervals. These stupendous hills, in comparison of what the traveller has been used to in his journey hither, raise both his pleasure and admiration, the prospects on both sides being beautifully romantic and singular.

Edward Hasted, *The History and Topographical Survey of the County of Kent* (1797-1801)

The landscape of the Kent Downs is widely appreciated for its flower-rich chalk grasslands yet for centuries these grasslands formed but just one part of a mosaic of traditionally managed grazing areas, many of which lay on the higher clay-capped uplands of the Downs. These areas of rough grazing once formed large tracts of waste and common land and are believed to date back to the Saxon and the early medieval period. Everitt (1986) suggests that they originated as 'boundary' lands, which provided a shared grazing area between neighbouring settlements. In the East Kent Downs these areas were commonly referred to as 'minnises'. The word 'minnis' is believed to derive from the Saxon word '(ge)maennes' meaning 'common land used as pasture.' Swingfield Minnis, for example, may well have formed an area of common pasture for the surrounding settlements of Alkham, Lydden, Wootton and Hawkinge. Over time some of these commons and minnisses came to support temporary squatters' communities which later developed into more permanent settlements.[17]

Situated on the upland clay and sand soils of the Downs, these areas traditionally supported a mosaic of plant communities characteristic of neutral and acidic soil conditions. Areas of open grassland probably existed in an ever-changing mosaic of heath and woodland. Lying on impoverished soils, these tracts of land had little agricultural value but nonetheless provided a much needed resource for the poorer rural inhabitants who depended upon their common rights to eke a living from these areas. These 'commoners' enjoyed a number of privileges that allowed them to graze livestock, collect firewood, forage for plants and to collect bedding and material to roof their houses.

Fig. 37 Rough grassland dotted with gorse and bracken at Ewell Minnis near Dover bears testament to the common that once covered a large tract of this area in times past.

As the 'ownership' of these commons gradually became absorbed into the manorial estates, the rights of the 'commoners' became more and more restricted. On Swingfield Minnis, for example, in the 1630s all commoners' livestock were to be branded, and the owners of any hogs and geese found on the Minnis were to be fined one farthing each. Naturally, for the landlords and wealthier farmers, keen to embrace agricultural reform, these commons represented little more than areas of 'waste' in dire need of improvement. The agricultural commentator John Boys writing in the eighteenth century described the waste lands and impoverished commons of Stowting Common, Swingfield and Stelling Minnis as, 'overdue for enclosure ... Our commons for livestock are generally much covered with furze, thorns and brakes, or heath with a mixture of plots of poor grassland; the cattle and sheep feeding on them are of course in a half-starved state'.[18]

Piecemeal incursion and reclamation of these commons by landlords and by the commoners themselves gradually reduced the extent of these areas over the centuries, often much to the disgruntlement of the more needy commoners. These incursions often took the form of 'casting up a dyke' (bank), and planting a hedge along the top and so making an enclosure. Local disputes and conflicts of interests occasionally led to local uprisings such as in 1548 when the commoners of Kent took the law into their own hands in an effort to stem the tide of enclosure and agrarian change.

Finally in the nineteenth century the introduction of the Parliamentary Enclosure Act provided the legal instrument to seal the fate of the few remaining unenclosed tracts. Within a space of thirty years the minnises and commons of Kent one by one succumbed to enclosure until, in 1848, only part of Rhodes Minnis and Stelling Minnis in east Kent were the last to remain. The year 1840 witnessed the enclosure of Swingfield Minnis, The Revd Barham, author of *The Ingoldsby Legends*, recording the event in a letter to his publisher, 'We have been rather busy of late carrying into execution the enclosure of Swingfield Minnis under the auspices of my Lord Radnor'.[19] Interestingly, as the heath and grasslands of this Minnis were broken into for cultivation for the first time, a great quantity of human bones were brought to the surface, local legend stating that these were believed to be the remains of some long-forgotten battle.

Fig. 38 Grazing has been reintroduced on Stelling Minnis in recent years to help conserve the unique heathland and acid grassland habitats. Hardy breeds such as Soay sheep are better adapted to grazing the coarser vegetation associated with these habitats.

Fig. 39 Harebell.

Today, all traces of these minnises and commons have disappeared, and only place names bear testimony to the former existence of these once common features of the downland countryside. Stelling Minnis in east Kent is an exception and remains the last unenclosed downland common, representing an unaltered relic of the medieval manors. Grazing of Stelling Minnis ceased in the 1950s and since then the common has changed much in appearance. Shrubs and trees that have grown up in the absence of grazing have gradually led to the demise of the former open character of this area. The once extensive tracts of heath and acid grassland have been reduced to a few relic areas, although practical conservation work in recent years has helped to preserve and secure a brighter future for these special wildlife habitats (Fig. 38). The minnis is particularly notable for its small population of western gorse (*Ulex gallii*) which is at its most easterly location here in southern England. Plants such as heath bedstraw (*Galium saxatile*), heather (ling) (*Calluna vulgaris*) and harebell (*Campanula rotundifolia*) can also be found here. The remnant areas of acid grassland provide a home for many invertebrates, notably twenty-two different species of butterfly[20] which include small heath, small copper and common blue, as well as a diverse range of beetles, dragonflies and moths.

– PARKLANDS AND WARRENS –

Traditional parklands are widespread throughout the Downs and contribute a distinctive thread to the rich fabric of the landscape. The characteristic parkland landscape of tree-dotted pastures provides a more formal dimension to the natural scenery of the downland that is elsewhere dominated by the irregular field and boundary patterns of an ancient countryside.

Abundant in trees and woodland, the Downs have always provided an attractive setting for the design and creation of parklands, a tradition that dates back many hundreds of years. Parklands are also extremely important in supporting one of the few remaining vestiges of 'wood pasture' habitat within the county. Characterised by the scattering of trees within a grazed pasture, this once widespread ancient habitat typically supports a unique assortment of insects and lichens associated with the mosaic of mature and veteran trees (Fig. 40) and grassland. It has undergone widespread decline in recent centuries as a result of changes in agricultural practices that have led to both the improvement (fertilising and re-seeding) of grasslands and to the neglect of old pastures (leading to the development of 'secondary' woodland).

Fig. 40 Veteran beech tree at Doddington Park.

THE AGE OF THE DEER PARK

The tradition of the earliest parks dates back to the post-Conquest period of the eleventh century and is rooted within the Normans' interest in deer farming. The introduction of the fallow deer at this time precipitated a dramatic upsurge in the popularity of parkland. These parks not only provided a functional role for the management of deer within the countryside, but also rapidly became a status symbol for the privileged and landed gentry. The characteristic feature of these estates was the boundary or 'park pale', an elaborate earth bank and ditch system, which was topped with cut branches (known as 'deadhedging') or hurdles to prevent deer escaping. Many small parks were formed by 'emparking' the whole of an existing wood.

Throughout the twelfth, thirteenth and fourteenth centuries England witnessed a dramatic increase in deer parks and at the peak of its popularity at the turn of the fourteenth century it is estimated that around 3,200 parks existed throughout the country.[21] Endowed with an abundant woodland cover, the Kent Downs would have offered an attractive prospect for the class of privileged and landed gentry keen to incorporate a mosaic of wood and pasture within the confines of the park pale.

By the later Middle Ages it appears that these deer parks gradually waned in popularity and many gradually went out of use and were 'disparked'. Although new deer parks were established from time to time, the conversion of farmland to park was a costly affair. The topographer and historian William Lambarde, writing in his *Perambulation of Kent* (1571) remarks:

> Parks of fallow deer, and games of grey conyes, it maynteneth many, the one for pleasure and the other for profit as it may well appear by this, that within memoire almost the one halfe of the first sorte be disparked, and the number of warrenys continueth, if it do not increase dayly.

The precise identification, location and lifespan of these early parks is clouded not least by the lack of documentary evidence. Some may have been short-lived affairs perhaps spanning a century or so while others persisted for many centuries before being abandoned. Lambarde's accounts provide some of the earliest documentary clues of the location and details of some of these early parks. Many within the Downs such as Knole, Cobham, Stowting and Postling remained intact at the time of his writing. Others such as Wrotham, Elham, Westwell and Folkestone were less fortunate and had been 'disparked' by this time.[22]

Edward Hasted's parochial visitations, some two centuries later, allude to a number of these earlier parks, commenting for example on the old park at Stowting, 'long before it was disparked and laid open there were several urns found lying in a trough of stone'.[23] Today all surviving traces of this park have long since disappeared although it has been suggested that Cage Farm which lies to the north of the village bears testament to its origins as a 'caged' enclosure area for the high-leaping fallow deer when the rounding-up of herds was required.[24]

THE DESIGNED PARKLAND

While the fashion for deer parks had almost disappeared by Lambarde's time, the eighteenth and nineteenth centuries witnessed a revival in parkland interest. The functional role of the medieval deer-parkland was replaced by the fashion of a parkland landscape valued instead for its aesthetic qualities.

This new surge of interest witnessed both the adaptation of existing deer parks to the new style as well as the creation of a suite of new parklands throughout the Downs as a result of an increasing number of country seats and estates of the smaller gentry embracing the new fashion. In some cases, such as at Torry Hill near Frinsted, clusters of neighbouring farms were amalgamated under single ownership to provide the resource and space needed to effect the design. Inspired by landscape designers such as Humphry Repton and William Kent, the layout of these new parklands was kept very much in harmony with the character and elements of the vernacular landscape. Thinning and removal of the trees was complemented by new tree-planting in other locations, incorporating, wherever possible, the natural woodland features of the existing landscape to frame far-ranging and channelled vistas and provide the sweeping and graceful curves that were characteristic of the contemporary style.

Some were modelled on the style of the earlier medieval parks, reviving the tradition of deer grazing. Most, however, were often simply intended to accommodate the grazing of sheep and cattle, avoiding the fuss and attendant problems of deer husbandry. As the fashion gained momentum, parklands became widespread throughout the Downs such that by the end of the eighteenth century, older established parklands such as Eastwell near Ashford and Knole near Sevenoaks, were joined by Bifrons, Charlton, Broome, Barham, Bishopsbourne, Chilham, Godmersham and Evington to the east of the Stour and Cobham, Torry Hill, Belmont, Chevening, Doddington and Lees Court to the west.

Over time the layouts of these original parklands have been modified to greater and lesser degrees to reflect the changing fashions and the ideals and whims of successive owners, each keen to mould the landscape to their own personal taste. Features such as ice houses were added, new avenues were planted and pathways, roads and carriageways were realigned. Interpreting the modern day parkland landscape is thus very much like piecing together a jigsaw with each feature reflecting a particular phase of evolution.

Fig. 41 Carriage drive arch at Torry Hill.

Torry Hill near Frinsted is characteristic of the many parks that owe their origins to the eighteenth and nineteenth-century style of parkland embraced by the gentry of the Downs. Often these parklands show a distinct evolution from enclosed farmland, through to small pockets of ornamented agricultural land and then to a fully developed parkland. Originally the core of the parkland area at Torry Hill was an enclosed mixed farm-holding typical of the Downs. Gradual amalgamation of neighbouring holdings in the eighteenth century set the scene for the initial phase of Georgian improvements undertaken by Osbourne Tylden in which the original vernacular farmstead was remodelled to an elegant Georgian 'villa' surrounded by pleasure grounds and a short 'ha-ha'. Subsequent rebuilding of the villa by Thomas Pemberton in the early nineteenth century, complemented by the acquisition of additional land allowed the creation of the core parkland area. The existing woodland and tree cover that was encompassed within the park was modified through tree 'thinning' in some areas and augmentation in others to achieve a more even balance of woodland and wood pasture. Subsequent expansion and phases of modifications throughout the nineteenth and twentieth centuries have furnished the parkland with a tree-lined carriage-drive (Fig. 41), specimen trees and an ice house. In common with many other parklands the onset of the Second World War prompted the conversion of many acres of pasture to arable land in the drive for self-sufficiency. Restoration schemes in recent years have enabled many parks in the Downs to be reverted to their former splendour through the reversion of arable land back to pasture and the restoration of parkland features.

ICE HOUSES

Up until the advent of railway transport in the nineteenth century, most big houses relied on an ice house as the main method of cold storage for food and produce. Acquiring a particular popularity in the latter half of the eighteenth century, these features were usually associated with larger houses that required a ready supply of ice for the bulk preservation of meat. They often took the form of a large ovoid chamber, two thirds of which lay submerged below ground level. The chamber normally contained a number of floors upon which produce such as meat was stored in alternate layers of barley and broken ice. According to the British Cyclopedia of 1835, chalk was considered to be the best soil in which to sink an ice pit which, if well-constructed, would keep ice for two or three years: 'In putting in the ice it should be rammed close and a space left between it and the wall packed with straw to facilitate the drainage of any moisture occasioned by partial melting'.[25] To aid preservation the stored produce was then saturated with a solution of salt.

Ice houses were often located at some distance from the main house and were normally situated close to a lake or a pond from which fresh ice could be collected. The absence of surface water in the Downs meant that regular and adequate supplies of ice in winter months may have been difficult to acquire. At Stede Hill near Harrietsham it is believed that the ice house was deliberately sited on the scarp at the elevated height of the 600ft (180m) contour line, in order to be supplied with snow which regularly fell at this height in winter months.

With the advent of the railway, ice soon became a commodity that could be easily transported, so heralding the demise of the ice house. At Godmersham Park near Canterbury a recent restoration project of the ice house (Fig. 42) revealed that the household waste that was used to fill it at the time of its abandonment dated to the 1840s, which, interestingly, corresponds to the time when the Ashford-Canterbury railway line was constructed through the valley.[26]

WARRENS

The rabbit was first introduced into Britain in early medieval times. Valued for its meat and fur, the rabbit, or 'coney' as it was then known, soon became an important commercial animal and was bred and carefully tended in much the same way as domestic livestock is farmed today. Unlike the rabbit of today the medieval rabbit, a western Mediterranean animal, was ill-adapted to the English climate and required artificial burrows and earthworks to be dug in which it could breed. These specially constructed 'warrens' would have existed on many estates and holdings before the rabbit began to evolve into the burrowing animal we are familiar with today. Evidence of the importance of rabbit farming can still be traced in the Downs in the form of place and field names associated with these former warrens. Queendown Warren near Chatham, for example, now valued for its diverse array of chalk grassland plants, was first managed as a rabbit warren and once supplied rabbits to markets at London.

Fig. 42 Ice house at Godmersham Park.

– FIELD NAMES –

The patchwork field pattern of the downland countryside provides one of its most distinctive and cherished features. The small irregular fields, which jostle for space in a countryside crowded with the detail of hedgerows, shaves, copses, woods and spinneys, have changed little over the centuries and provide a fascinating insight into the past and lives of the generations of families associated with these places (colour plate 1). Within the hollows, chalk pits, banks and ridges of these fields lie the stories and memories of the people who lived and worked in this countryside. These visible traces, left by the continuous succession of many generations, provide valuable clues for the landscape historian in piecing together the story of the landscape. Equally revealing is the rich cultural heritage associated with field and place names. In an age when people's lives revolved around the villages they lived and worked in, the local detail of field and place names provided the familiar reference points for the whole community. The world seen by most people was at most twenty or thirty miles across, where meadows became parishes and parishes became counties, and features such as old trees and chalk pits became intimately known. Shared folk memories, oral histories and legends, passed on from one generation to another, perpetuated the sense of cultural attachment to each field, bank and wood within the parish.

Over the centuries some field names were gradually corrupted and have perhaps lost their original meaning, while others were, in turn, re-named to reflect a new relationship and identity of a field perhaps with a new owner or a different land use. The Tithe Survey maps, produced in the 1840s, provide a valuable record of field names for each parish of the county. Many names originated simply to indicate the size of the field or position of the field within the farm. Field names typical of many downland parishes include 'Hither Field', 'Hither Ten acres', 'Further Ten acres' and 'Middle Ten acres'. The element 'Shott' or 'Shot' is frequently found within field names of the Downs and derives from the old English word 'sceat' which is believed to simply represent a division of land as is found at Temple Ewell in the field names of 'First shot', 'Second shot' and 'Third shot'.

Many field names are associated with the nature of the field's shape, topography and aspect. Field names such as 'Long Meadow', 'Bottom Ten acres', 'Broad field' and 'Sunny Hill' occur throughout the downland parish tithe maps. The shape of the field was variously expressed in names such as 'Pan Field' to indicate a field that sat in a round depression as in the parish of Temple Ewell. The name 'Gore' as in 'Gore Land' at Barham and 'Gore Field' at Bredgar is an old term used to describe a triangular remnant of land that was left after two field boundaries met at a sharp angle.

Throughout the downland parishes it is evident that many field names came into being to reflect the contemptuous nature of the poor impoverished soils. These were variously expressed in common field names such as 'Stony Field' and more obscure names such as 'The Clouts' in Alkham, which may derive form the old Kentish dialect word 'clout' meaning a 'clod' or lump of earth in a field. The chalky nature of the soil in many fields gave rise to field names such as 'White Lands' in Ash near Meopham, and 'Silver Downs' at Bishopsbourne.

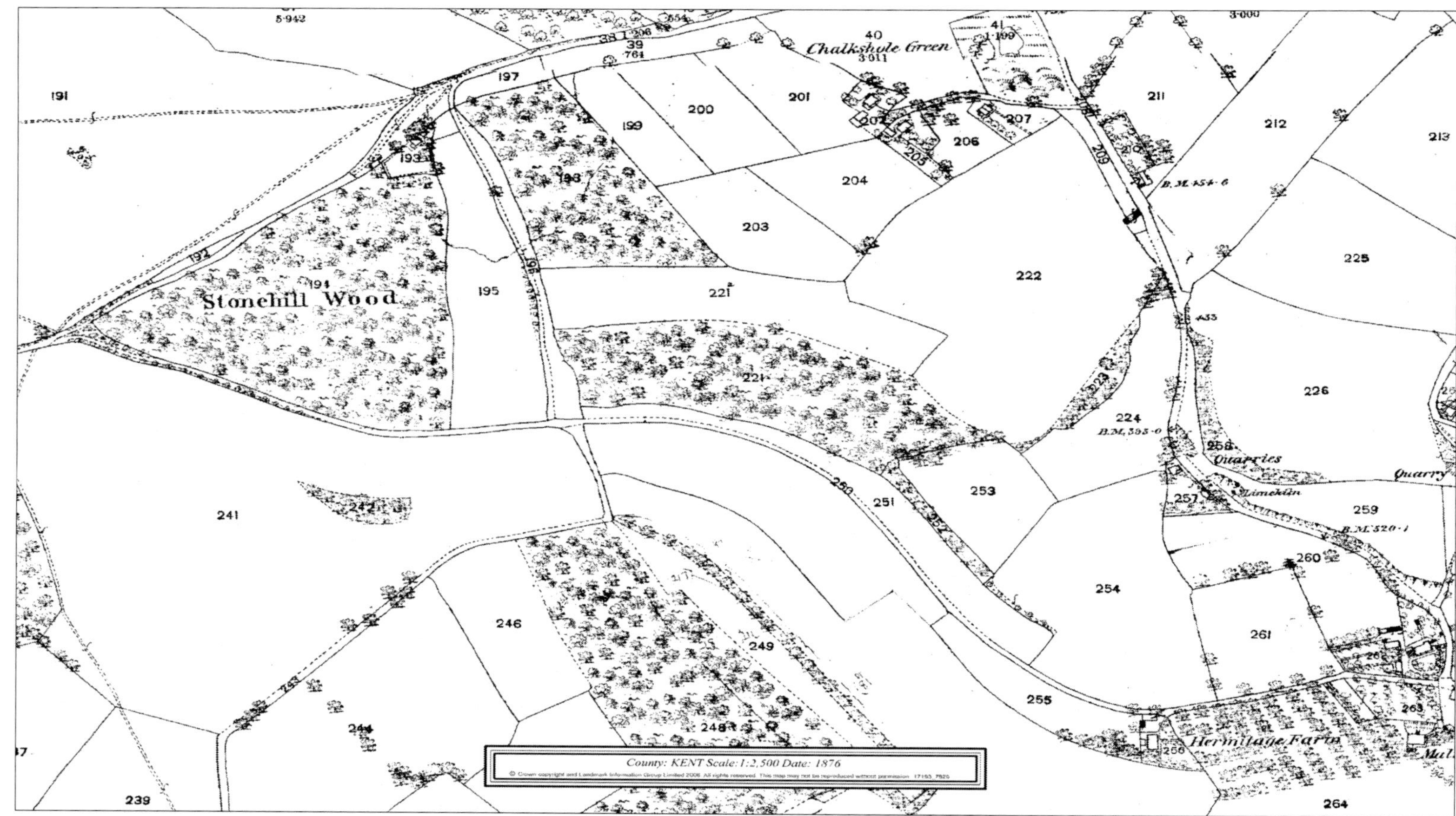

Fig. 43 The irregular and patchwork field pattern of the downland countryside provides an insight into the lives of the people who, in ages past, drew their livelihood from these hills. Extract of Alkham parish from OS County Series published 1876 © Crown copyright and Landmark Information Group Ltd (All rights reserved June 2007).

Often the despairing nature of the infertile soils was conveyed or described as a sense of hunger in field names such as 'Hunger Downs' in River. Similar variants with the prefix 'Starve' as in 'Starve Crow' and 'Starve-all' are common throughout the Downs. 'Starve Acre' appears in Bredgar, Burham, Meopham and Wrotham while 'Starve Crow' is found in Hollingbourne, West Kingsdown and Wrotham. 'Small Gain' as at Longfield and 'Small Profits' as at Acrise and Meopham have similar connotations. 'Bedlam' such as at Temple Ewell may well refer to land that only a madman would attempt to cultivate. 'Starving Sitlings' in Wrotham is a particularly evocative field name and, like 'Devil's Kitchen' in the same parish and 'Devil's Bowling Alley' in Shoreham may again represent land that was either notoriously poor crop-growing ground or land that was especially difficult to cultivate.

The use or function of a field also often came to be embodied within the field name. The popularity of crops such as sainfoin (Fig. 47), tares and lucerne grown within the Downs in times past is particularly revealing through many field names. 'Sainfoin Field' at Brabourne, 'Old Sainfoin Hill' at Buckland, 'Dover Sainfoin' in River and 'Lucerne Spot' in Swingfield all bear testament to the extent and importance of legume break-crops within the traditional four-course rotation of downland farming. The origin of field names such as 'Hop Garden', 'Ice House Bank', 'Chalk Hole Field', 'Kiln Field', 'Mill Field', and 'Saw-pit Field' is self evident. Many too are connected with the name of a former owner or occupier such as 'Cooper's Foin' in Lydden and 'Page's Field' in Barham.

Clues as to the former extent of common and waste land are also evident in field names such as 'Minnis Field' at Lydden and within names which are associated with gorse or 'furze', a common shrub of commons and unenclosed land (Fig. 44). 'Old Furze Field' at Charing and 'Furzes' at Cudham number among the many 'furze field' variants. Corruptions of the word 'Gost', the old English name for gorse, may also account for names such as 'Ghost Hill 'at Temple Ewell, rather than allude to any supernatural phenomena.

Many field names within the Downs are connected with the old Kentish dialect. Field names containing elements derived from the word 'Brack' such as 'Brake' or 'Brakey' refer to a 'tear' or a 'crack', in this case features that appear to 'slice' the land. 'Carvet' and 'Corvet' as well as 'Shave' and 'Shaw' frequently appear within field and wood names. 'Carvet' was a Kentish term used for a thick hedgerow often on a piece of land carved out of another. 'Shaw' and its corruption to 'Shave' were similarly used to describe a small copse or wood. 'Close' is also another old term commonly found as in 'Horse Close' and 'Stack Close' in Lydden. This normally referred to an enclosed yard or field often adjoining a farmstead.

Perhaps far more intriguing are the more obscure names that may relate to long-forgotten local folklore lost over the passage of centuries. 'Cats brain', as at Alkham, is a name which occurs with some regularity throughout the southern counties and has been found to often relate to fields that contain a soil-type of rough clays mixed with stones. One suggestion is that the name may have originated as a local name to describe the appearance of certain types of fossil found within the field.

Many parishes possess more fanciful field names that conjure up intriguing images. 'Catch me Jack' in Lydden and 'Rob Jack' in Barham perhaps suggest romantic or sinister associations yet their meaning may allude to the 'Jack-a-Lent' figure, once common in local tradition and folklore. This was a figure associated with the start of the forty-day period of Lent (Shrovetide) in which activities normally forbidden during Lent were practised as a means of confessing one's sins. In this case the figure, represented by a puppet or sometimes a living person, was pelted with heavy sticks and then burnt on Easter Sunday.[27]

Fig. 44 Gorse, once commonly known as 'furze', gives its name to many field names within the Downs.

FOUR

Fields, Folds and Furrows

Farming in the Downs

For a landscape so diverse in landform, soil type and aspect, the Kent Downs have always supported a rich heritage of mixed farming, typified by a seasonally changing patchwork of grassland and arable crops. Whilst the agricultural advances of the last fifty years have witnessed the demise of the farm practices and traditions of yesteryear, the diversity of enterprises and the mosaic of arable, grassland and fruit orchards remain an enduring part of the landscape today. Orchards, though fewer in number, are still a prominent feature of the northern fringes of the mid-Kent Downs dipslope, where the chalk is overlain by brickearths and well-drained gravels. Hop gardens (colour plate 11) too have witnessed a dramatic contraction within the last few decades, but a few still remain, notably in one or two of the sheltered valleys to the west of Canterbury. Far more widespread however is the patchwork field pattern of tilled land and grass that is perpetuated through the strong tradition of livestock and arable farming.

Unlike other areas of the county that have been blessed with light and easily-worked soils or fertile lush pastures, farming in the Downs has never been an easy or straightforward affair. Lack of surface water, steep gradients, and the impoverished and poor-yielding soils, have persistently thwarted the attempts and toils of man to eke a living on these hills. The lighter chalky soils of valley sides and bottoms may have been relatively easy-going for plough and harrow, yet their impoverished and flinty nature, coupled with the absence of surface water, offered little consolation. The early accounts of farming within the county from the agricultural commentators of the eighteenth and nineteenth centuries provide a fascinating insight into the difficulties faced by the downland farmer.

John Banister, a Horton Kirby farmer, whose *Synopsis of Husbandry* (1799) was published towards the end of the eighteenth century wrote of these downland soils:

> Though chalks may be numbered among the lighter kinds of soil, yet a much greater strength of horses is required in the tilling of them, than either of gravels or sands, not only on account of their hilly situation, the superior depth of mould, and of the large flints which are generally to be met with beneath the surfaces, but from the impenetrable quality of the understratum, which deadens the draft of the plough and causes it to work much heavier.

Clearing the fields of these flints and stones was a back-breaking task and became a routine part of the farming year for villagers young and old. The older generations recall that before the First World War, stone-picking was a routine task for children as soon as they were old enough to walk:

> There would be several families out there. You'd have a strip to do. We had a galvanised bucket to put the stones in … stones were tipped into a square yard frame and we were paid by the yard.[1]

Once a field had been cleared by these 'flint grubbers' the task of working the soil down to a fine tilth and seed bed was the next challenge. For those unfortunate to farm the heavy, sticky and intractable clay-with-flints soils of the high plateau lands of the Downs, these field cultivations were a particularly arduous affair. Here the ploughmen had to contend with 'clays by their nature so stiff and tenacious as not to be meliorated with by tillage or manure, bid defiance to the most skilful of husbandry and can never be brought to yield of sufficient quantity of earth to heal the seed, unless in a season the most propitious'.[2]

Prior to the introduction of mechanisation, multiple cultivations were often needed to break down these heavy-going soils to a state ready for seeding. This involved ploughing the ground two or three times before the sowing of the crop. Even when conditions were right to produce a relatively healthy crop, the slightly higher altitude of the downland districts, when combined with an exposed aspect to the elements, sometimes meant that crops were slower to ripen. Best known for his observations of farming practices that were published as a series of regional studies, the agricultural writer William Marshall (1745-1818) noted in his *Rural Economy of the Southern Counties* (1798) that in 1795 the harvesting of crops on the east Kent downland areas was a fortnight behind that of the Isle of Thanet.

Such obstacles to cultivation, however, did not necessarily mean that extensive areas of the Downs were given over to grassland. The wide tracts of sheep-grazed open downland, perhaps more commonly associated with other English chalklands, are few and far between on the Kent Downs and historically it appears that even these were never of any great extent and largely confined to the steeper banks of valley sides and the escarpment. Of these areas, the Wye, Brabourne, Chartham and Barham Downs probably numbered among the largest, perhaps originating as 'sheep

Fig. 45 Sheep on Wye Downs.

walks' from the days of the medieval manors. Today, most of these former extensive tracts of grassland have all but disappeared, their former existence preserved only in place names such as at Chartham Downs. Wye Downs, near Ashford, is an exception, its steeper banks too steep for plough and harrow, and as such has remained over the centuries one of the largest tracts of open downland within the county. At the latter end of the sixteenth century this area amounted to some ninety-one acres of sheep pasture 'in the demesne of Hampton near Brook', constituting the two largest enclosures on the chalk downs of Kent,[3] which, in general, could only boast a relatively small area of perennial sheep walk. Chalklin (1965) estimated that, in the seventeenth century, the areas of permanent pasture amounted to only about a third of the land under arable crops. It appears that, even then, sheep flocks of any size were still curiously rare on the Downs, in contrast to other areas of English chalkland such as the South Downs where the sheep-corn husbandry was supreme.

Instead, it is evident that the range of soil types encountered throughout the Kent Downs has always encouraged a farming system based on a far more mixed range of enterprises. Livestock farming has thus always gone hand in hand with a strong arable tradition, where sheep and cattle have formed an integral part of a crop rotation system based on cereals, root crops, legumes (peas, beans, and vetch) and fallows. The origins of this system of inter-dependent livestock and arable farming go back many centuries. The dramatic rise in population that characterised the twelfth and thirteenth centuries undoubtedly brought much of the marginal land of the downland region into cultivation at this time. More people simply meant more hungry mouths to feed. Crop growing during the medieval period became so profitable that large areas of pasture were converted into arable ground, whilst areas of woodland were cleared to make more land available for both grazing and crops. In order to enhance and sustain the fertility and condition of the soils the medieval farmer relied principally on the practice of grazing sheep on the cereal stubbles, tares and vetches so that the nutrients from their dung cold be returned back to the soil. In addition, legume crops also helped to add nitrogen organically to the soil.

Within the last few hundred years this system evolved to loosely follow the traditional 'Norfolk four-course rotation' although it is evident that such rotations practised in the Kent Downs were very rarely fixed and were adapted to each particular farm and soil type. Barley, wheat, followed by a fallow was a typical rotation on the lighter chalky soils while heavier clay soils often favoured a rotation of wheat, peas and a fallow. Traditionally wheat and barley were the popular cereal crops of this arable rotation system with barley more common in the east Kent area.[4] Chalklin (1965) calculated that these two crops amounted to 68 per cent of the total arable acreage between 1600 and 1620.

The traditional means of harvesting crops such as wheat, barley and oats was by hand, with sickles and long-handled scythes. A group of men and women would take on the role of 'reapers', cutting the corn about 8ins below the ear, and a second group would follow up with long-handled scythes cutting the long stubbles down to ground level. Some would act as 'binders', gathering the cut crop and binding it for drying, storage and threshing. Much of the grain fell to the ground and there would often be enough for peasants or 'gleaners' to gather and feed their families. Samuel Palmer's 'The Gleaning Field', of around 1833 (colour plate 15), set in the Darenth valley, records this long-forgotten tradition which was once an important part of life for the poorer inhabitants of the Kent Downs.

Faced with the adversities of unforgiving and impoverished soils, the downland farmer has long sought ways to overcome these difficulties through careful husbandry of soil and crop. Some of these practices were no doubt borne from the wave of innovations that swept the country under the agricultural revolution of the eighteenth century, yet for a district that had remained, by and large, remote from the intensive agricultural pressures of the county's more fertile lands, it is likely that the uptake and embracing of new practices in the Downs was a slow and piecemeal affair. Investment in machinery and changes in husbandry were costly undertakings and beyond the means for many cottagers, smallholders and tenant farmers. Instead, many simply relied on the tried and tested age-old traditions that had evolved to fare best with the unforgiving soils of the Downs. The plain and ordinary implements employed on these farms were symptomatic, in the words of William Marshall, of the 'torpid state in which agriculture has remained for a century or centuries past'.[5]

One of the earliest traditions of soil husbandry was the practice of spreading chalk on fields to improve the soil condition. First noted by the Roman historian Pliny, this practice was clearly in use for many hundreds of years, the legacy of which can still be seen today in the many **chalk pits**, **chalkwells** and **deneholes**, which form a distinctive part of the Kent Downs landscape. Agricultural commentators of the eighteenth and nineteenth centuries were well-acquainted with the beneficial effects of 'chalking' or 'marling' land, principally to aid the breakdown of heavy clay soils. Even, as W.M. Mathew (1993) suggests, that scientific knowledge had yet not advanced by this time to fully explain the chemical benefits that 'chalking' gave in reducing the acidity of soils, many agricultural commentators of the time were nevertheless still able to observe these effects. John Boys, a farmer from Betteshanger, near Deal, whose survey *A General View on the Agriculture of Kent* (1794) was written at the request of the Board of Agriculture, was evidently well-acquainted with this practice, noting that on the downland of Kent, 'chalk is used to great advantage as a manure on some wet stiff soils from 50 to 80 cart loads per acre … its beneficial effects are said to last 20 years'.

Another traditional means of increasing fertility of arable fields was the practice of keeping or 'folding' sheep on fallow land after harvest, so that nutrients could be added to the field in the form of dung. Often this was achieved with the use of a fodder crop, undersown into the stubble upon which the sheep fed. The nutrient-rich dung was then ploughed back into the soil in the spring to provide the fertility for the next crop. Usually sheep were folded by means of constructing an enclosure of wooden hurdles which could be moved around the fields through the seasons. William Marshall noted that:

> in folding, the ordinary calculation is three sheep to a hurdle. The hurdles of these hills vary of seven to nine feet, each sheep has a space of eighteen or nineteen square feet … I have measured on a fold for two hundred six-tooth Wiltshire wedders, which was pitched twenty-four yards by twenty; thus allowing twenty-two square feet to each sheep.[6]

John Boys estimated that 200 sheep would fold an acre in one week.

When grassland was being 'broken into' (ploughed) for the growing of crops, the practice of 'turf-burning' was employed by many as a means of enriching the soil. This method, also locally known as 'paring and burning', appears to have acquired popularity on many of the downland farms, John Banister observing in the eighteenth century that 'of all the improvements in cultivation of lands that have hitherto been made in Kent, this stands foremost … poor chalky downs, of scarcely any value in their original state, are by paring and burning made to produce good turnips and clover'.[7]

The practice involved firstly the removal of the turf, known as 'paring', by means of a beating-iron (an adze-type implement) or a breast-plough (a pointed shovel pushed by hand – see Fig. 46). Once the turf had been removed it was gathered into beehive-like heaps to dry and these were ignited to smoulder, leaving a pile of ashes which was then scattered or ploughed into the field. Field (1993) notes that evidence of the practice is often revealed in field names which may allude to one or both stages of the process. For example names such as 'Burnt Close' may often refer to a field that had been 'pared and burned'. In Kent the field name 'Denshare' which occurs on a number of downland parish tithe maps, such as at Alkham, is believed to be associated with 'paring and burning'. This name is thought to be a corruption of the word 'Devonshiring', another term for the 'paring and burning' practice which arose from the belief that the custom originated in Devon.

TURNIPS, TAR-GRASS AND TURN-WREST

The eighteenth century witnessed the revival and widespread uptake of the use of fodder crops and legumes as a form of 'break crop'. Whilst the growing of legumes as a means of enriching the soil with nitrogen was a practice that had been adopted since at least medieval times, the renewed interest in this practice was spurred on not least from the growing popularity of a range of new herbage and root crops that could incorporated within the traditional rotation. These crops were used as an integral component of the cereal crop rotation as a means of maintaining fertility, having the dual benefit of refreshing or 'cleaning' the land, as well as providing fodder for livestock. Within the Downs it is clear that a variety of crops were used for this purpose, ranging from 'herbage' leys (temporary crops) of clovers, sainfoin and tares, to root crops such as turnips, swedes, peas and beans. Turnips were, in all likelihood, a new idea borne from the agricultural revolution. They were rarely found in the county prior to 1700 yet by the mid-eighteenth century they had become a popular 'break' crop on the Downs, more prevalent on the lighter free-draining soils and serving as a valuable fodder crop for sheep in the winter season.

A wide variety of legumes, collectively known in Kent as 'tar-grass', were also grown as popular break crops. This family of plants which includes clovers and trefoils had the added value of fixing nitrogen into the soil. Tares were important for summer fodder, being either mown and fed in racks, or 'folded off' for grazing straight from the field. One particular legume which acquired much popularity in the latter half of the seventeenth century was sainfoin (Fig. 47), which was particularly well-suited to lighter, free-draining soils of the Downs. John Boys noted that, 'Sainfoin is the most valuable of all grasses cultivated in this county: and is much grown on the chalk-land of the eastern part ... the produce is sometimes very abundant'.[8] William Marshall similarly remarked on the popularity of this crop which was 'much more prevalent on this than on the other divisions of the chalk hills of the southern counties. It is grown even on the deeper clayey lands with success'.[9] Sainfoin was often sown with wheat and barley at Lent and with good management would yield as much as 60 cubic weight of hay an acre and last for ten or twelve years.[10] The Pre-Raphaelite artist John Samuel Raven captured the distinctive pink hue of this crop that would have once covered large swathes of the Kent Downs countryside in his 'Sainfoin in Bloom: View near Cobham in Kent' (1857) (colour plate 16).

Elsewhere, experimentation with other herbage crops evidently met with some success. Cinquefoil, for example, was a popular crop at Acrise, near Elham in the 1690s, while lucerne acquired a reputation in many other areas. By the end of seventeenth century, sainfoin, clover and trefoil were widespread throughout the Downs.

For grass crops, the commonly sown species were ryegrass and 'Kent Wild White' clover but other grasses such as timothy, fescue grasses and cocksfoot also produced good forage crops on the heavier clay soils.

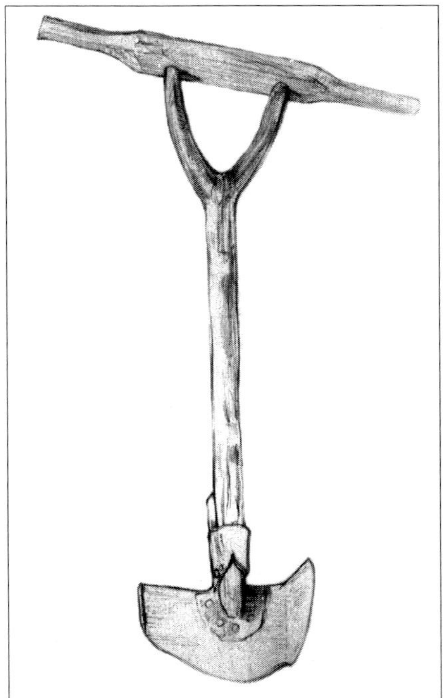

Above left: Fig. 46 Pencil drawing of a 'Breast Plough' used for manually paring turf, drawn by Kent Downs artist and writer Thomas Hennell, *c.*1930s. Taken from an original pencil drawing. Hennel's mentor A.S. Hartrick described the use of the breast plough as 'the hardest work I ever saw'.

Above right: Fig. 47 Legume crops such as sainfoin, grown here at Luddesdown Court Farm, once formed an important part of crop rotations and were ideally suited to the light chalky soils of the Kent Downs.

Once these break crop 'leys' had been grazed-off or mown, the task of ploughing began in earnest in order to prepare the seed bed for the following crop. For the unforgiving and tenacious clay soils of the Kent Downs, the 'turn-wrest' plough long occupied a special place in the downland farmer's armoury of implements (Fig. 48 and colour plate 13). Widely adopted throughout Kent, Surrey and Sussex, it is fitting that the birthplace of this distinctive plough is believed to lie within the scattered farms of the Kent Downs, where the flinty nature of soils and uneven steep-sided hills rendered conventional ploughs largely ineffectual. The most remarkable feature of this plough was its size and weight. With a main beam of oak some 10ft (3m) in length and a pair of wheels 'fully as large as the fore-wheels of a moorland wagon',[11] it was particularly suited for working the hillsides and difficult soils of the Downs. Unlike the fixed mouldboard style of plough used elsewhere, the 'wrest' of the 'turn-wrest' could be adjusted to lay the soil on either side. This enabled the ploughman to plough along one furrow and down the next, laying the soil flat rather than creating a single furrow which had the advantage on clay soils of preventing moisture loss. This differed from the conventional fixed mouldboard style which only allowed a ploughman to plough down a central ridge, giving rise to the distinctive ridge and furrow field pattern more characteristic of the Midland counties. Its sheer weight required as many as six horses to pull it yet it appears that occasionally even the most daring and ambitious farmers were prone to misjudgement and error, William Marshall recording that the plough was sometimes used on surfaces 'so extremely steep, that, on being overturned!, the plow, horses and the plowman, have been known to roll down, from the top to the bottom of the hill'.

Fig. 48 A Kentish Turn-wrest plough (in Brook Agricultural Museum).

THE NINETEENTH CENTURY

The changes of the agricultural revolution that filtered down through the eighteenth and nineteenth centuries began to witness a new period of restructuring on the downland farms. Dependency on the small-scale corn-sheep economy had always perpetuated a general trend of modest farm sizes. Yet, as the impact of the new technology associated with the advances in agriculture began to make their mark throughout the late eighteenth and nineteenth centuries, change was inevitable. Investment in the new agricultural machinery was desirable but beyond the means of many small farmers and thus land began to change hands as the smaller yeoman farmers, unable to afford the investment in new technology, sold off their land to the wealthier gentryman farmers. Between 1770 and 1885 Godmersham Park near Canterbury, for example, acquired large tracts of land in surrounding areas and these were occasionally redistributed amongst existing farms, with newly bought farmhouses being turned into tied cottages for farm workers. A similar sequence of events occurred in the countryside around Elmsted and Waltham, in the East Kent Downs, where homes and land were sold to the Evington estate. Once in the estates' ownership, the age-old tradition of family farms passing from one generation to another came to an abrupt end. This was replaced by a much less rigid system of land inheritance and occupation whereby farms were rented out to tenant farmers. This in turn heralded a period of greater mobility within the rural population, with farmers perhaps moving on from one farm to another every ten or twenty years.

For the small-holders and tenant farmers who managed to eke a living from the land, the economic hardships that were to set in following the Napoleonic Wars witnessed an unparalleled era of hardship and poverty. During this period, at the turn of the nineteenth century, the demand for local home-grown grain increased as imports from enemy-held territory became more and more restricted. It is this era that marked a renewed assault on the marginal crop-growing areas of the Downs. Woodland was cleared and grassland ploughed to make way for an increasing area of arable production to feed a steadily growing population.

The situation was exacerbated by a spate of poor harvests at the end of the eighteenth century, pushing the price of wheat beyond the reach of much of the rural population. As these prices rose, it was the wealthier farmers who gained most by increasing rents and land prices which forced many small-holders to sell up. The end of the Napoleonic Wars saw wheat prices fall dramatically yet this was of little consolation for a poverty-stricken rural workforce. With an increasing number of mouths to feed, many farm labourers' families had already been displaced from their rented cottage and were no longer able to rely on a discounted supply of meat and wheat from the landlord. The mechanisation of farm machinery also witnessed the demise of the seasonal and winter hand-threshing jobs, leading to even greater hardship. By the 1830s, many of the villages in Kent and East Sussex were filled with people living on the edge of starvation. The Poor Relief that had provided some hope for the needy rural inhabitants in previous centuries could not keep pace with the growing demand. The donation of Sir John Honywood who gave beef and bread to 652 families in Waltham and Elmsted in one particular year stands testament to these desperate times.

It was against this background of depression and poverty that the uprisings known as the 'Last Labourer's Revolt' or 'Swing Riots' broke out at Lower Hardres, near Canterbury in 1830. These riots were a disorderly attempt on the part of labourers and farm workers to secure better wages and more constant employment at a time when developments in machinery and technology began to replace the traditional manual farm tasks. This unrest was exacerbated by the growing trend of importing more foreign wheat which had the knock-on effect of putting even more labourers out of work. Up until the early nineteenth century the threshing of corn had been undertaken by farm labourers keeping them gainfully employed over the winter months, yet with the newly introduced horse-drawn method this task was soon completed by early November, leaving many without work until the following spring. The destruction of threshing machines in 1830 at Upper Hardres and other locations in East Kent marked the culmination of perhaps two or three years of ever-increasing acts of desperation and discontent on the part of farm workers and labourers. The numerous reports that filled the pages of local newspapers of the time tell of farm incidents, such as mysterious building fires, the cutting of hop bines and livestock rustling, and stand testament to this period of great unrest. The village of Shoreham was one of the worst affected areas in the west of the county, a newspaper of September 1830 recording that 'scarcely a night passes without some farmer having a corn stack or barn set fire to'.[12] The disastrous harvest of 1829, followed by a cruel winter, was the final straw for many farm labourers and open revolt ensued with the burning of hay ricks and farm machinery, sometimes accompanied by sinister letters in the name of 'Captain Swing' (colour plate 14).

The hard times that set in after the Napoleonic War set in motion a large-scale exodus of the rural workforce which continued throughout the century. Mechanisation of farming had made crop growing more profitable, yet the average farm labourer enjoyed only a limited share of this prosperity and many took the decision to emigrate.

Fig. 49 The nineteenth-century mechanisation of traditional namual farm tasks left many agricultural labourers out of work and led to a period of great social unrest.

THE TWENTIETH CENTURY

The persistence of the simple and traditional sheep and corn enterprise that had sustained generations of downland farmers over the centuries was, in part, due to the marginal nature of this part of the county. Remote and distanced from the changing fortunes of farming on the more fertile lands elsewhere in Kent, there were probably few other alternatives for those who wished to earn a living from the land. Little could be done however to safeguard this simple way of life from the unprecedented economic pressures and technological advances in farming of the twentieth century.

The traditional four-course rotation that underpinned the sheep and corn economy, and that relied upon a plentiful supply of labour for the handling of sheep and cultivation of root crops, was unable to survive the changing economic conditions that marked the start of the twentieth century. From 1890 onwards the prices of barley, mutton and wool began to fall in the face of imports, and the period of agricultural affluence ended as markets were overwhelmed by cheap grain from the rapidly expanding American corn-belt. At the same time, farm workers began to demand an increase in their wages. This resulted in men leaving the land and labour became difficult to obtain and expensive in relation to the sale price of farm products. The value of corn and fat lambs continued to fall throughout the early twentieth century culminating in the agricultural depression of the 1930s when commodity prices sank even further leaving many in financial ruin. Those that struggled on reacted in two ways. Some continued and persevered with the traditional rotation system, trying new variations of the rotation whilst others remodelled their farming enterprises entirely. Pig farming witnessed a new lease of life on some farms while on others, such as those on the clay plateau lands above Lenham and Charing, poultry rearing became an attractive enterprise.

Many began to consider the new opportunities that were opening up within the dairy farming industry. The need for a ready supply of milk and butter had always necessitated the keeping of cattle on downland farms, yet traditionally the size of these herds was small, principally because of the lack of surface water and the impoverished nature of the downland pastures. Chalklin (1965), for example, estimated that average herd sizes had historically been much lower in the downland region, numbering around six and a half cows per farm towards the end of the seventeenth century, compared with twenty-two per farm on the marshlands of Kent, and fifteen per farm in the Wealden districts of the county.

The gradual introduction of mains water supply in the early twentieth century overcame the problem of the lack of surface water and precipitated a widespread uptake of dairy farming throughout the Downs. Aided by the Government's wartime policy of the offer of attractive prices for milk, many farmers began to replace sheep flocks with dairy herds. Throughout the Downs fattening yards were converted into cowsheds and milking parlours, which paved the way for a lucrative dairy enterprise that has persisted on many farms up until recent years.

For some, the Second World War brought a return of prosperity, based on the higher prices for home-grown corn and the reduction in cattle and sheep numbers. The drive for self-sufficiency led to the 'breaking up' of much grassland into arable ground spurred on by incentives and the 'dig for victory' campaign. This was naturally seen as an ideal means of rebuilding the nation's agricultural industry to some of its former glory, after the depression of the 1930s. Throughout the county huge tracts of grassland were brought under the plough. The minutes of a mass meeting of farmers at Maidstone in April 1940, presided by Lord Cornwallis, Chairman of the Kent War Agricultural Committee, record the scale of this transformation and the enthusiasm with which this new challenge was embraced by the farmers of Kent:

> The Minister had asked the farmers of Kent to plough up 30,000 acres of grassland. Thanks to the untiring efforts of the District Committees and the parish representatives they had been able to schedule for ploughing up to 37,000 acres.[13]

Publications such as *The Kent Farmers Journal* devoted considerable space to dispensing advice and guidance on the best husbandry methods that should be employed to bring these impoverished pastures back into good productive land for crops, drawing on the knowledge of local farmers and on the experience of those who had reverted grasslands for crops during the years of the First World War.

For many farms this period heralded the onset of changes which were to have far-reaching consequences for the traditional farmed landscape of the Kent Downs. Advances in farming technology, coupled with the drive for efficiency and increased food production, most notably since the United Kingdom joined the European Common Market in 1972, have had a profound impact on the way of farming. With the replacement of the horse-drawn plough by the tractor, fields that were set aside for the growing of hay and oats for horse feed were no longer needed. The widespread development and adoption of agro-chemicals to combat disease and pests have allowed farms to become more specialised and the development of higher yielding winter crop varieties has witnessed the demise of spring cropping. Financial support through subsidies has favoured some crops such as cereals, oilseed rape and linseed, while enterprises that have not benefited from support have suffered, particularly those requiring higher labour costs such as orchards and hops. Changes too in the structure of farms has seen the loss of medium-sized mixed farms and a move to increasingly larger land units farmed by 'contract' or 'share' arrangements. Where small farms continue to exist the farm income is often supplemented by non-farm activities.

In recent years, however, the tide of maximising production has begun to turn. A review of the Common Agricultural Policy has now put in place a new system whereby farmers are rewarded for delivering environmental benefits rather than being subsidised for growing crops. Building on the success of the Government's Countryside Stewardship Scheme, introduced in 1991, the new 'agri-environment' schemes provide payments for protecting and managing farmland habitats for wildlife, and protecting the cultural and historic heritage of the farmed landscape.

These changes coupled with falling farm incomes and the volatility of agricultural commodity prices are also encouraging many farmers to diversify into activities such as horse-keep and stabling, field sports, and alternative crops such as lavender growing and vine cultivation.

Despite the post-war changes in agriculture, the mixed farmed landscape has remained, in many places, largely intact over the last forty years (see Fig. 50) and in so doing has helped to preserve the natural beauty of the Kent Downs for which it is now celebrated. It is a fitting tribute to the generations of farmers who have helped shape and mould this unique landscape. The future will undoubtedly hold many challenges, but with care and thoughtful custodianship, there is no reason why the Kent Downs cannot continue to evolve to adapt to these challenges and still retain the distinctive features that are cherished today.

% of farmed landcover	1961	1972	1990	1999
Arable	53	64	58	55
Grassland	37	27	35	30
Grassland with scrub	0	0	1	9
Orchard and hops	7	6	4	4
Parkland	3	3	2	2
Area of farmed land (ha)	64,227	64,295	64,141	64,546

Fig. 50 Changes in patterns of agricultural land use in the Kent Downs AONB. (Kent Downs AONB and Kent County Council)

~ DEWPONDS ~

This pool that mirrors the green April sky
And the windflattened thorn at fall of day,
Is also a symbol of that older mystery
That is our perilous self, and ancient history.

The pond holds the dregs of daylight, darkly deflecting
The image of the budding thorn, refracting
The last rainclear crystal brightness, the last
Twilight which now flames yellow in the West ...

Jocelyn Brooke, 'Dewpond' from *December Spring* (1946)

Fig. 51 Dewpond at Lydden near Dover.

Dewponds have a long association with the chalk country of southern England. The porous nature of the chalk bedrock has inevitably meant that naturally occurring ponds and pools are few and far between, and consequently in times past this has necessitated the construction of simple clay-lined depressions as a means of watering livestock.

The term 'dewpond' is perhaps a misnomer since it is believed that dew, in the strictest meaning of the word, would not be of sufficient quantity to be able to keep a pond supplied with water. In fact, the term 'dewpond' was not known of much more than a century ago and these features were often locally referred to as mist ponds, fog ponds and cloud ponds. In all likelihood it is probable that the ponds are simply fed by the run-off of surface water from the surrounding area occasionally supplemented from water accumulating in the form of mist and low cloud.

The origin of dewponds is a matter of much conjecture and some have speculated that the practice of dewpond construction may date back to Neolithic times. Place name evidence suggests that the stock-watering ponds of the Kent Downs, natural or artificially constructed, have long been a familiar feature of the countryside. Research shows that of the Kent place names containing the element 'sole' (an old word for 'pond' or water pool'), around 90 per cent are found in the Downs.[14]

It appears that they were sufficiently commonplace throughout the Kent Downs in the eighteenth century to warrant comment from the agricultural writer William Marshall who was able to report on the method of their construction:

> Drinking pools are formed, on these hills, with chalk and lime ... The bason being formed, agreeably to the situation, and the intention, it is bottomed or lined with a coat of chalk, six or eight inches thick. This being beaten with rammers, so as to give it a degree of firmness, and smoothness, a grout, or batter, of pounded chalk, and lime hot from the kiln, is prepared, and spread regularly over the surface of the chalk; covering it perhaps half an inch thick. When the first coat of cement is sufficiently dry, another is added. Thus closing the pores of the chalk, and glazing the bottom of the bason; so as to make it perfectly tight; and, at the same time, effectually preventing the mischiefs of earth worms.[15]

Another method employed to ensure that the basin retained water was to 'puddle' the bottom with clay and straw. A writer for the Kent County Journal records:

> Some years ago I met an old fellow who, as a lad, was one of the dewpond craftsmen. His father before him had plied the same ancient trade, travelling from farm to farm, making new ponds and repairing the old ones. He told of the days when a dewpond was essential for some farms situated in the 'dry' country ... First we used to dig a hollow in the hillside about 40 feet wide and 5 feet deep. When we'd stamped down the earth we'd strew straw over it and cover it with 6 inches of puddled clay ... strew a layer of soot between clay and straw to prevent worms from doing damage.[16]

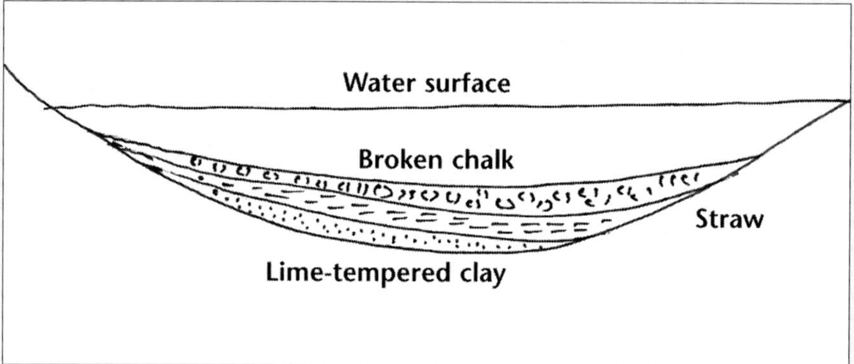

Fig. 52 The construction of a dewpond.

Evidence suggests that dewponds continued to be dug well into the twentieth century with records of professional dewpond makers practising the art at least into the 1920s. Occasionally these ponds also served to supply water for domestic needs, long before the days of mains water. A former resident of the farmstead at Podlinge near Hastingleigh in the 1920s, recalls the two dewponds at the farm, one serving the livestock and the other for the family:

> ... that was called the Tea Pond. It was fenced off to keep the animals out and there were a few hazel trees around to shade it. Of course the leaves fell in but otherwise it was clean although we were never allowed to drink the water before it had been boiled.[17]

With the introduction of mains water in the twentieth century many of the dewponds of the Downs fell into disuse. Today, whilst many of these ponds have disappeared from the countryside, it is still possible to find original dewponds surviving here and there in field corners and copses (colour plate 17). A good example of a dewpond can be seen at West Hougham, near Dover. Known as Soval Pond, this feature can be viewed from the nearby public right of way that runs along the top of Whinless Down.

– CHALK PITS AND LIMEKILNS –

The practice of quarrying for chalk has been an important part of the local downland economy for over 2,000 years. Documentary and archaeological evidence suggests that chalk and lime were used for building and construction work as far back as Roman times, whilst the tradition of quarrying chalk for use in its raw state, as a means of 'improving' soils for agricultural purposes, may well extend to a far earlier period of time.

Two principal methods of obtaining chalk have been widely adopted throughout the Downs over the centuries. The first was by 'uncallowing a piece of ground'[18] and making it convenient for an open-cast pit, and the second involved the sinking of vertical shafts now known as **deneholes** and **chalkwells**. The latter method was largely associated with the extraction of chalk for agricultural purposes, but it is probable that both techniques have been in everyday use for hundreds of years. The advantage of the denehole and chalkwell method of extraction lay in the ability to gain access to what was regarded as the higher quality and purer chalk at depth, with minimum disruption to the fields and crops above (see Deneholes and Chalkwells). Their limited yield however, coupled with the extra effort involved in their excavation, made them less attractive for large-scale chalk quarrying purposes. Instead, where local topography allowed or, where more plentiful amounts were needed to supply a limekiln on site, the quarrying of chalk from an open-cast pit became the preferred method of choice. It is also evident that chalk pits sometimes developed from deneholes and chalkwells that had fallen in or collapsed, leaving exposed shafts or chambers which could then be mined from the surface.

Many chalk pits date to the eighteenth and nineteenth centuries when the use of lime on the land increased and the growth in house building fuelled the demand for lime in the production of mortar. The importance of this industry continued up until the turn of the last century when Kent was by far the most important chalk-yielding county in the kingdom, many of the quarries producing more than 100,000 tonnes annually.[19]

The exposed working face is a characteristic feature of all chalk pits where chalk in its natural state was hacked away with picks and loaded into carts ready for carrying away. Although most chalk pits are now long abandoned many still show a clear access point, often evident as a break in the 'lip' of a pit where carts were brought in to be loaded up.

The transformation of raw quarried chalk into lime necessitated the construction of a kiln in which the charge of chalk was burnt in a chamber to produce 'quicklime'. This product could be used to improve the condition of clay soils or, if mixed with water, became 'slaked lime' for use as lime mortar in building work. While the origin of lime production for building construction can be traced back to Roman period, the practice of applying it as an agricultural fertiliser may not have originated until the sixteenth century. Prior to this time the 'manuring' of fields simply involved the application of chalk in its raw state, being quarried from open-cast pits and deneholes. Normally the dressing of chalk would have taken place in the autumn and been left on the field for some considerable time to allow the weather to dissolve the lumps. According to a seventeenth-century farmer, 'you chalke your ground and let it ly a year or two which is the way used in Kent; that it may be matured and shattered by sun and raine, otherwise, if it be turned in presently, it is apt to ly in great clods'.[20]

From the sixteenth century onwards, the 'flare kiln' became a popular means of obtaining lime for agricultural purposes, particularly in rural areas such as the Downs. This type of kiln was a small dome-based structure in which fuel such as wood was lit below the charge of chalk. These were often temporary structures and perhaps served one or two farmsteads whenever the need for fresh lime arose. For this reason field evidence of their former locations is now difficult to trace.

As demand for lime increased for building work through the eighteenth and nineteenth centuries a more permanent form of field kiln, known as a 'draw kiln' was adopted on many farms. These consisted of a brick-lined 'pot' or 'chimney' sunk some 6-8m into a bank, narrowing at the bottom to a 'drawhole' (Fig. 53). Usually fed with alternating layers of fuel (bundles of coppiced wood known as 'faggots'), the chalk would be poured into the 'pot' and burnt to produce lime. This would then be drawn from the bottom via arched brick-lined cavities and then loaded into carts for transporting away (Fig. 54).

With its readily accessible supplies of chalk, the downland of Kent would have at one time supported a wealth of kilns producing lime for both local and county-wide use. A trader's account of 24 September 1624 illustrates the importance of the Kent Downs as a source of chalk for many farms outside the district: 'Nicholas Toke of Godinton in Great Chart payd Faierbeard of Kennington for digginge 38 loades of chalke at Beamestone downe (in Westwell) which I brought to my kell (kiln)'.[21]

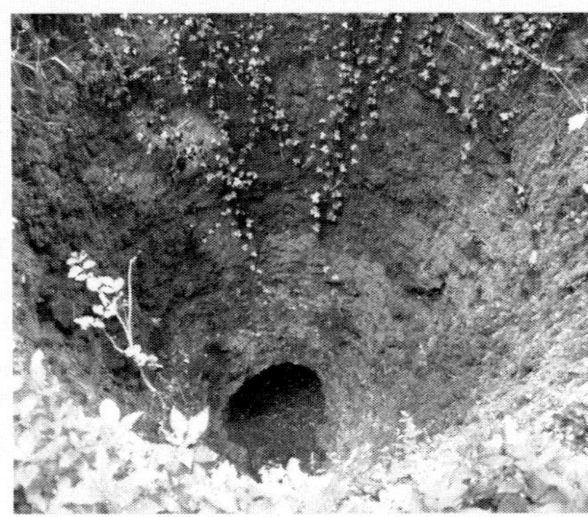

Above left: Fig. 53 A kiln pot (chimney). The draw-arch can be seen at the bottom of the pot.

Above right: Fig. 54 Draw-arch on kilns at Charing Beech Hangers' Wood near Westwell.

With the advent of modern technology and the availability of alternative farm and industrial products over the last century, the quarrying industry has now virtually disappeared from the county. The cement manufacturing industry in the Medway valley area provides one of the last vestiges of the chalk quarrying tradition, the large open-cast pits here still very much an important part of the industrial heritage of the valley.

Today the hundreds of long-abandoned chalk pits are an enduring and characteristic part of the landscape. Pock-marking the woods, fields and copses of every downland parish, they have always held a unique and deep-rooted association with place and locality for the villagers and farmers of these areas. In a gradually changing landscape these pits and quarries have become steadfast companions, indelible features of the countryside, imprinted on the memories of the generations who have grown up in the Downs. In times past they provided convenient reference points for field names as tithe maps of any downland parish will testify. Field names such as 'Chalk Hole Field' and 'Pit Field' abound throughout the downland parishes. Often these pits acquired local names such as 'Croker's Pit' and 'Wimble Pit' in Wrotham, 'Crow Pit' in Hollingbourne, 'Abbot's Hole' in Temple Ewell, and 'Old Mother Brompton's Pot' in the Elham valley.

To stumble across a long-forgotten chalk pit, half hidden in a shady overgrown dell, is a memorable experience, for it is here that the more familiar gentle gradients of the downland give way all at once to an enchanting world of white-washed chalk walls, creeper-clad banks, and tangled masses of briars and ferns, a land of solitude and peace enfolded from the outside world. Poetically captured within the words of nineteenth-century essayist Henry Gay Hewlett:

> When these have been deserted long enough for a growth of green lichen to encrust their broken surfaces; when the hollows are filled up with a thicket of elder and bramble, and sprays of ivy and clematis fringe their mouths and trail down their sides, few features of the landscape are more picturesque.[22]

For many who have spent their childhood in the Downs, the chalk pit will hold many fond and cherished memories, a magical microcosm, captured within the words of Hilaire Belloc who described them in his journey of *The Old Road* (1904):

> These pits which uncover the chalk bare for us show us our principal treasure and the core of our lives, and show it us in grand facades, steep down, taking the place of crags and bringing into our rounded land something of the sudden and abrupt. Everyone brought up among the chalk pits remembers them more vividly than any other thing about his home and when he returns from some exile he catches the feeling of his boyhood as he sees them far off upon the hills ... I know and love them all. The chalk gives a particular savour to the air, and I have found it good to see caked upon my boots after autumn rains, or feel it gritty on my hands as I spread them out, coming in to winter fires.

The celebrated nature-writer and poet Edward Thomas (1878-1917) who lived in Bearsted for a few years of his life, was well-acquainted with the chalk pits on the Downs above Maidstone, likening their overgrown and peaceful interiors to, 'little islands of copses, some brimful of rosebay flowers in the midst of corn, others a riot of bramble, curtains of travellers joy and overhanging roots'.[23] Others who have drawn on the chalk pits of the Downs for inspiration include the author Joseph Conrad who used the Hampton Hill chalk pit at the foot of the downland escarpment near Postling, with its 100ft (30m) drop, as the scene of Flora de Barral's meditated suicide in the novel *Chance* (1914). It was also used in his previous book *Romance* (1904), written in collaboration with Ford Madox Hueffer, in which it provided the setting for the smugglers and excise men episode.

FLORA OF CHALK PITS

Abandoned chalk pits provide a unique and fascinating oasis of chalkland flora and fauna. The thin skeletal soils, exposed chalk ledges and areas of chalk rubble and scree provide ideal conditions for a range of wildflowers able to tolerate the nutrient-poor soils, while the damper quarry floors and sheltered nooks and crannies support a range of shade-loving plants.

Well-adapted to these impoverished soils are kidney vetch (*Anthyllis vulneraria*), mouse-ear hawkweed (*Pilosella officinarum*) and common rock-rose (*Helianthemum chamaecistus*) with its sulphur yellow blooms, as well as many orchid species. Here too can be found wild basil (*Clinopodium vulgare*) and wild marjoram (*Origanum vulgare*) (colour plates 24 and 27). The delicate, small purple and lilac blossoms of wild basil appear in July and August. Both wild basil and wild marjoram are relatives of the commonly grown cultivated varieties, although their aromatic fragrance and tastes are far more subtle than their culinary counterparts. In the damper shady areas of chalk pits the distinctive hart's tongue (*Phyllitis scolopendrium*), a true 'wall fern' and a member of the spleenwort family can be found.

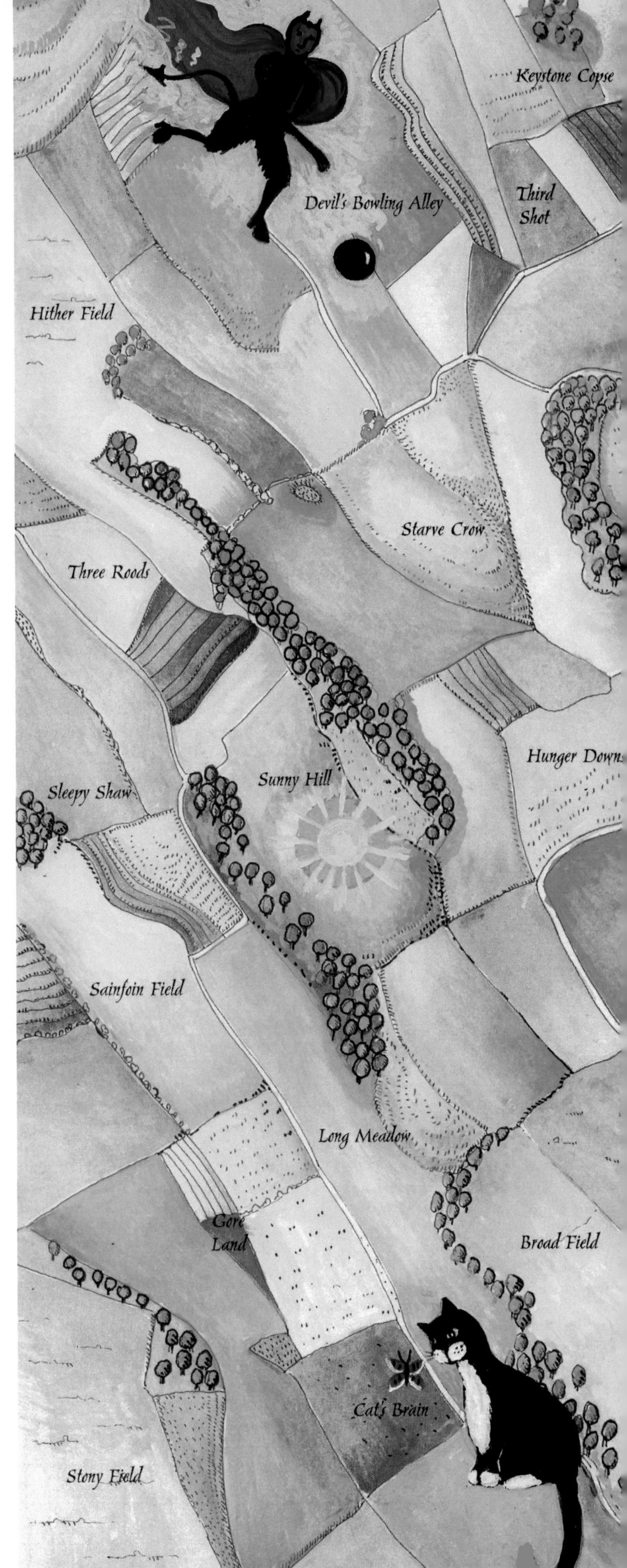

001 Field-names offer a unique insight into the history and stories of the patchwork of fields, meadows, banks and woods of the Downs.

Left: 002 Warren Banks near Lydden.

'Later as the day merges into evening and departs to the world beyond the further most hills, the valley mist begins its ethereal journey over the pastures and through the freshly stacked corn to the downlands which remain even yet, and but slowly yield up their warmth, whilst shadows rise and fall to the flitting clouds capricious call.'

With the Valley Below, Martin D. Austin, 1944.

Opposite above: 003 The ridges, lynchets, hollows and sheep terraces as at Lydden National Nature Reserve are characteristic features of the long-established chalk grasslands of the Kent Downs.

Opposite below: 004 The fertile and lighter soils of the gentler footslopes and valley bottoms have been attractive for crop growing since the first Neolithic farmers settled in these areas.

005 Bronze Age barrow at Great Watersend near Dover.

006 Kit's Coty long barrow on the footslopes of the Kent Downs near Maidstone.

'Thou haughty relic of a bloody day
unchanged the standest; save the vest of grey
The cold, damp, mouldring of hand of Time hath thrown,
Around thee - and that marks thee for its own …'

The Amicii, 'To Kit's Coty House'.

007 Spindle.

008 Wayfaring tree.

009 Traveller's joy.

010 Rosehips, known in Kent as 'Canker-berrys'.

011 Hops were once grown throughout the Kent Downs and sustained a thriving sweet chestnut coppice industry, the straight stems of which were used for hop poles.

012 The patchwork field pattern is characteristic of the Kent Downs and led the agricultural writer William Marshall to remark at the end of the eighteenth century,

'The appearance of a country, diversified in surface, and amply wooded, as are the hills under view, cannot fail to interest: especially, where the vallies are cleared, and the hills remain capped with woods which bend over their brows and fall with irregular outlines down their sides of the vallies: passages of beautiful scenery, which not unfrequently meet the eye…'

William Marshall, *The Rural Economy of the Southern Counties*, 1798.

013 The origins of the Kent turn wrest plough are believed to lie in the Kent Downs where the steep hillsides and heavy clay and flint-ridden soils rendered most conventional ploughs ineffectual.

208

[illegible] Street Hotel de France

French — Very spelling is bad but de French are not in English.

I write you these few lines merely to give you warning. I'm one of 3 thousand who mean to pull down to de ground your house which is called [illegible] next week and [illegible] your [illegible] de horse feet [illegible] you think dat soldiers will [illegible] us no no [illegible]. Monsieur with his [illegible] will [illegible] red herrings. You may [illegible] to your heart dat we will come. Monsieur will not [illegible] de English [illegible] upon it, if we do not come de moon does not shine nor de stars look bright to night. [illegible] shoot 50 of your special constables — — — —

— The Lane down to your farm is dark — we will light it up.

All your tenants farms are dark ditto

Sulphur & Wheat [illegible]

[illegible]

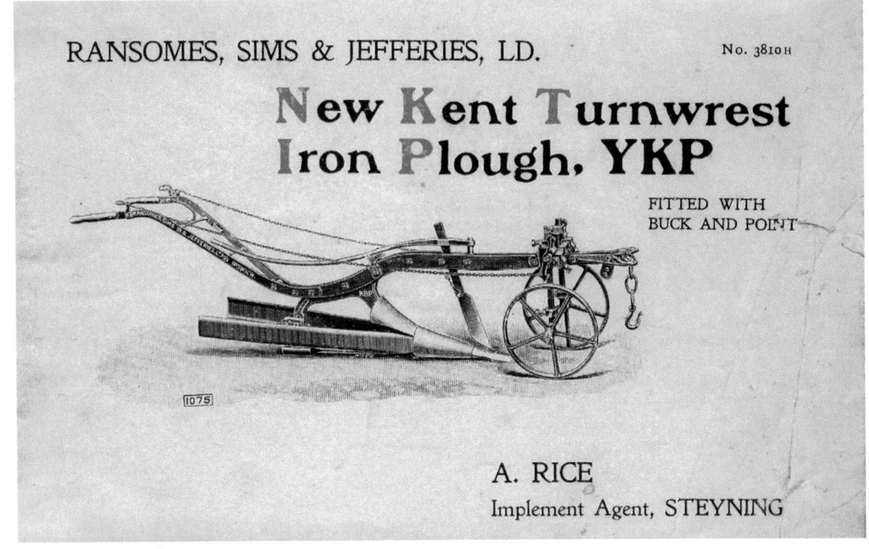

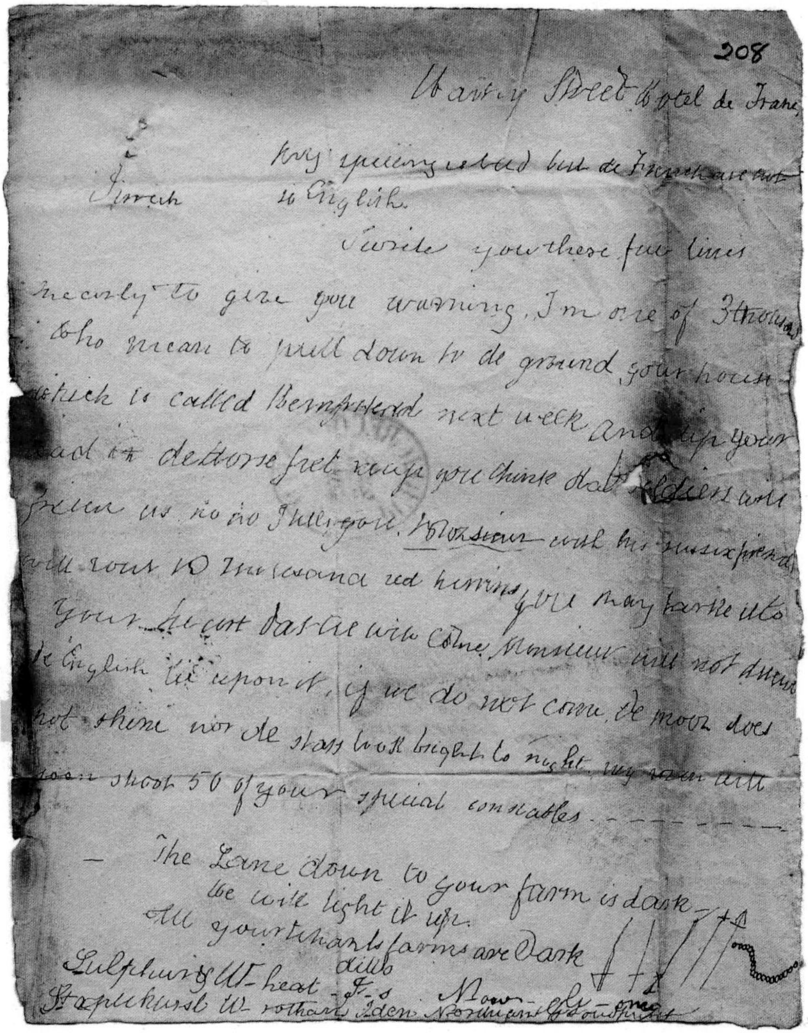

014 A 'Swing' letter threatening a local farmer in Kent with arson, *c.*1830. (courtesy of The National Archives, Catalogue reference: HO 52/8, f.208)

Opposite above: 015 'The Gleaning Field', Samuel Palmer (*c.* 1833) © Tate, London 2007.

Opposite below: 016 'Sainfoin in Bloom: View near Cobham in Kent', John Samuel Raven, 1857. (© Tate, London 2007)

Above: 017 Dewponds and 'soles' were traditionally constructed to provide water for livestock. Today they remain a distinctive feature of the Kent Downs countryside.

Right: 018 A view of a denehole shaft. The shaft descends some thirty metres and opens into three chambers at its base from where the chalk would have been mined and extracted. Some deneholes still retain the original foot-hole marks which the diggers would have used to climb in and out of the shafts.

Left: 019 Chalk pits can be found throughout the Kent Downs countryside and are a legacy of the once-thriving chalk quarrying industry. Today they provide a refuge for many species of wildflowers that thrive on chalk soils.

'The quarry itself is vastly picturesque. The quarrymen have cut away a sheer cliff of white chalk … at night when the kilns are lit and cast a reddish glow on the towery white mass beyond, the scene is uncomfortably weird.'

Ford Madox Hueffer, *The Cinque Ports*, 1900.

Below: 020 Winter scene on Wye Downs.

Above: 021 An autumn scene in the Stour valley.

> 'If these uplands are more beautiful at one time than another, it is, perhaps under two different conditions of the atmosphere. On a summer's afternoon, when a south wind is blowing freshly and the sky is full of diffused light and floating masses of cumulus, there is no lovelier sight than to watch the cloud-shadows chasing one another in endless succession down the slopes, and, caught for a moment in the valley, disappearing into space. On a still autumn evening the gradual suffusion of the hillsides with a sleepy glamour of mist, and the lengthening shadows of the trees slowly stretch eastward before the westering sun, compose a picture beyond the reach of art.'
>
> H.G. Hewlett, *Studies in Kentish Chalk*, 1880.

Below: 022 The interchangeable nature of chalk grassland and arable land that has typified the downland countryside over the centuries is illustrated by a comparison of current day land use with that of the mid-nineteenth century. The Tithe Maps of the early 1840s for the parish of Ewell (Temple Ewell) near Dover show that much of the downland now part of the Lydden and Temple Ewell National Nature Reserve (shaded light green) was once arable land.

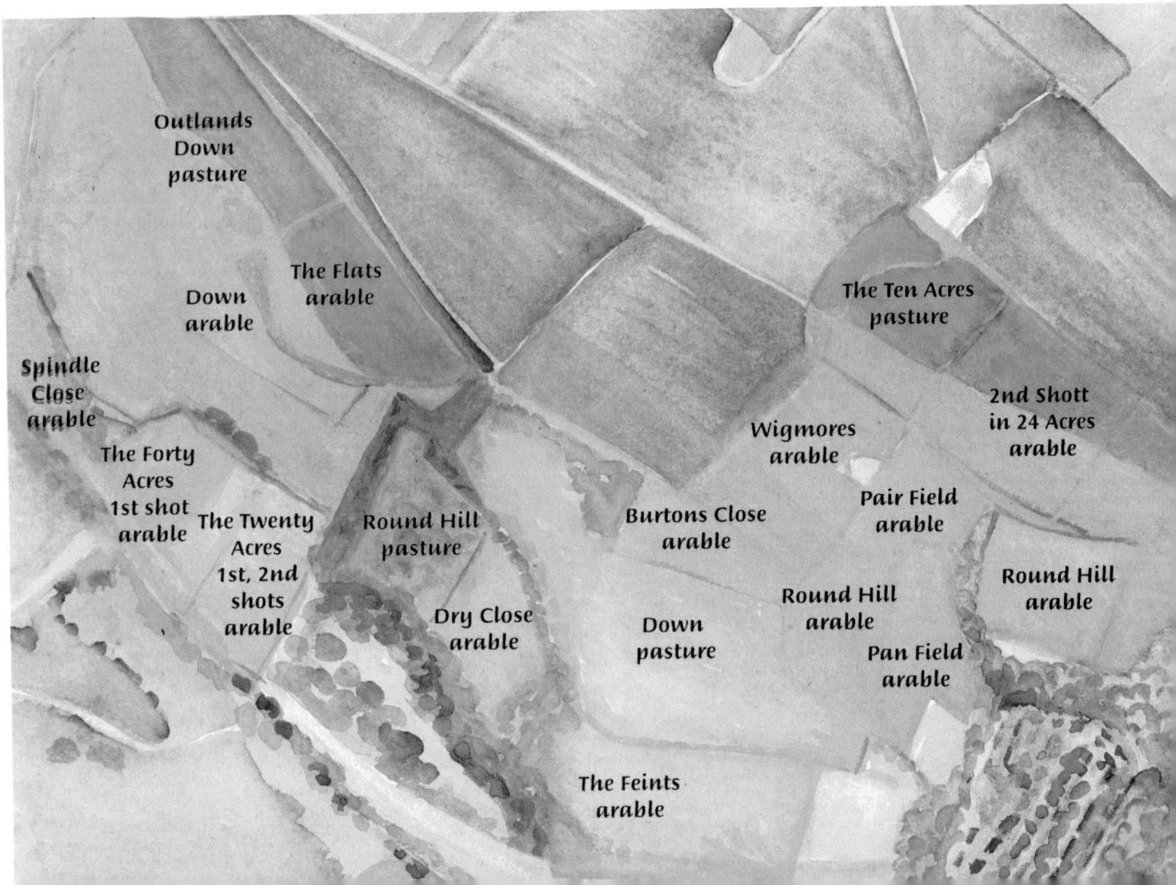

Opposite above: 023 Flower-rich chalk grassland on 'The Flats' at Lydden Downs, an area that was under arable crops in the mid-nineteenth century.

Opposite below left: 024 Wild marjoram provides an attractive source of nectar for many downland butterflies.

Opposite below right: 025 Cowslip, a familiar plant of the downland country, used in times past for its medicinal properties.

Right: 026 Lady's bedstraw earned its name from former times when the floors of houses were commonly strewn with hay.

027 Wild basil is an upright pink-flowered herb often found on chalk grasslands.

Overleaf: 028 Wild Thyme & Dyer's Green-Weed from Anne Pratt's *Wild Flowers*, published in 1853. The Victorian botanist Anne Pratt drew much inspiration for her illustrations in the downland of Kent.

WILD THYME.—*Thymus Serpyllum.*

Class Didynamia. *Order* Gymnospermia. *Nat. Ord.* Labiatæ.—The Labiate Tribe.

It is pleasant to wander over the "bank whereon the Wild Thyme blows," and to breathe the air which, in July and August, is fragrant with the odour of its purple flowers and aromatic leaves. It is very abundant on dry hilly pastures, and Dr. Armstrong, in his celebrated poem on the Art of Preserving Health, recommends such spots as peculiarly salubrious.

> "Mark where the dry champaign
> Swells into cheerful hills; where Marjoram
> And Thyme, the love of bees, perfume the air,
> There bid thy roofs, high on the basking steep
> Ascend; there light thy hospitable fires."

Doubtless the pure air of such places strengthens the human frame, and we know well that sheep flourish where Thyme is plentiful. It was long thought that the value of the animal was increased by feeding on Thyme, but this is generally known to be an error. Mr. Bowles, the author of the "Sheep-walks in Spain," says that sheep are not fond of aromatic plants, and that they will carefully push aside the Thyme to get at the grass growing beneath. He adds that they never touch it, except when walking upon it, when they will catch at anything.

The odour of the Wild Thyme is increased when we tread upon it, and its flavour is very similar to that of the kind cultivated in the kitchen-garden; like that plant, too, it yields a strong essential oil. It was owing to its grateful aroma that the genus derived its name from the Greek word signifying mental vigour, its balsamic odour being supposed to strengthen the animal spirits. Country people make the Thyme into tea for curing head-ache, and also consider it a certain cure for nightmare. Few wild plants vary more than this in size. When growing on dry exposed downs it is small and close to the ground, but when springing up among the Furze and Broom and Ling, and other plants of the Heath land, its stalk is often a foot high, and its cluster of flowers much larger. The leaves, too, are in some plants hairy, and in others quite smooth. It is the only British species of the genus.

DYER'S GREEN-WEED.—*Genista Tinctoria.*

Class Diadelphia. *Order* Decandria. *Nat. Ord.* Leguminosæ.—Pea and Bean Tribe.

Another familiar name for this plant is, Woad-waxen. It is frequent in England, on pastures, field-borders and thickets, and is common, too, in the Lowlands of Scotland. Its pale yellow butterfly-shaped flowers open in July and August. The stem of the plant is about one or two feet high, and in some specimens the blossoms become double, as in those which grow on the rocks near Ilkley in Yorkshire. The plant yields a good yellow colour, and is used by dyers. The author of the "Journal of a Naturalist" says, "Our poorer people, a few years ago, used to collect it by cart-loads, about the month of July, and the season of Woad-waxen was a little harvest to them; but it interfered greatly with our hay-making. Women could gain about two shillings a-day clear of expenses by gathering it." The collecting the Dyer's-weed is a very laborious employment, as the roots extend a good way into the soil. The writer referred to adds that the trade is not so common now, and is discouraged by the farmers. This plant is seldom eaten by cattle. It grows in most countries of Europe, and is, by people in villages, used as a medicine for various maladies.

We have three wild species of Genista. The Needle Green-weed, or Petty Whin (*Genista Anglica*), is not unfrequent on moist heaths and moory grounds. It is a low shrub, its stems are tough, about a foot high, and studded at intervals with sharp thorns. The flowers are very similar to those of the engraving. The Hairy Green-weed (*Genista pilosa*) is a more rare plant. It has no thorns, and its yellow flowers are smaller than those of the other species. They bloom in May, and again in Autumn. The stems are much gnarled and branched, and the leaves are often covered on the under surface with silky hairs.

The genus received its name from the Celtic Gen, a small bush, whence also is derived the French name of the plant, *Genet*. From the same origin is the name of the Plantagenet family.

PUBLISHED UNDER THE DIRECTION OF THE COMMITTEE OF GENERAL LITERATURE AND EDUCATION, APPOINTED BY THE SOCIETY FOR PROMOTING CHRISTIAN KNOWLEDGE.

Price ½d. Plain; 2d. Coloured.

R. CLAY, PRINTER, BREAD STREET HILL.

029 Lady orchid.

030 Man orchid.

031 Pyramidal orchid.

032 Burnt-tip orchid.

033 Woodlands cover a significant area of the Kent Downs and are an important component of the natural beauty of the landscape.

034 Yellow archangel.

035 Sanicle.

The range of conditions, from exposed chalk faces to grassland, scrub and woodland habitats is equally important for a diverse array of insects, mammals and reptiles. Many pits such as at Cuxton Pit now provide a useful refuge and habitat for glow worms, a creature which is in fact a carnivorous beetle. It feeds on snails that thrive in these calcium-rich environments. Chalk pits also occasionally provide homes for hibernating bats where they area able to find cool dark crevices in cavities and small caves that have been excavated into the chalk face.

– DENEHOLES AND CHALKWELLS –

> ...There are to be seen ... near ... this town ... sundry artificial caves or holes in the earth, whereof some have ten, some fifteen and some twenty fathoms in depth at the mouth, narrow like the tunnel of a chimney or passage of a well: but in the bottom large, and of great receipt: insomuch as some of them have sundry rooms one within another, strongly vaulted and supported with pillars of chalk, and, in the opinion of the inhabitants, these were in former times digged, as well for the use of chalk towards building, as for to marle their arable lands therewith ...
>
> William Lambarde, *Perambulation of Kent* (1570)

One of the most intriguing features of the Kent Downs, the features known as 'deneholes' and 'chalkwells' have long attracted curiosity and interest not least for their alarming tendency to suddenly appear in previously unknown locations with sometimes hazardous consequences: In September 1912 a Mr Trull of Hextable was picking apples when he heard a rumble beneath him. Looking down he was alarmed to see that a yawning and seemingly bottomless pit had opened beneath him and his ladder was resting on a single tree root, one inch in diameter. Gingerly he climbed down to safety. Other victims were less lucky such as a Mr Glossop who stepped back into one while nut picking in 1881. Missing for three days he was eventually discovered but later died of his injuries at the age of twenty-eight.[24]

Scattered throughout the Downs, these 'wells' have come to refer to underground structures characterised by a vertical shaft that opens at the bottom into a series of chambers (colour plate 18). Sometimes reaching depths of up to 40ft (12m), and typically 3-6ft (1-2m) in diameter, they often simply exist as individual holes, although they can also occasionally be found in groups and clusters of three or more.

Seemingly unique to south eastern counties, their mysterious nature was clearly sufficient to warrant wonder and comment from the topographers and antiquarians of former times. William Camden was among one of the early topographers to record these features noting in his *Britannia* (1637), 'Near Faversham are found as elsewhere throughout the county pits of great depth; which being narrowed at the mouth and very spacious beneath have in certain districts rooms or chambers with their several supporting pillars of chalk'.

Above left: Fig. 55 A denehole chamber.

Above right: Fig. 56 A chalkwell chamber.

Theories as to their origin and use have ranged from Roman underground grain pits, hiding places, flint mines, places of worship, ice houses, underground dwellings, animal traps, oubliettes (dungeons) as well as a belief that they have been formed naturally. Much of this speculation that has been discounted in recent years.

The pioneering research of J.E.L. Caiger followed by the work of the Kent Underground Research Group and Kent Archaeological Society, suggests that the majority of these shafts were dug for the simple means of extracting chalk to spread on surrounding fields as a form of 'manure'. That chalk should be dug from a depth of twenty feet or more, when logic may suggest that it would have been far easier to extract from open-cast pits has remained a perplexing issue. The reasoning behind this appears two fold: Firstly, given that the business of transporting chalk by cart over any distance was a costly and troublesome affair, a shaft or well had a distinct advantage in that it could be sunk on the edge or close to the very field that was to be dressed with chalk without the disruption and loss of land that an open-cast pit would have involved. The vast majority of deneholes and chalkwells that survive today appear on the edge of woodland, in shaves and hedgerows where mining could be undertaken without disturbance to the land above. Chalkwells and deneholes that today appear in the middle of fields may thus provide clues as to the evidence of former field boundaries that have long since disappeared.

The second reason lay in the belief that chalk mined at depth was of a much superior quality than that at the surface. John Banister's *Synopsis of Husbandry* (1799) written at the end of the eighteenth century explains, 'The best chalk is that which is white and hard; and the deeper it lies beneath the surface, the more efficaceous is the dressing supposed to be as partaking less of the nature of the soil whereon it is applied as a manure'.

Studies of the depth and layout of these structures has enabled a distinction to be drawn between two types of underground structure. The term 'denehole' refers to the narrow shafted structure of about 3ft (0.9m) in diameter often sunk through a surface layer of Thanet Sand, and opening out into six chambers arranged in a double 'trefoil' (clover leaf) pattern (Fig. 57). These are believed to have been dug up until the late fourteenth century. The term 'chalkwell' is used to describe the wells sunk normally in areas overlain by a heavier soil such as clay-with-flints, where the shaft is wider, up to 4-6ft (1.2-1.8m) in diameter and opening into two, three or four roughly cut chambers that radiate from the base of the shaft. This type of well generally applies to those dug from the late seventeenth century onwards.

The evolution of the efficiently designed medieval denehole and its replacement over more recent centuries with the cruder designed chalkwell bears witness to the fluctuating pressures on agricultural land in times past. The art of sinking the medieval denehole which seems to have peaked in development around the late medieval period may well have been lost following the drastic decline in rural population after the Black Death. With little demand for new arable land over the subsequent centuries, it was not until perhaps the seventeenth century that population levels were once more sufficient to necessitate the clearance of marginal land, scrub land and wood for arable crop production. This in turn rekindled the need for a regular supply of chalk and so revived the practice of chalkwell sinking, albeit of a cruder design.

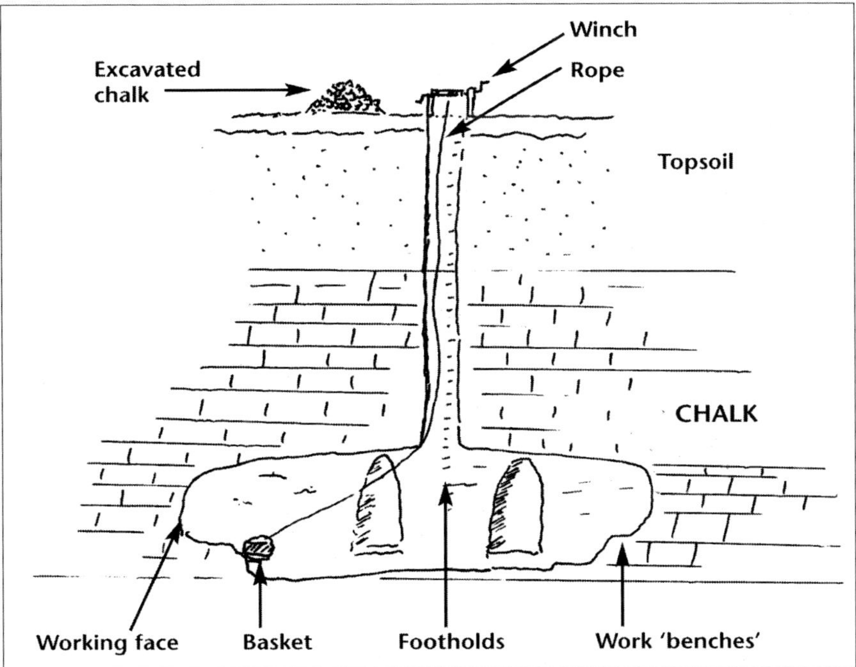

Fig. 57 Cross-section of a denehole.

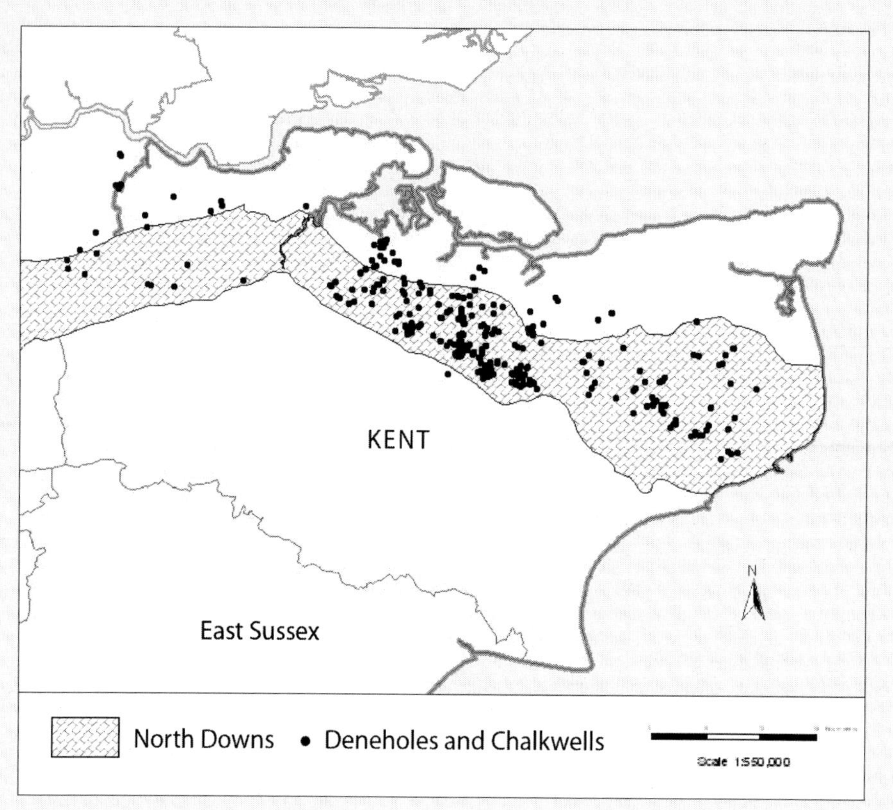

Fig. 58 Map of known denehole locations in Kent. (From records documented by The Chelsea Speleological Society, 1966)

The work of Chelsea Speleological Society and Kent Underground Research Group in recent years has enabled a wealth of information to be gathered on the distribution, type and locations of many deneholes and chalkwells. Anecdotal evidence gathered from local inhabitants as well as field research and aerial photography study has provided evidence for well over 300 deneholes and chalkwells in the Downs, the vast majority of which have now disappeared through infilling and subsidence. It is clear that chalkwells and deneholes were once a common landmark of many downland parishes as is shown in Figure 58. Some parishes such as Challock and Ospringe in the Mid Kent Downs area appear to have supported high concentrations of these structures, although whether this indicates a higher demand for chalk in these areas or simply that these more remote downland parishes have been fortunate in retaining and preserving these features over the centuries is unclear. Given that many deneholes and chalkwells were associated with boundary features such as shaves and hedgerows, the fashion of field enlargement and boundary clearance associated with the agricultural improvements of the last century have undoubtedly resulted in the disappearance of many of these wells.

At a local level the abundance and distribution of these wells within the countryside may have reflected the nature of farming and soil type as much as the limitations imposed by the practicalities of mining at depth and the difficulties of carting chalk over any great distance beyond the surrounding fields. Le Gear (1979) estimates that the average chalkwell would have supplied approximately 360 tons of chalk which would be spread over 6 acres equating to a dressing of about 60 tons to the acre. Important too of course was the cost involved in the sinking of a pit and the fee charged to the landowner. Evidence certainly seems to suggest that craft of sinking a denehole was not a job to be undertaken by anyone and required the services of a skilled and fearless breed of man. John Banister noted of these men:

> The people who undertake this business, having been brought up to it from the cradle, perform it with great facility, and without any timidity, though attended with much danger... Accidents render this profession extremely hazardous, but as the people who embark in it entertain little thoughts of a future period, and since the chief end of their pursuits is the obtaining of a liberal supply of drink; if this end be answered they bestow small attention to the hazards of their profession.[25]

The method of extracting the chalk would have been by rope and basket and many deneholes and chalkwells still exhibit a groove in the lip of the well where a rope would have been used to haul up a basket. The mining team probably comprised three men, one to cut the chalk below ground while the other two hauled the basket to the surface.

The tradition of chalkwell sinking naturally died out with the introduction of alternative products for improving and fertilising soils and the last known chalkwell was dug in 1904 near Doddington.[26] No longer needed, many deneholes and chalkwells were filled in and 'capped' or were left to collapse naturally. As a result many wells have now long since disappeared, although clues to their location are occasionally provided by small depressions or hollows in fields and woodlands which mark the top of the in-filled shaft. Occasionally, subsidence leads to the dramatic reappearance of the denehole shaft and evidence shows that as well as the occasional unfortunate human-being, livestock, dogs, and farm machinery have all been victims of the sudden appearance of a long-forgotten well.

Some chalkwells are deneholes are still remarkably well-preserved and exist with their shaft and chambers largely intact. It is evident that the abandoned deneholes and chalkwells have always provided an important winter roosting habitat for bats, that find the cool stable temperatures of the underground chambers ideal for their winter hibernation. A denehole close to the village of Luddesdown was once locally known as 'Flittermouse Hole' on account of its regular use by bats, 'Flittermouse' being the old Kentish word for bat. Today, the deneholes and chalkwells that remain in the landscape continue to provide this important habitat. One particular denehole near the village of Lynsted provides one of the most important hibernation sites in the county for Natterer's, Daubenton's and Long-eared bats, three of sixteen bat species that have been recorded within the county. These sites are carefully monitored by Kent Bat Group.

~ FLOWERS OF THE CORNFIELD ~

The long tradition of arable farming in the Kent Downs has provided ideal conditions for a rich and diverse range of flora associated with tilled and cultivated ground. These cornfield annual plants depend on the seasonal cycle of disturbed and bare ground to provide the right conditions for their seed to germinate. Often regarded as weeds and unwelcome contaminants to the crops in which they grow, it is only in recent years that the widespread decline in their populations has been recognised and given cause for concern. Prior to the introduction of agriculture it is likely that these species would have evolved to take advantage of ground disturbance brought about the trampling effect of large herbivores and by natural events such as fires which provided areas of open bare soil. The introduction of farming and regularly tilled ground in Neolithic times provided an ideal niche which these plants were able to exploit.

While drastic population declines have been associated with intensification of farming over the last fifty years, the fate of many can be traced back to the improvements in crop husbandry and the mechanisation of farm technology associated with the late-eighteenth and nineteenth centuries. Improvements in the speed and efficiency of farm operations, coupled with the more recent impacts of widespread herbicide use on farms, have now rendered the remaining populations of many of these 'arable weeds' seriously under threat and in many cases extinct.

The chalky soils of the downland fields were once home to a host of annual plants that lived alongside the corn, beans and peas. An indication of the richness of these cornfield flowers is provided by early herbalists such as Thomas Johnson who, in the mid-seventeenth century, was able to record corncockle (*Agrostemma githago*), corn marigold (*Chrysanthemum segetum*), thorow-wax (*Bupleurum rotundifolium*), cornflower (*Centaurea cyanus*) and shepherd's needle (*Scandix pectin-veneris*) in a leg of one of his many excursions around Dartford.[27] Hanbury's *Flora of Kent* (1899) is a sobering reminder of the diversity of plant life which once adorned the cultivated fields of the Downs, yet even by this time it appears that the increasing impact of agricultural mechanisation had begun to take its toll on many of these cornfield flowers. Some species such as the scarlet-flowered pheasant's eye (*Adonis annua*), recorded as being plentiful in the county in 1666 was by the end of the nineteenth century 'well-established in some places on the chalk, but often only a casual; rather rare.' At this time it was recorded at Keston, the hills about Cuxton, and in cornfields in the vicinity of Dover and Maidstone. Today the species is restricted to just a few localities, centred around the districts of Meopham and Longfield in the West Kent Downs.

The cornflower (*Centaurea cyanus*), known as 'bluebottle' in former times (Fig. 59), and a notorious contaminant of grain, appears in nineteenth-century flora guides as 'a common weed in cornfields' and appears to have had its strongholds in Kent on the free-draining chalky soils of the North Downs and the North Kent Plain. By the time of Hanbury's *Flora of Kent* its appearance was less common, it being found in 'fields, especially on the chalk; not unfrequent and found in every district, though it

Fig. 59 Cornflower.

can scarcely be called a common Kentish plant'. Yet by the mid-twentieth century the advancement of agricultural mechanisation had clearly made a lasting impact, the local author Jocelyn Brooke lamenting its demise in his beautifully written *The Flower in Season* (1952):

> I can only say I have failed, for the last thirty years or so, to come across it – it is now so scarce that it can scarcely be counted as a British plant at all.

Today the plant is confined to just a few localities in the Kent Downs although new populations have been known to occasionally come to light when earthworks associated with road developments or farm operations disturb dormant seed in the soil.

Fig. 60 Corncockle.

Corncockle (*Agrostemma githago*) was once another widespread cornfield plant (Fig. 60), although botanical accounts suggest that even by the late nineteenth century, it was sparsely distributed throughout the county. Ranscombe Farm near Cuxton is one of the few sites in the Downs that still supports a thriving population of corncockle. The farm and its neighbourhood, situated on the slopes of the Medway valley, still provide one of the richest sites for arable flora within the county. The rolling chalky fields of this area are home to other scarce annual species including rough mallow (*Althaea hirsute*) and the Kent speciality, ground-pine (*Ajuga chamaepitys*), which, as far back as the eighteenth century was recorded as being more plentiful in Kent than in any other county.[28]

Today, despite the widespread declines and losses of many of the once common cornfield flowers, the chalky soils of the Kent Downs still provide a refuge for a number of more widespread species that have managed to persist in less intensively farmed field edges and corners. These include venus's-looking-glass (*Legousia hybrida*), several members of the fumitory family (*Fumaria spp.*) and poppy family (*Papaver spp.*), and both round- and sharp-leaved fluellen (*Kickxia spuria* and *Kickxia elatine*).

FIVE

THE SPIRIT OF THE DOWNS

THE DOWNS IN ART AND LITERATURE

If you would know me, you must know the Downs,
The chalk hills of Kent, stretching across the county,
Shaking themselves free from roads and smoke and towns;
I am theirs, and they are mine, for here
From the Down dust there came,
Resting in the chalk once more now,
Generations of my name.

Rhoda Cutbush, 'The North Downs' from *In Black and White* (1950)

From the shady depths of tree-muffled holloways to the airy expanses of open down and wind-swept scarp, the Kent Downs have long been treasured as a landscape of immense beauty. Just as its mysterious, secluded coombes and hollows secrete a hidden and un-sung beauty, this modesty of character is reflected in a cultural heritage that belongs not so much to the more widely celebrated authors and artists, as to the generations of local poets, writers and painters whose empathy with this landscape is conveyed in a strong and real attachment to a 'sense of place.' The scattered associations of William Shakespeare, Alfred Tennyson, Jane Austen and J.M.W. Turner bear testament to the many who have drawn inspiration through visiting the more accessible areas of this area yet it is only by delving into the deeper cultural legacy of those who have walked and wandered the remote valleys and hills that the true spirit of this countryside can be found.

Fig. 61 Downland at Lydden near Dover.

A SENSE OF PLACE

Many have found a strong sense of attachment here, where the solitude, peace and beauty of the landscape is enshrined within a very personal sense of place and belonging with the landscape. Captured within the words of east Kent author Mary Laker, who poetically reminisces of the countryside of Eastwell Park, at the foot of the Downs near Ashford, 'what is there about this place that draws me back and back again for one last look, for the last glimpse? ... the hills seem long familiar to me ... '[1] is a sentiment echoed time and time again by those who cherish this special area of the county.

It is within the work of the author Jocelyn Brooke (1908-1966) that we find this strong empathy and affinity, his novels and poems littered with nostalgic recollections and reminiscences of a countryside steeped in mystery and a haunting beauty. Inspired as much by his childhood years of growing up in this countryside as by his passion for botany and orchid hunting, his lyrical prose draws heavily on his memories and experiences of the East Kent Downs. Much of his early childhood was spent wandering the hills and woods of the Elham valley and Bishopsbourne area where his parents owned a holiday cottage (Fig. 62). It was here where his nature rambles and quest for elusive orchids imprinted an everlasting sense of attachment where each wood, down, field and place became imbued with a unique association.

Fig. 62 Ivy Cottage, Bishopsbourne, the holiday home of Jocelyn Brooke who spent many of his childhood summers searching for elusive orchids in the Downs thereabouts.

Writing of his first and unpublished 'novel', *Clouds* (*c.* 1923), set in the countryside of Bishopsbourne and the Elham valley:

> … it was as though a new dimension had been added to those remembered fields and woodlands so that when we returned to the cottage, for our summer holidays, it seemed to me that Gorsley and Forty-acres, the water-tower and Mr Adams's farm had acquired a deeper and poignant reality … they had now become, as it were, a part of 'literature', I saw them through the romantic haze of a novelist's imagination … the Elham Valley, in fact, had become for me already, as it were, the Brooke country. [2]

Brooke used the term 'Month's Mind' to describe this sense of belonging to the Downs:

> … a country of the mind to which I find myself returning, with a recurrent nostalgia, over and over again. The dominant image evoked is of a wooded and remote countryside, silent and frost bound in the early twilight of a winter's evening. It is the dead season, yet there is a subtle, half-realised feeling of spring in the air: a stirring of bird-life in the woods, the catkins lengthening upon the hazels, the first celandine, perhaps, gleaming precociously in the sheltered hedgerow … a broad rift of brightness palely green over the humped outline of the woods … the beech-crowned hill, where the cromlech rises stark against the rainy sunset …[3]

Others too have been touched by this sense of belonging to a particular locality that holds a cherished memory or experience. For London-born author Richard Church (1893-1972) the downland around Otford became deeply associated with the childhood times that he shared with his brother, where 'on that hillside of lark song and dazzling light coming down from the sky and up from the chalk through the pores of the thin surface soil, I have had, in the past, moments of spiritual feast in a companionship so complete that it was wordless'.[4]

THE RURAL IDYLL

For many, the Kent Downs have come to epitomise a distinctively English landscape identity, a romantic vision of England with its spiritual roots deeply entrenched within an archetypal countryside of rolling hills, small fields and woodlands.

For the Victorian 'Romantic' movement who sought to recapture the ancient English pastoral idyll in a time of urbanisation and expansion of the London metropolis, the Kent Downs provided the perfect arena for poets and artists wishing to extol the virtues of natural scenery, and the traditional ways of rural life. Struggling to preserve this bucolic existence against the onslaughts of modern civilisation, they saw their mission in religious terms, celebrating nature as the product of divine creation. One of the most widely celebrated artists of this era was the painter Samuel Palmer (1805-1881) who lived in Shoreham between 1826 and 1833 and was profoundly touched by the serene splendour of the Darenth valley, which he named 'The Valley of Vision'. It was here during these seven years that Palmer's art reached its creative heights, producing vision-inspired landscapes of unprecedented boldness and poetic richness [5](see colour plate 15). Many of Palmer's early works here are of pastoral scenes, often depicting shepherds and their flock, protected by enfolding hills and often combined with exuberant and dramatic nocturnal effects such as magnified stars and a vast waning moon as in 'A Shepherd and his Flock under the Moon and Stars' (*c.*1827), and 'Shepherds under a Full Moon' (*c.*1826-1830). The varied topography of the downland hills and valleys of the Shoreham area was used to great effect by Palmer in many of his works to capture the light and shadow and textures of the landscape cast by an illuminated moon and stars as in 'The Flock and the Star' (*c.*1831-1832) and 'Cornfield by Moonlight, with the Evening Star' (*c.*1830). Palmer's time in Shoreham also marked the period when the artistic group known as 'The Ancients' were at their height. The Ancients, one of several artistic practices that became common in the nineteenth-century, were a group of like-minded fellow artists who drew inspiration from the art of the Middle Ages. For a time they formed a community in Shoreham, led by Palmer, where they roamed the hills and valleys, often by night, dressed in archaic costumes.

In many of their ideals the Ancients foreshadowed the Pre-Raphaelites who came to the fore as an artistic group in the mid-nineteenth century and who sought to record the beauty and detail of the natural world before it succumbed to the material advances of mankind. Their work was fired by a passion for the natural world, but was also deeply rooted in the scientific and religious ideas of the day. Like many of the young artists of this era, John Samuel Raven (1829-1877) fell under the spell of the Pre-Raphaelite movement and strove to capture the intricate colour and detail of nature in paintings such as 'Saintfoin in Bloom: View near Cobham in Kent' (colour plate 16). Painted in 1857, this picture captures in intricate detail the wayside flora of poppies and field scabious, bordering a field of sainfoin.

The romantic spirit that lingered on into the later nineteenth and early twentieth century provided an expression for many to capture the enthralling beauty and antiquity of the Kent Downs landscape. The tiny villages of Denton and Wootton in the East Kent Downs have strong associations with the seat of the Bridges family and in particular the Poet Laureate, Robert Bridges (1844-1930). Bridges was greatly influenced by the beauty and antiquity of the countryside in which he grew up, perhaps most eloquently expressed in his poem 'The Testament of Beauty', 'a gallery of local watercolours, landscapes and seascapes in words, to be recognised again and again in the corners and open sweeps of this land where the poet was nurtured'.[6]

Born in the remote and peaceful countryside of the small village of Ash in the west Kent Downs, the artist, poet and writer Thomas Hennell (1903-1945) developed a strong and deep empathy with the rural way of life from an early age. In the same way that the Victorian 'Romantics' sought to portray and celebrate the beauty of the natural environment at a time of urban and industrial advancement, so Hennell used the medium of watercolour and verse to record in intimate detail the

Fig. 63 'Landscape: Flint Heap, Road-Making' by Thomas Hennell (c.1937-41). The scene is believed to be the field opposite Hennell's own Orchard Cottage at Ridley in the West Kent Downs, the flints raked and gathered from the plough-land ready to be used for road-making.

dying traditions, practices (Fig. 46) and country ways of life that had fallen victim to the ever-increasing march of technological progress. Growing up in the Downs at a time when grass and corn was, here and there, still mown with scythes and oxen and horse were still used to pull ploughs, Hennell was acutely aware that he was witnessing the end of an era that had persisted for centuries. His fear was that rural Britain was as much threatened by mechanisation and urban civilisation as by the possibility of invasion from Germany. His prose and verse reveal his deep fascination and knowledge of rural traditions and crafts, the best known of which *Change in the Farm* (1934) is an eloquent tribute to the generations who were deeply attached to the land and drew their livelihoods from it. Rural activities appear at the forefront of much of his watercolour work and pen and ink sketches such as 'Stacking Wheat' (1941) and 'Landscape: Flint Heap, Road Making' (*c.*1943) (Fig. 63) both painted at New Street Farm, Ridley near Ash.

The renowned author Joseph Conrad (1857-1924) dwelt for a time in Essex and Bedfordshire yet it was Kent alone which really aroused and kept his affections. There was something in the landscape and atmosphere of this county which spelt for him the very essence of England. He lived in the county for twenty years in various places but spent much time in Postling at Pent Farm and later settled in Bishopsbourne. The countryside of the Kent Downs had a lasting impression on

Conrad who would often take car trips out into the countryside, exploring the small lanes and villages of the area. Naturally this deep empathy for the downland countryside can be found in several of his works, including the novels *Chance* (1914) and *Romance* (1904) which feature the chalk pit at Hampton Hill, near Postling.

Local author and editor of the Kentish Express, Sir Charles Igglesden (1861-1949), became popularly known for his *Saunters through Kent with Pen and Pencil* series, but also wrote a number of works of fiction, including *Downs Valley Farm* (*c.*1940), a story of rural life in wartime Kent. The countryside of Hastingleigh, Wye and Godmersham provide the perfect backdrop for this tale which follows the idyllic country life on a farm nestled in the depths of the Downs, with the ever-present threat of invasion from across the channel. *Crimson Glow* (1925) by the same author is in a similar vein, the picturesque countryside of Godmersham, the Stour valley and King's Wood providing the setting of the pastoral English countryside during the fatal years of the First World War. Igglesden used the local scenery of the Kent Downs to great effect to convey the charm and antiquity of the English countryside which stood as symbol of the green and pleasant land so dear to heart of the nation. Others too have touched upon this association. In her *Kentish Memories* (1989), local author, Mary Laker, recalls walking in the peaceful, 'benign and ever-enticing Downs' during the wartime years, which for her became an enduring symbol of the unspoilt and beautiful countryside that was under threat.

The spiritual power of the downland landscape is equally apparent in the work of film maker Michael Powell (1905-1990). Born at Bekesbourne, near Canterbury, Powell developed a passionate love for the English countryside, using the natural imagery of landscape in the same vein as the author Thomas Hardy. His film *A Canterbury Tale* (1944), produced by Emeric Pressburger, is regarded by many as the most complete expression of the mystical power of landscape. The film is set in the fictitious wartime village of 'Chillingbourne', a cinematic collage of countryside and village scenes from Chilham, Chartham, Fordwich and other locations in the Stour valley, and follows three modern day pilgrims to rediscover their lost spiritual heritage. Evocative of Chaucer's *Canterbury Tales*, Powell uses the strong sense of antiquity of the Kent Downs landscape to portray a vision of England with its spiritual roots in the countryside. The film was intended to add a spiritual dimension to the propaganda messages of earlier films such as *One of our Aircraft is Missing* (1942), serving to reinforce the power of the English identity against the dark forces of Germany. Some of the most memorable scenes feature Chilmans Downs and Julliberrie's Grave near the village of Chilham (Fig. 64)

The pastoral scenes that caught the imagination of landscape artists of the nineteenth century have continued to provide inspiration for artists of more recent times. Brian Walters (1935-1999) used watercolours to capture the ever-changing moods of this remote and peaceful landscape. Much of his work portrays east Kent rural downland scenes in the autumn and winter seasons when the fickle play of light and shade capture the depth and beauty of the landscape, as in 'Returning Home across the Downs' (1998), 'On the Hillside' (1997) and 'Snow Cluster' (1998).

Fig. 64 Scene on Julliberrie's Grave from *A Canterbury Tale*, 1944.

REMOTENESS AND ISOLATION

Of all the individual qualities of the Kent Downs, the sense of remoteness and isolation of the landscape has been a recurring theme for many writers. Lost within the network of narrow wood-shrouded lanes, the overpowering sense is of being immersed and enfolded in a countryside where the twisting roads and paths afford only occasional glimpses into the countryside beyond. It is this sense of the 'unknown' that continually beckons the traveller. Poetically expressed by local author H.E. Bates:

> To know what lies on the other side of the hill-this feeling inevitably draws you up to the deep carved lanes … the depth of silence here on hot summer days, when there is no wind and the chalk is blinding on the eyes and the rock-roses are brilliant lemon in the sun, can be immense, the feeling of isolation splendid.[7]

Brooke too was equally fascinated by the lure of this countryside where:

> ... in this country of hills, there was never what could properly be called a 'view': one reached the summit of one hill, only to be confronted by another. Somewhere, one felt, one would come one day upon the focal centre of this land: see it stretched out around one, the familiar hills and valleys falling into position, making a completed pattern. But this never happened: the gentle hills rose in their long undulations and sank again, the dark crest of woodland masked the further valley; one was perpetually enclosed, there was always something "just beyond" which one could never reach.[8]

Just as this sense of isolation is able to convey a sense of peace and solitude, it has been equally apt to evoke a more sinister or haunting atmosphere to the landscape. The Kent author Richard Church, is one of many who have experienced this foreboding nature to the countryside. Reminiscing on his childhood exploration of the wooded hinterland country around Bromley in his book *Kent* (1948) he recalls the discovery of a derelict cottage in a wide stretch of deserted wooded country, 'grooved with valleys of a slightly ominous nature.'

Few areas have evoked such a haunting atmosphere as the remote network of valleys of the East Kent Downs. On the Barham Downs, the juxtaposition of the wind-swept open downland to the north and the wood-shrouded valleys that stretch away to the south cannot be more apparent. The network of valleys that penetrate the hinterland of Kingston, Lynsore, Petham, Stelling Minnis and Elham are some of the most remote throughout this stretch of countryside. Joseph Conrad, regarded as one of the greatest writers of English fiction, spent the last years of his life at Bishopsbourne and drew much inspiration from this area, the remote 'forgotten' valleys around Stelling Minnis and Upper and Lower Hardres providing the perfect backdrop to the opening scene of his novel *The Inheritors* (1901):

> We were sauntering along the forgotten valley that lies between Hardres and Stelling Minnis; we had been silent for several minutes. For me, at least, the silence was pregnant with the undefinable emotions that, at times, run in currents between man and woman. The sun was getting low and it was shadowy in those shrouded hollows.

For Jocelyn Brooke the isolation of this area imparted a mysterious and haunting power to the landscape, deeply rooted within a childhood fascination with the weird and wonderful place names of the Downs. His autobiographical novel *The Dog at Clambercrown* (1955) recollects his childhood adventure to discover a lonely and isolated inn at a place called 'Clambercrown' in the remote hinterland country of Bishopsbourne and Elham a name, 'so pregnant with strange echoes, seemed to have absorbed into its mysterious syllables ... the mystery of all those other place names ... The Dog ... acquired for me ... a vague, rather frightening yet perversely seductive aura of evil'.

Of all his works it is perhaps his poem 'California'[9] (1946) which captures the very essence of this malevolent quality to the landscape, manifest in a deep sense of foreboding and menace that can suddenly overcome the solitary traveller, 'among the thickets, watchful and unfriendly', and that he also experienced in the countryside around Gorsley Wood near Bishopsbourne.

David Hewson's novel *Native Rites* (2000) draws too on this same powerful atmosphere of the remote and wooded 'desolate hill country' of the East Kent Downs to provide the backdrop to a tale of mystery and suspense within a small downland village community.

SIX

Customs and Legends

Kent has traditionally boasted a rich and colourful history of folklore and customs. The insular nature of its hinterland districts, coupled with the evolution of a distinctive social and economic structure have perpetuated an interesting mix of traditions some of which continue to the present day. Passed on from generation to generation through the centuries, folklore and superstition once formed an important part of village life. Many traditions were simply regional and local expressions of deep-rooted widespread customs whose origins extend far back into pagan society. Like all other villages, downland communities would have observed and celebrated the familiar seasonal customs, Saints' days and festivals associated with the renewal of life, crops and the farming year. The four agricultural festivals of Plough Sunday, Rogantide, Lammas and Harvest Thanksgiving were widely observed festivals when farmers and all others working on the land would join in asking God's blessing on their endeavours.

Plough Sunday traditionally took place on the first Sunday after the Twelfth Day and involved the ceremony of 'plowlode' in which the plough was taken to the village church and blessed. The following day, Plough Monday, celebrated the blessing with the ploughmen carrying the plough around the village in the company of musicians. Variations of this tradition were carried out in each village. At Crundale, near Canterbury, the tradition was for the plough-boys to lead the horses round the farms and large houses, in order to collect donations of meat, eggs and butter which they then took to the local inn to be cooked. This was then followed on Plough Monday night with a custom in which they would pull an old ploughshare around the village with their faces blackened and their coats turned inside out, and asking for donations of money.

Rogantide involved a similar perambulatory custom commonly known as 'Beating of the Bounds' in which villagers would join clergy and churchwardens in walking the boundaries of the parish. This ancient custom, which can be traced back to Roman times, traditionally involved acts and gestures which would help keep fresh the collective memory of the boundaries. In some parishes, as at Stowting, this involved the symbolic beating of the ground and of the younger generation with sticks of hazel. In others, young males were symbolically bumped on boundary markers such as stones and pollards.

Lammas Day marked the first day of August and of the harvest, one of the most important events in the village year when families, young and old alike, would help in the harvesting and bringing-in of the crops. The cutting of the last sheaf of corn on the farm was a particularly symbolic event as this sheaf was believed to embody the harvest 'spirit'. This was treated with special respect and straw from this sheaf was often used to make corn dollies known as 'Ivy Girls' in Kent, which were used to preserve the spirit of the corn through the winter. On Plough Monday the dolly would be ploughed back into the soil to release its spirit and so ensure a good harvest. The changing practices associated with nineteenth and twentieth-century farm mechanisation sadly witnessed the demise of the corn dolly tradition, the West Kent Downs artist Thomas Hennell recording the last vestiges of this age-old craft in his pen and ink sketches of 'rick' dollies (a dolly made to decorate a hay stack) made in the 1920s and 1930s in the Ridley and Ash areas.

Harvest Thanksgiving marked the occasion when the last cart loads of sheaves were brought in. Often the cart and horses were decorated and the last sheaf was placed on the top. The cart would make its way to the farm passing at inns and ale houses where everyone involved in the harvest would celebrate the 'Harvest Home'.

A number of traditions are associated with the religious festival of Easter. The period of Shrovetide, before Lent, still widely celebrated by the making of pancakes on Shrove Tuesday, was also observed in Kent with the 'Jack-a-Lent' tradition. This involved the beating of a scapegoat figure known as the 'Jack-a-Lent', which would sometimes take the form of a puppet or effigy and on other times would be represented by a living person dressed in costume. Traditionally the effigy was then burnt on Easter Sunday.

According to some accounts, Easter also appears to have been associated with a variation of the 'Ivy Girl' corn dolly tradition. In this tradition the 'Ivy Girl' referred to the ivy branch Christmas decorations that were kept in houses until Shrove Tuesday which were then made into bundles, known as 'Ivy Girls', by the girls of the village. A similar practice was undertaken by the boys of the village who gathered the holly Christmas decorations and constructed 'Holly Boys'. These figures were then carried off with much noise and acclamation and burnt on Shrove Tuesday. Ash Wednesday was popularly celebrated by the carrying of a branch of an ash tree.

Fig. 65

One particular Easter custom celebrated in Kent was that of 'going a-pudding-pieing', in which it was fashionable for people to visit hostelries and inns which served pudding-pies. These were flat, pastry-like cakes made with a raised crust to hold a small amount of custard scattered with currants. Apparently it was common to see the inns along the old Watling Street offering these cakes to travellers as they journeyed from London to Canterbury.

Many downland villages had their own Easter customs. At Wye, a tradition that dated back to at least the early eighteenth century was the distribution of six crown pieces to six elderly men and women of the village who attended the morning service on Good Friday.

May Day marks the beginning of summer and has been traditionally celebrated with May garlands and maypoles. May garlands were made by children of the village and carried from door to door. Kathleen Pilcher of Stowting recalls:

> You know those big hoops what you knock along with a stick? We got two of those and put 'em through one another and decorated 'em all with flowers and hung a dolly or a fairy or something inside; covered it up with a sheet; put a stick through it so one could hold one end and one the other; and then we took it round the houses to show people. You took the sheet off for them to see and then they'd give you a penny or twopence or something. So we had all one day picking primroses and violets and decorating them all up.[1]

The May Day celebrations at Chilham traditionally included a trial race. Charles Iggelsden records that this custom apparently dated back to the seventeenth century when, under the will of Sir Dudley Digges, twenty pounds was left as a prize for a race between two young men and women. The bequest provided that 'four of the best freeholders should choose a young man and young maiden of good conversation between sixteen and twenty-four and these two men and women should run a tie at Chilham and the young man and young maid who prevail should each of them have ten pounds'.[2] This custom persisted for many years, Iggelsden recording in the early twentieth century that the race was still run 'amongst a great concourse of the neighbouring gentry and inhabitants who assemble there on this occasion'.[3]

Races on foot appear to have been a regular part of village life in times past. Newspaper accounts as far back as the eighteenth century record events such as at Barham where 'a ladies match of running' was held in August on Barham Downs by young women of the parish with twelve on each side.[4] These running events were known in the nineteenth century as 'goal running' and it appears that most villages had a 'goal running' club based at a local village inn. The game involved teams from neighbouring villages competing against each by running around flags set up at a fixed distance from a boundary line. Old accounts suggest these matches were often lively affairs with always a strong competitive spirit. At Crundale, near Canterbury the Compasses Inn was the home of the local goal running club.

The celebration of Bonfire night has been a popular tradition for many centuries. In east Kent the night was a traditional occasion for masquerading in fancy dress and calling on the houses of the village. Many villages have always had familiar fields and places to celebrate particular events such as Bonfire night. At Lydden near Dover the local hills, known as 'Catch me Jack' and 'Green Hill' became popular places in times past from which to celebrate Guy Fawkes Day and the associated Dover Regatta,'when the whole village would gather as dusk fell to view the pyrotechnics in Dover harbour'.[5]

The curious mid-winter festival of 'hoodening', traditionally associated with the north-east corner of the county, was practised in some of the downland country to the south of Canterbury. This tradition was a 'peramubulatory' custom, involving a seasonal good luck visit to each of the houses of a parish, whereby the performers, normally comprising a 'rider', a 'wagonner', a 'hoodener' and a 'mollie' acted out a set ritual at each house, accompanied by singers and instrumentalists. The centrepiece of this ritual was

Fig. 66 Hooden horse figure now adopted by the East Kent Morris Men.

the 'hooden horse' which was a specially made wooden horse's head with an articulated lower jaw, affixed to a pole. This was operated by the 'hoodener' to make a loud snapping noise, who performed the part of the horse under a covering of sack or cloth. Each locality appears to have had its own variation of the ritual and type of horse. At Lower Hardres near Canterbury the hooden horse's covering was a black glossy material and the horse had a distinctive neck with a white streak down its forehead. Anecdotal evidence gathered in the early twentieth century suggests that the tradition of the Lower Hardres hoodenors, who also visited the villages of Petham, Waltham and Stelling, died out towards the end of the nineteenth century. One amusing tale recorded by Percy Maylam (1909) tells of a particular visit in 1859 when the hoodenors called at the rectory at Lower Hardres to perform the ritual. A German lady who was staying at the rectory and who had not walked for seven years was wheeled out to the lawn to watch the performance. When the hooden horse made a feigned jump, the lady's fright was so great that she sprang out of her chair and ran into the house and miraculously found herself able to walk thereafter. The hooden horse was given to the lady as a gesture of remembrance and the following year a new horse had to be made. There is also some evidence to suggest that Elmsted, Elham and Chartham once had their own hoodening tradition. Although animal disguise customs are common throughout midwinter customs of Britain, the origins of this particular custom are unknown, some suggesting that it may have been a relic of an ancient festival associated with the Anglo-Saxon cult of the horse. Today the custom continues in a few localities where the tradition has been revived. Local Morris Men teams such as the East Kent Morris Men have helped preserve the tradition by adopting the hooden horse as a mascot (Fig. 66).

In west Kent the custom of 'mumming' or 'plays of the seven champions' was commonly practiced as a mid-winter festival. The custom similarly involved a visit to each house of the parish by performers in traditional costumes adhering to a well-rehearsed themed play. Subtle variations in the characters and dialogue reflected local adaptations from village to village. The Darenth valley appears to have been a particular focus for this custom in the west of the county and evidence of variations of mummer's plays has been discovered at Brasted, Shoreham, Riverhead and Sutton-at-Hone.

The mid-winter tradition of 'youling' or 'apple wassailing' was practised in many villages in the county as a means of bringing luck for a good harvest of apples. This involved the gathering of young men in the village who, when assembled, would run to each nearby orchard shouting and singing. Upon arrival they would encircle each tree and chant the rhyme:

Stand fast root, bear well top
God send us a youling sop!
E'ry twig, apple big
E'ry bough, apple enow!

The owners of the orchard were then expected to give money and drink to the participants.

An important event in the calendar of all villages were the annual stock fairs and fetes which became popular gatherings for all to enjoy rustic games, dancing and revelry well into the night. Stelling Minnis fair for horses, cattle and pedlars was one of the most important in east Kent, existing since Elizabethan times. Sir Charles Igglesden, writing in his parochial visitations, recorded that in times past, visitors flocked in from all neighbouring towns and villages and dancing went on far into the night. Badlesmere near Faversham also once held a fair for toys and pedlary that would attract thousands to enjoy the games and revelry.

Elham market, once a flourishing weekly event, dates back to 1251 when Edward I first granted a market. Pedlars would be joined by stock traders who would bring their hides from neighbouring homesteads for sale, a tradition which gave it the local name of the 'leather market'. The wide part of the High Street in the village also marks the site of the annual horse fair which was held every Monday before Easter until about 1840.

Many villages had their own individual traditions and customs associated with other trades. At Lenham, an old custom for the men who transported the lime from the many limekilns and chalk pits in the area was to receive free ale on their nightly runs from the local village inns. In order to avoid being disturbed after he went to bed it is told that the landlord of the Chequers Inn put a pot of beer for the lime-carriers' benefit outside his door every night.

While many of these traditions and customs have now disappeared, the resurgence of interest in old customs in the 1960s, and more recently through initiatives led by the Kent Downs Area of Outstanding Natural Beauty (AONB) Unit, has ensured that this rich cultural legacy is able to continue and provide inspiration for future generations of the Downs. One recent project led by the AONB unit, called 'Sounds of the Downs', has encouraged young people to record and produce music inspired by the local countryside

SUPERSTITIONS

The springs along the footslopes of the Downs have naturally attracted a wealth of folklore in times past. At Thurnham there was a spring known as the 'round well', which flowed throughout the year, never running dry in summer months. The well had the local name of 'Christ's Tears', the tradition being that it was caused by the tears shed by Jesus when he wept and from that day it has never ceased. Another local country belief recounted by Iggelsden tells of a superstition in Badlesmere in which it was believed to be unlucky for a newly appointed domestic servant to enter the place of her working before midday.

The belief and fear of witchcraft goes back to the pagan societies of pre-Christian times but reached a peak in England in the sixteenth and seventeenth centuries. As a means of protecting themselves against witches, many people placed charms in their houses to deter witches. Salt and iron were believed to be particularly effective weapons and were sometimes put at the bottom of a bed of a newborn child. A

Fig. 67 Witchcraft superstitions. Many people believed in the use of charms to protect themselves against witches, such as the placing of salt and iron at the bottom of a newborn child's bed.

common form of protection was the burying of jars and bottles containing items such as bent pins, iron nails, hair and cloth. These were usually buried at the entry points of a house such as beneath the door sill or hearth of a chimney stack. In the downland village of Charing the recent discovery of jars beneath the hearths and sills of three houses in the High Street, containing, amongst other things, round-headed pins, locks of hair and bone flakes, is believed to be associated with the story of a seventeen-year-old girl named Mildred Norrington who in 1574 spread panic and fear amongst the inhabitants of the nearby village of Westwell. After developing fits she claimed to be possessed by the Devil and accused her mother of witchcraft. The jars discovered at Charing, which appear to be contemporary with this time, suggest that the fear in the community was enough for people to step up their house protection.[6]

Many customs and superstitions were associated with the plants and animals of the land.

Fig. 68

'Bee whispering' was also a well-known superstition in rural districts of the county. This was based on the belief that when an owner of a hive of bees died, then the bees must be told at once, otherwise they will swarm and the spirit of the man will never leave the earth. There were various ways of telling bees, the simple way being to walk straight to the hive and whisper 'Bees, bees! your master's dead!' In some places the tradition was to place some sweet cake outside the hive whilst at others it was necessary to tinkle a bell before chanting the words.

A superstition particular to east Kent asserted that one way of avoiding rheumatism was to catch a mole and cut off all four feet.

PLANT LORE

Long before the seventeenth-century apothecaries first began to document the names of plants and herbs of the countryside, the flora of the downland hills and pastures provided a wealth of resources for a range of everyday needs, much of which was steeped in a rich tradition of plant folklore and superstition that had been passed down through the centuries. Many plants provided the natural remedies for common complaints, illnesses and disorders, while others were gathered and collected for their use in food preparation, flavouring and drinks.

Cowslip (*Primula veris*), known variously in Kent as 'paigles' (from which is derived the old Kentish expression 'as yellow as a paigle'), 'fairy cup', 'cove keys', 'culverkeys', or 'horsebuckle' is a characteristic plant of the chalk downland of Kent (colour plate 25). The leaves of this plant were often boiled for the table and the flowers were once used to make a medicinal wine which was said to be beneficial for giddiness and nervous disorders. Another old practice associated with this plant, and a particular source of delight for children, was the making of 'cowslip balls' in which clusters of flowers were picked from the stem and hung on a string between two chairs. The flowers were pressed together and the string drawn up so as to bring them into a ball.

Other plants were prized for their roots. The dried tubers of dropwort (*Filipendula vulgaris*), for example, were a good substitute for bread flour while those of restharrow (*Ononis repens*), when boiled, were sweet and flavoured of liquorice.

Among the many wild plants that were collected for their medicinal properties, the low growing, white-blossomed herb, common eyebright (*Euphrasia nemorosa*) had a reputation for improving the eyesight (Fig. 69). The purple flower of devil's bit scabious (*Succisa pratensis*), when ground into a powder, was used to heal bruises. Burnet-saxifrage (*Pimpinella saxifraga*), a species belonging to the carrot family (umbellifers), was once used to treat stomach problems. Selfheal (*Prunella vulgaris*) had a multitude of uses from treating wounds to curing sore throats and mouth ulcers. Another denizen of the downland turf, fairy flax (*Linum catharticum*), is a delicate white-flowered plant which was once known as 'purging flax' because of its former use as a purgative.

Several plants were highly prized for the dyes that could be obtained from their leaves and flowers. Dyer's greenweed (*Genista tinctoria*) is a member of the 'whin' family which, like gorses and brooms, have yellow flowers that 'explode' when insects such as bees alight on the lip. The particles of pollen that are showered out are then carried by the insect to another plant. Once found in abundance on the Downs, the plant was also known as 'woad waxen', and was commonly gathered in July for making a yellow dye, although its long roots made harvesting a laborious affair. When mixed with woad (*Isatis tinctoria*), which yields a blue dye, a good colour of green could be obtained. Weld (*Reseda luteola*) also known as dyer's rocket was also gathered extensively for its yellow dye.

A number of plants were particularly renowned for their ability to act as natural barometers. The pale-yellow flower heads of carline thistle (*Carlina vulgaris*), for example, were locally known as a good indicator of atmospheric changes, opening fully in advance of dry bright weather and closing to herald damp unsettled weather (Fig. 70). The scarlet pimpernel (*Anagallis arvensis*) a common plant of waysides and cornfields, is another flower sensitive to changes in weather conditions, earning it in times past the name of 'shepherd's weather glass'.

Those who were well-acquainted with the medicinal properties of plants were often held in high esteem. One local tale in the Kent Downs tells of a 'witch', well-versed in plant lore, who once dwelt in a hovel on Swarling Downs near Petham in the late eighteenth century. Her local reputation was such that villagers would often visit her to buy charms and receive herbal cures for their ailments. On one occasion, however, her popularity quickly disappeared when she allegedly took it upon herself to act as a surgeon and cut off the leg of a boy who had developed a septic wound from an adder bite. The story goes that despite much protestation from the local villagers, the boy suffered no ill effects and lived out a full life, the witch having probably saved his life.

Above: Fig. 69 Common eyebright

Right: Fig. 70 Carline thistle.

WINDMILL LORE

Windmills have long held a rich association with the countryside of Kent, and were once familiar landmarks in many of the downland parishes. Their prominence as landmarks on the hill-tops and ridges of the Downs in times past was such to earn them the local name of 'Ships of the Downs'. In their heyday of the mid-nineteenth century, it has been estimated that over 400 mills existed throughout the county with many downland parishes such as Waltham, Swingfield, Petham and Elham boasting two or even three mills. Mourning the loss and deterioration of the mills in the agricultural depression years of the 1930s, William Coles Finch (1933) noted that at one time ten mills could be seen from the top of the mill at Stelling Minnis.

Just as local and seasonal events were expressed in customs and celebrations, windmills too became a medium to express community life. Often the windmill was dressed to celebrate a particular event. On the feast of Whitsuntide the mills in Kent were once often decorated with a bucket or pale containing a small tree, suspended from the top of one of the arms (sweeps), and a basket containing bread and butter from the other. The mill also became a useful means for the miller to communicate with the villagers. Different positions of the sweeps would indicate for example whether the miller was at home. If the owner of the mill died all the twenty boards in each sweep were taken out and the mill stood motionless for a given time. When the wife of the miller died it was tradition for nineteen boards to be removed, and for a child thirteen boards were taken out. Often when the daughter of the miller married, the mill was decorated and bedecked with bunting.

LEGENDS

Generations of downland dwellers, journeymen and travellers have handed down a rich resource of local folklore and tales. Few places are so steeped in legend and fable as the area surrounding the Barham Downs situated between Canterbury and Dover. Straddling the ancient thoroughfare of the 'Old Dover Road', the wind-swept and open, desolate country of these Downs in former times was littered with tales of long-forgotten battles and eerie happenings. The musings of the early twentieth-century travel writers bear witness to the mysterious nature of this tract of country long before the pressures from agriculture, roads and development made their mark:

> Standing here beside the road at evening when the sun is going down and these bleak and unenclosed uplands grow dark and mysterious, the centuries pass away like a fevered dream. Here and there the solemn expanse of the barren land is diversified by a few trees; here and there a few yards of hedge, beginning nowhere in particular and ending with equal strangeness skirt the way; weather beaten signposts start suddenly out of the moorland and occasional haycocks take on a dead and awful blackness as the evening light dies out of the sky in long and angry streaks of red.[7]

One of the earliest legends of this district is that of the 'golden calf'. This legend claims that a calf made of pure gold was buried by the early Britons in this district when they were being driven back by Roman soldiers of Caesar's army in AD 56. They buried it, intending to return, but the opportunity never arose and since then it has remained lost somewhere beneath the fields and woods of this area. Sir Charles Igglesden, in his *Saunters in Kent with Pen and Pencil* series (1900–1946), recounts that a resident of Derringstone disclosed the secret hiding place of the calf to her maid when she was on her death bed, which she claimed had been passed down from generation. It was also said that a holly tree was planted on the spot where the calf lay buried, though to this day the resting place of the calf remains a mystery.

The haunting quality to this landscape is immortalised in the work of Reverend Richard Harris Barham who, in the early nineteenth century and under the pseudonym of Thomas Ingoldsby, wrote a series of fictional tales and poems collectively known as *The Ingoldsby Legends* (1885). Born in 1788, of a family deeply rooted within the east Kent area, Barham blended his passion for antiquarian research and a mastery of prose and wit to great effect in this collection of tales. Tappington Hall Farm, near Denton, was the manor house of the Barham family and provided a fitting situation for the backdrop of the legends. Supposedly haunted by the spirits of two brothers, one a royalist and the other a follower of Cromwell, the beautiful Tudor building provides the scene of the opening legend, 'The Spectre of Tappington'. The nearby Barham Downs provided the backdrop for the 'Hand of Glory' legend. Perhaps of all the tales it is 'The Witches' Frolic' that best captures the mysterious beauty of this 'magic-ridden patch of country'. Barham used the remote and isolated building of St John's Commandery (Fig. 71), near Swingfield, for the setting of this tale, a story read by the character of 'Grandfather Ingoldsby' and within whose words the depth of Barham's affection for the 'grey ruin' is so strikingly apparent:

I love thy tower, Grey Ruin
I joy thy form to see.
Though reft of all, Cell, cloister, and hall,
Nothing is left save a tottering wall …

The storm came at last,-loud roar'd the blast,
And the shades of evening fell thick and fast;
The tempest grew; and the straggling yew,
His leafy umbrella, was wet through and through …

Revd Richard Harris Barham, The Witches' Frolic, *The Ingoldsby Legends* (1885)

As far back as Elizabethan times when the roads of Kent became notorious for highway robberies, the wooded districts of the Kent Downs have been associated with the haunts of highwaymen and thieves of all descriptions. Long Beech woods at Westwell were the supposed retreat of a highwayman known as 'Robert the Wizard', earning the name from his remarkable ability to evade capture. It was said that his success was due to the assistance he received from the local villagers who he paid in kindness by never robbing or molesting them.

Fig. 71 St John's Commandery near Swingfield provided the setting for Revd Richard Harris Barham's 'The Witches' Frolic', one of the tales of *The Ingoldsby Legends.*

Fig. 72 The tale of the phantom horsemen.

Perhaps the most notorious highwayman of the Canterbury to Dover Road was 'Black Robin', a highwayman who terrorised unsuspecting travellers on the roads and lanes of Barham Downs. The pub now known as the Black Robin was allegedly his hideout, taking its name from the black mask that he always wore. It is said that when he was eventually captured and executed, his horse refused all food and starved itself to death. The old sign of the pub once bore the legend:

Rigden Dellman ales are sold,
Where once did live Brave Robin bold.

The remote and secluded countryside of the Downs abounds in stories of the supernatural. Among the many is the tale of the ghost of Lord Rokeby, an eccentric eighteenth-century nobleman who lived at Monks Horton near Hythe, who was said could often be seen careering down Stone Street in a wagon pulled by four 'coal-black' horses and with his decapitated head in his lap. Phantom horsemen also appear in the legends of other downland parishes. Near Lydden in 1597 a German traveller, Paul Hentzner, set out at night with post horses for Dover when, after becoming separated from the rest his party, came to a junction in the road. While contemplating which path to take, 'all on a sudden on our right hand some horsemen, their stature, dress and horses exactly resembling those of our friends' came galloping past. 'We determined to set out after them, but it happened, through God's mercy, that when we called to them, they did not answer us, but kept on down the marshy road at such a rate, that their horses' feet struck fire at every stretch... there were a great many Jack a Lanterns' ('will o' the wisps'-a natural occurrence formed by self-igniting marsh gas) 'so that we were quite seized with horror and amazement.' When they were eventually reacquainted with their companions further down the path, they asked them if they had seen the horsemen, to which they replied "not a soul"'.[8]

Another story tells of the strange affair of Thomas Page, a journeyman carpenter, living in the nearby parish of Temple Ewell in 1815 who dreamt that if he dug in a certain place near the junction of the turnpike road with the road to Sandwich, he would find great treasure. Accordingly he proceeded to the spot that he had dreamt and with his knife unearthed several silver ornaments, believed to have belonged to a Roman warrior.[9]

Hollingbourne Manor was also believed to be haunted by Catherine Howard who stayed at the Manor when she was young. Beheaded by Henry VIII, it is said that her spirit was seen in the guise of a headless body who walked the staircase.

– BEACONS AND HIDE-OUTS –

For centuries the Kent Downs have held a strong association with the defence and protection of the nation. Affording far-ranging views over the lowlands and channel coast, the high ridges and wooded hinterland of this countryside have offered both a naturally strong defensive position and a refuge in times of war. The cliff-tops above Dover and Folkestone are littered with the remains of defensive structures from a range of historical periods such as the Second World War gun batteries on the Dover cliffs and the Norman motte and bailey of Caesar's Hill Camp above Folkestone. The cliffs themselves conceal a labyrinth of passages, caves and cells, some dating back to Napoleonic times which were later extended and adapted to accommodate the complex and ingenious nerve centre of channel surveillance and defence during the Second World War.

BEACONS

The high hill-tops of the Kent Downs played an important role for the beacon network in the county, which was used as an early warning system to signal the approach of hostile ships since Saxon times. The antiquarian William Lambarde provides one of the earliest references to this system noting that, 'before the time of Edward the Third they were made of great stacks of wood, but about the eleventh yeere of his reign, it was ordained, that in our shyre they should be high standards with their pitchpots'.[10] In 1372 an order was made that common signals 'called 'beknes', by fire upon hills and other high places in the said county, shall be made where as shall seem best'.[10] In the sixteenth century the beacon network was strengthened to provide an effective early warning system

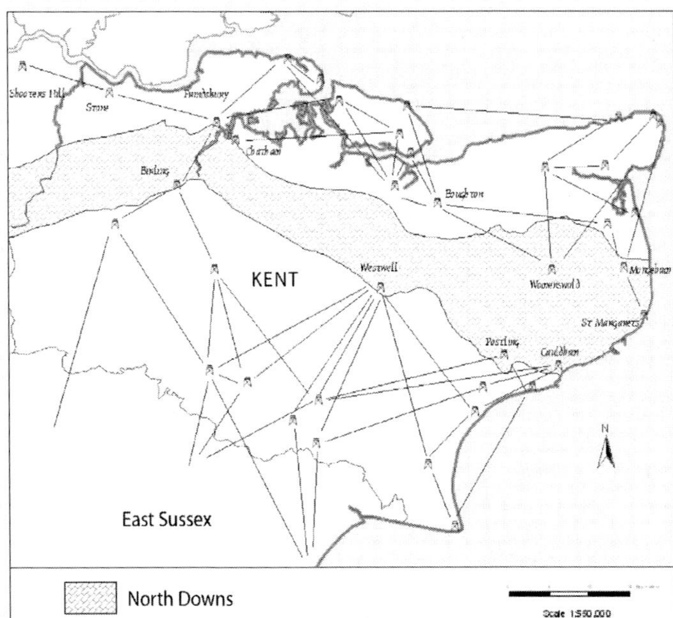

Fig. 73 The Armada Beacons in the Kent Downs (from Lambarde, 1570).

against the Spanish Armada. Hill-top beacons were constructed at Postling, Westwell, Cauldham (near Capel) and Birling, most of which were kept in a good state of repair until the middle of the seventeenth century (Fig. 73). Later in the eighteenth century the beacons received a further phase of reinstatement and upkeep with the threat of Napoleonic invasion. The network in the Downs at this time included Barham, Postling, Westwell and Wrotham. These were adapted to send semaphore messages, allowing a far speedier system of communication. It was said that a message could be sent from Deal to London in two minutes using the line of beacons from Betteshanger, Barham Downs, Shottenden Hill, Beacon Hill, Gad's Hill, Swanscombe and Shooters Hill.

SMUGGLERS

The remote and obscure wooded valleys of the Downs have offered an ideal setting for more clandestine activities. Notoriously difficult to traverse and wayfind on foot, these remote valleys were a particularly favourite haunt for smugglers. Within easy reach of the cliff-tops, areas such as the Alkham valley soon acquired a notorious reputation with the smuggling trade where the remote and lonely farmsteads were often used by smugglers to store their contraband. The farmstead of Hockley Hole in the valley became known as Smuggler's Hall from its rich associations with the smuggling trade. In 1773 French silks and laces to the value of £15,000 were seized from the hall by Excise officers. The smuggling trade was so rife in these valleys that local farmers often struggled to find a workforce as so many farmhands and labourers had become involved in the trade.

Stone Street Farm at Petham was the former abode of 'Slippery Sam' the notorious east Kent smuggler. Born in 1730, he earned his name from his wily and ingenious means of escaping from the hands of the Excise men, usually eluding them by disappearing into the thick woods of the Downs while running a smuggling 'line' from the coast to his abode.

At Magpie Bottom, near Otford, the remote lanes made ideal thoroughfares for smugglers to transport their contraband from the coast to London. Ever grateful for local assistance, smugglers often relied on the watchful eyes of villagers to forewarn them of approaching customs officers. Local legend states that a hole in the wall of the farm cottage at Magpie Bottom was a 'brandy slide', a secret cavity where smugglers rewarded the goodwill of the helpful locals with a payment in kind. The nearby field known locally as 'Pig and Whistle' is believed to be a corruption of the phrase 'peep and whistle' a reference to the clandestine collaboration between locals and smugglers.[11]

The cavern-riddled chalk pits above Lenham have similar connections and legend has it that they were used by smugglers to store contraband who leagued with local villagers and disposed of it to the gentry and farmers in the district.

WARTIME

In wartime the remote valleys and woods of the Downs were ideally suited to the more covert activities of the home forces. A secluded valley near King's Wood at Godmersham Park became the mooring-out sub-station for a 140ft (42m) long surveillance airship that undertook regular forays over the English Channel to reconnoitre for German submarines. According to local accounts the airship was hauled by large chains into the valley, secured by buried yew stumps, and the cockpit berthed in a large entrenchment. The original hole measured 60ft (18m) long by 30ft (9m) wide and 30ft (9m) deep, much of which still remains to this day and is known locally as the 'airship hole'.

During the Second World War the remote countryside of the Kent Downs provided the ideal theatre of operations for the select unit of men known as the 'Secret Army'. This unit comprised local farmers, labourers, foresters, gamekeepers and poachers who acted, in the event of invasion, as a resistance unit, drawing on their intimate knowledge of the woods, hills and marshes to sabotage and cause havoc with German forces. An elaborate network of hide-outs, camps and surveillance points was set up in the Downs to provide 'foxholes' from which small units of men would operate to sabotage supply and communication lines and disrupt enemy operations. Such was the risk of capture that their life expectancy was only a matter of days. Their hideouts were ingeniously constructed and great pains were taken to keep their locations secret, often involving elaborately constructed entry points. The airship hole at Godmersham Park was adapted as a hide-out for resistance men on the run and was designed to accommodate 120 people. This cunningly contrived hide-out was constructed beneath the existing airship berthing entrenchment and was accessed by an underground shaft and secret 'trapdoor' entrance, operated by a movable tree trunk.

SEVEN

SKYLARKS, SKIPPERS AND SCABIOUS

THE FLORA AND FAUNA OF THE DOWNS

> Against the hot blue sky, the terraced knoll loomed enormous, its summit lost in a shimmering heat-haze. The grassy flanks seemed to radiate a reflected heat, enfolding us in a weighted, thyme scented silence, enhanced rather than disturbed by the monotone of a thousand insects. On the banks at the hill's foot, the cropped turf was gemmed with the small downland flowers … in that moment I encountered a new love – the chalkdown flora.
>
> Jocelyn Brooke, *The Military Orchid* (1948)

The Kent Downs are renowned as the home of some of the richest chalk grassland plant communities within the British Isles, for it is here, where the influence of a distinctly continental feel to the climate, provides the conditions for a range of flora and fauna on the edge of their northern and western continental ranges. The current day area of chalk grassland in the Kent Downs, characteristically comprising rich and intimate mixtures of wildflowers and fine grasses, amounts to some 1,650 hectares, contributing towards approximately 5 per cent of the United Kingdom resource of this habitat. The United Kingdom itself holds a staggering 50 per cent of the world's lowland calcareous grassland area. Much of this habitat in Kent and elsewhere in the southern chalklands of the country, exists as scattered, isolated and fragmented pockets of grassland that have escaped the damaging effects of agricultural intensification, development and abandonment to woodland, either through good fortune and sympathetic management, or more commonly, by virtue of their often steep and inaccessible locations. Here and there in Kent, larger contiguous tracts of traditionally managed grassland persist, but these are chiefly confined to steeper areas of the escarpment such as at Wye Downs

Left: Fig. 74 Chalk downland flora.

Below: Fig. 75 Squinancywort.

and Folkestone Downs and also in the parts of the eastern dipslope country such as at Lydden and Temple Ewell Downs and the grasslands around Folkestone and Dover.

For their botanical interest alone the chalk grasslands of lowland England have long attracted attention and interest for the sheer richness and exceptional diversity of plant species that they are able to support. Lousley (1950) has estimated that calcareous grasslands support more than half of the total 1,550 or so different species of plants and ferns growing in the United Kingdom. These herb-rich plant communities have evolved to tolerate the stress-inducing conditions imposed by the shallow, free draining and impoverished calcareous soils which restrict the growth of more competitive nutrient-demanding plant species. Some plants such as dropwort (*Filipendula vulgaris*) and wild thyme (*Thymus drucei*) have deep and extensive root systems that help them to tap into sources of moisture deep within the soil. Salad burnet (*Poterium sanguisorba*) has also adapted in this way, its sprays of cucumber-scented, dark green leaflets once used to flavour salads. The roots of restharrow (*Ononis repens*) are so tough and deep that, in times past, they were notorious as an impediment to plough and harrow.

Lady's bedstraw (*Galium verum*) (colour plate 26) and fairy flax (*Linum catharticum*) are examples of the numerous chalk grassland plants that have evolved with small leaves to minimise transpiration loss. First documented in Kent by the herbalist Thomas Johnson in 1629[1], the name of lady's bedstraw is thought to hark back to a long-forgotten age when floors of houses were strewn with hay as a natural bedding. It also had the local name of 'rennet' or 'runnit' owing to the belief that milk would curdle if mixed with this plant.

Common eyebright (Euphrasia nemorosa) (Fig. 69), common rock-rose (*Helianthemum chamaecistus*), milkwort (*Polygala vulgaris*), and squinancywort (*Asperula cynanchica*)(Fig. 75) are typical of many of the plants that thrive on shorter grazed turf, their low growing habit perfectly adapted to take full advantage of the more humid atmosphere that lies immediately above the surface of the soil. Some plants such as rock-rose have the added

Fig. 76 Devil's-bit scabious.

advantage of having waxy leaves which help to retain moisture on the plant and so minimise water loss. Others which have adapted in a similar manner include mouse-ear hawkweed (*Pilosella officinarum*), the dense covering of hairs on the underside of its leaves providing an effective means of conserving moisture.

Horseshoe vetch (*Hippocrepis comosa*) and kidney vetch (*Anthyllis vulneraria*) number amongst the several legume species found on downland pastures, a family of plants able to tolerate the low nutrient conditions by 'fixing' nitrogen from the atmosphere through their leaves. Yellow-wort (*Blackstonia perfoliata*), with its sulphur-coloured flowers is another denizen of the chalk (Fig. 80), first recorded in the county by the herbalist John Gerarde in 1597 and named in honour of John Blackstone (d.1753), a botanist and apothecary of the eighteenth century. This plant is well-adapted to the drought-stricken chalky soils having evolved pairs of fused leaves along its stem which form a natural cup to collect overnight dew droplets, thereby providing the plant with moisture to photosynthesise in daylight hours.

The mosaic of short and long grass, bare ground and low bushes (scrub) is characteristic of traditionally managed chalk downland and provides a varied vegetation structure attractive to a diverse array of insects, mammals and birds. Where grazing pressure is less intense, such as on the fringes of thickets and bramble patches, taller herbs are able to thrive. Colourful plants such as wild marjoram (*Origanum vulgare*), greater knapweed (*Centaurea scabiosa*), wild carrot (*Daucus carota*), wild mignonette (*Reseda lutea*) and devil's-bit scabious (*Succisa pratensis*) can often be found in these areas. The conspicuous purple button-head flowers of devil's-bit scabious (Fig. 76) were once ground down into a powder that was supposedly used to kill worms. The flower was also used in medicine to heal bruises. Wild carrot was also once commonly known as 'bird's nest' because the upright cluster of flowers give the appearance of a concave nest. Its white umbrella-like flower head is often easily distinguished from other umbellifers by the purplish-red coloured centres of the inner flowers.

Low bushes and shrubs, both solitary and in groups or 'clumps', provide an additional chalk grassland habitat and create a varied structure of vegetation that appeals to a wide range of insects and mammals. Typically this scrub vegetation includes species such as hawthorn (*Crataegus monogyna*), dogwood (*Cornus sanguinea*), spindle (*Euonymus europaeus*), bramble (*Rubus fruticosus*) and gorse (*Ulex europaeus*). In times past it is evident that Juniper (*Juniperus communis*) was once more widespread on the Kent Downs. The herbalist William Turner noted in his *Herball* of 1562 that this plant 'groweth most plentuously in Kent' and even at the end of the nineteenth century it was recorded as being frequently found within the downland areas of the county. Being slow growing, susceptible to grazing in its early years and requiring thin skeletal soils on which to establish, its demise has naturally been attributed to the many factors which conflict with these conditions. Rabbit grazing, the impact of repeated fires, habitat loss, woodland encroachment, and the demise of chalk quarrying (where it once thrived on bare chalk soils) have all contributed to the decline of this plant in the county and across much of southern England. Today, the remaining population in the county is believed to number around 130 and is centred in two distinct enclaves; one around the White Hill area near Shoreham and the other on the coast around Dover and Folkestone.

As well as a diverse array of wildflowers, chalk grassland supports a range of highly adapted grasses, rarely found on other soils. These include crested hair-grass (*Koeleria macrantha*), downy oat-grass (*Avenula pubescens*), yellow oat-grass (*Trisetum flavescens*), upright brome (*Bromus erectus*) and tor grass (*Brachypodium pinnatum*). In areas particularly where grazing is absent or sporadic, the more unpalatable grasses, notably tor grass and upright brome can soon begin to dominate the sward, gradually shading out the fine-turf plant species. Tor grass is a familiar component of chalk grasslands east of the River Stour, often forming extensive tussocky patchworks through its creeping rhizomous rootstock, such as at Wye and Crundale Downs. Sheep's fescue (*Festuca ovina*) and red fescue (*Festuca rubra*) are also common species on dry grasslands. Of all the chalk-loving grasses, special mention must be made of course to the enchanting quaking grass (*Briza media*). Its triangular-shaped green spikelets hang down on slender stalks and dance and tremble in the slightest breeze. It once had the old country name of 'dodder' or 'dawther' grass in Kent.

Features sometimes known as 'fairy rings' can also be occasionally found on old grasslands of the Downs. These are formed by a soil fungus which gradually spreads in an ever-widening concentric circle and in so doing affects the growth of plants, giving the sward a darker appearance.

Anthills, or 'emmet-casts' as they were once known in Kent, are another characteristic feature of long established chalk grasslands and add much to their aesthetic appeal. These mounds are formed by the yellow meadow ant, each 'hill' supporting a colony of ants that raise their brood within galleries just beneath its surface. The micro-topography of an anthill-studded downland contributes much to the diversity of plant and invertebrate life for the soil of anthills is structurally finer, more free-draining and subject to greater fluctuations in temperature. Fine-turf plants such as rock-rose and wild thyme thrive on the close cropped sward and bare earth conditions of these miniature hillocks. The warmer south-facing sides of the mounds are also attractive to a range of insect species.

DOWNLAND FAUNA

Flower-rich chalk grassland supports a wide range of insect species. The larvae of many butterflies find their foodplants here on the Downs, notably those of the family of blue butterflies. Of all the blues, the adonis blue holds a special place in the Kent Downs where it has traditionally maintained a stronghold of the United Kingdom population. It has been fittingly adopted as the emblem of Kent Wildlife Trust. Like many other butterfly 'specialists' of the Downs, this vivid blue butterfly depends on the warm microclimates of south-facing slopes. The eggs, always laid on horseshoe vetch, produce beautifully camouflaged green and yellow caterpillars that have a special association with ants. In return for a sugary substance that is secreted from its glands, the ants tend and protect the caterpillar while it feeds on the vetch during the day. This is one of several butterfly species that produce two generations of butterflies each year, the first emerging in late May and the second in late August. At the turn of the last century, adonis blue was recorded as being locally abundant on the chalk hills near Shoreham, Folkestone, Dover and Chilham, but is now largely confined to just a few localities on the escarpment and more extensive tracts of dry valley chalk grassland.

Small blue and chalkhill blue are also denizens of the warm slopes of the Kent Downs. The small blue is dependent on kidney vetch as its foodplant and is more commonly found on the close-cropped turf of chalk pits and embankments where the vetch thrives on skeletal soils. The chalkhill blue is another feeder of horseshoe vetch, although is less fussy in its choice of egg laying sites and, like the adonis, its caterpillar is often betrayed by the presence of ants which milk its honey-like secretions.

The rare silver-spotted skipper is another Kent Downs speciality, confined chiefly in its habitat requirements to the close-cropped turf of warm south-facing slopes. The caterpillars of this butterfly feed exclusively on sheep's fescue which, whilst common enough, may not always provide the right conditions for an egg-laying site. Females seek out small isolated tufts of fescue growing beside bare ground for egg-laying and consequently butterfly populations are relatively susceptible to extinction where there is lack of suitable habitat. Like many other species, this butterfly has witnessed severe declines in recent times and is especially vulnerable when the extinction of neighbouring colonies leads to isolated populations becoming isolated which area less able to repopulate when numbers decline. The Downs are home to several other members of the skipper family. Large, Essex and small skipper are plentiful throughout the downland country and the stronghold populations of the less common dingy skipper and grizzled skipper are also found here.

Fig. 77 Marbled white, a distinctive butterfly of chalk grasslands where it can often be found feeding on knapweed, scabious, marjoram and thistles.

Many butterfly species prefer areas of longer grass, either in open downland or around the margins of scrub and woodland. These include more common species such as the distinctive black and white chequer-board patterned marbled white (Fig. 77), as well as gatekeeper, ringlet and meadow brown. A number of species rely on the dappled-light conditions associated with woodland glades and scrub. The evocatively named Duke of Burgundy is typical of several butterfly species that have adapted to the dappled light conditions provided by the traditional practice of woodland coppicing. This butterfly depends specifically on foodplants of the primula family but also requires the mix of light and shade provided by young trees and bushes. Traditionally this type of transitional habitat, often occurring on the margins of grassland and woodland, was more abundant in the Downs. A century ago this butterfly occurred 'in many woods near Canterbury, Dover and the Blean'[2] but is now confined to the Wye, Crundale, and Denge Wood area south of Canterbury. The black-veined moth is a similar specialist of this type of habitat, requiring coarse and tussocky grassland where it feeds on herbs such as wild marjoram. Loss and fragmentation of rough grassland sites has contributed to the decline in this species and today a small tract of country in the Stour valley supports the sole five remaining colonies within the United Kingdom.

The pearl-bordered fritillary was once present throughout the woodlands of the Downs, its existence largely dependent on the habitat conditions provided by regular coppicing. Its foodplants are members of the violet family and like many other 'specialists' it requires a particular set of conditions for egg laying afforded by the nature of the vegetation on the woodland floor and the degree of light and shade.

The decline in traditionally managed grassland and woodland habitats has inevitably taken its toll on many butterfly species. Much effort has been made in recent years to arrest these declines. Unfortunately for some such as the pearl-bordered fritillary, with the sad demise of its last surviving colony in the downland woods near Bishopsbourne, it seems that this may be too late. For others however, the outlook appears brighter with several species showing signs of population recovery. This is largely due to sites being brought back into favourable condition through the dedicated work of conservation organisations, farmers and landowners. Both the adonis blue and silver-spotted skipper butterflies have been the focus of attention for reintroduction projects in recent years. Considerable success has been made at sites such as Burham Down near Maidstone and Wye Downs near Ashford where in 1997 Kent Wildlife Trust introduced the silver-spotted skipper from Lydden Downs. Similar reintroductions occurred in 2002 when adonis blues were released on Queendown Warren near Rochester. Today these sites boast growing populations.

The insect- and seed-rich habitats of chalk grassland provide an attractive haunt for many bird species. The distant melody of skylark and the call of meadow pipit and yellowhammer are perhaps some of the most evocative sounds of the Downs in the summer months. Skylark, deprived to a large degree of its former rough grassland nesting sites, is still in healthy numbers throughout the Downs, making use of spring-sown cornfields and areas of fallow land where the low growing vegetation affords attractive nest sites. Meadow pipit is now largely confined in its breeding areas to the remaining areas of chalk grassland especially near the coast where it can often be seen rising into the sky and then 'parachuting' back down to the ground with its distinctive song. Records suggest that the pipit bred more commonly along the Downs in times past. The open windswept expanses of the newly created Samphire Hoe near Dover also support some of the few remaining breeding localities of the stonechat within the county which appears to have been more widespread in times past particularly along the gorse-clad crests of the Downs between Dover and Maidstone. Its relative, the whinchat, was also formerly found on the rough, bush-dotted grasslands of the Downs but is now only seen on migration through the county in spring and autumn months.

The native grey partridge was once in large numbers across the open farmland of Kent and large coveys were once familiar sights in the downland countryside. The early-twentieth century ornithologist Dr. Norman Ticehurst wrote of this bird as 'numerous' and even by the mid 1970s this popular game bird occurred in healthy numbers throughout the county. The rolling tracts of arable land at Luddesdown were once well-known for their partridges, Sir Charles Igglesden noting in the 1930s that the bird thrives here 'as in no other part of Kent'. Its demise in the last thirty years or so has been attributed to the loss of its feeding habitat of weedy and insect-rich field edges and corners that were once common in traditionally managed cornfields prior to the widespread introduction of pesticides.

Lapwing, too, was once a common sight on many areas of the Downs nesting on open spring-sown ground, its characteristic call earning it the name 'peewit'. Another bird of open farmland, the corn bunting, still maintains stronghold populations in some parts of the East Kent Downs where it can often be heard, perched on a telegraph wire or lone tree, its song resembling the jangling of keys. Historical records suggest that the open chalk country of east Kent has long been a favoured haunt of the corn bunting within the county. Its relative, the cirl bunting, has fared less well. It appeared to have bred with some regularity in times past, particularly in the West and Mid Kent Downs, as is evidenced by nineteenth-century breeding records in Shoreham, Knockholt, Boxley, Wye and the Westwell areas. In common with many other areas of southern England, this species witnessed a widespread decline in Kent in the twentieth century and today the sole remaining breeding populations occur in south-west England.

The hedgerows and thickets of the Downs, less affected by changes in farming practice, provide the attractive nesting sites for birds such as yellowhammer, linnet and lesser whitethroat as well as many of the more common species such as chaffinch, wren and whitethroat. Woodland birds too have generally fared well within the Downs, with species such as nuthatch, treecreeper, nightingale, willow warbler and chiffchaff well-represented in the deciduous woods of this area. It is reasonable to assume that in former times the more open tree-dotted commons of the downland plateau provided an attractive haunt for birds such as tree pipit.

Traditionally the river valleys of the Kent Downs provided extensive areas of damp grasslands, ditches and ponds attractive to birds such as yellow wagtail, reed warbler and snipe. The Darenth valley in particular appears to have been a regular haunt for breeding snipe where their 'drumming' was once a familiar sound every year in April and May. The water meadows and hay fields of the Downs also once supported the corn crake or 'land rail', a bird that today is largely restricted to the damp grasslands of the Scottish Isles. The steady decline of this ground-nesting species from Kent was noted in the early twentieth century, and was attributed to the mechanisation of agriculture and the effect mechanical mowing. Mourning their demise from the fields and farmland around the tiny hamlet of Crundale in the Stour valley, local farmer Jim White remembered their harsh call as a familiar sound within the cornfields each year before harvest, described in his enchanting account of farmland life of yesteryear, *A Countryman's Year on the North Downs of Kent* (1985).

Whilst many of these wetland species have disappeared with changes in land use, the river corridors themselves are still frequented by birds such as kingfisher and heron. Chilham Castle and Park, situated in the Stour valley, is famous for its long-established heronry dating as far back as the thirteenth century, reputedly the oldest in the western world. Records indicated that in the early twentieth century the number of nests averaged around eighty per year.[3] Local legend states that if the herons do not return from their winter migration to nest each year by Saint Valentine's Day, then disaster will befall the lord of the castle.

The wind-swept chalk cliffs of the South Foreland between Kingsdown and Folkestone deserve special mention, for this area has become home to a unique range of birds in times past. Both chough and raven are known to have once held long-established nesting sites upon the rocky and turf-clad ledges of the cliffs. The chough, now largely confined to the western coastline of England, is believed to have had its last colony here in the mid-nineteenth century. The peregrine falcon has also had a long standing association with the cliffs around Dover, regularly numbering six to eight breeding pairs in the early 1900s. The impact of persecution and poisoning contributed to the decline in numbers and by the 1960s the bird had disappeared from the county as a breeding species. More sympathetic attitudes in recent decades have now seen this charismatic bird of prey return to nest on the cliffs and the number of breeding pairs is now once again estimated at six to eight pairs.[4]

THE ORIGIN OF CHALK GRASSLANDS

Chalk grasslands, in common with other grassland communities, are only able to persist where the natural and inevitable succession to scrub and eventually woodland is kept in check. To some degree, natural events such as fires and storms may have helped to keep the development of woodland at bay in times past, but by far the most important mechanism is the action of grazing and browsing by herbivores. The domestication of livestock by early farmers in Neolithic times undoubtedly played

Fig. 78 Highland cattle, believed to be a descendant of the extinct European wild ox (auroch), grazing on downland.

an important role in providing this grazing mechanism, yet what has not been clear is how the plants of chalk grassland were able to persist prior to this time.

At the end of the last Ice Age, the gradual warming of the climate across present day southern England witnessed the colonisation of grassland and woodland plant species from the European continent. The nature of this colonisation is poorly understood although understanding of the migration routes for the British Isles flora was greatly advanced by Rose (1972) who highlighted the continuity of the chalk grassland system with the Boullonais area in northern France. His study compared the relative abundance of chalk grassland species on either side of the English Channel and led him to suggest that colonisation of the British Isles was most likely along the corridor of the Somme valley, prior to the English Channel forming.

Recent studies by the Dutch ecologist Franz Vera have now begun to shed new light on the post-glacial landscape which traditionally had been viewed as closed-canopy lowland forest. This work has highlighted the instrumental role that wild herbivores would have played in perpetuating and 'managing' a 'parkland' or wood pasture mosaic of habitats with open clearings and glades of grassland in a mosaic of tree-dotted grassland and woodland.[5] The wild breeds of horse, forest cattle, wild ox (auroch) boar, bison, deer, and elk that roamed the hills and valleys during this time were the natural browsers and grazers that shaped this ever-changing vegetation structure of trees, grasslands, glades, mires, fen and bogs. It is likely then that chalk grassland in these earlier times was simply one component of a dynamic natural system where different soil and drainage conditions, coupled with the continual impact of browsing and grazing allowed a wide range of species and habitats to exist side by side.

In terms of the current day resource of remaining chalk grasslands in the Downs, it was popularly believed that these originated from the grazing of formerly cultivated land that was converted to pasture at various times between the Neolithic and late-medieval periods. Detailed studies on the evolution of species-rich chalk grassland swards suggests that such processes could take considerable time to develop stable species-rich plant communities, dependent on the interaction of many factors such as soil conditions, grazing pressure, nutrient levels and species competition.[6]

Recent times have however witnessed a re-appraisal of this assumption and it is now becoming increasingly apparent that many of today's chalk grasslands are not as 'ancient' as previously thought. Undoubtedly there are those downland areas that have perhaps remained under grassland for many centuries such as the steeper banks that once formed part of the medieval 'sheep-walks' as at Wye Downs, yet there are equally many areas of apparently 'old' chalk grassland that have now proven to have been under cultivation as recently as the mid-nineteenth century. Research by the landscape historian Dr Nicola Bannister, in particular, highlights a number of such sites within the Kent Downs and draws attention to the dynamic nature of the landscape over time, in which chalk grassland should be viewed as simply one state of an interchangeable cycle of arable, pasture, scrub and woodland.[7] A study by Cornish (1964) similarly demonstrates the cyclical nature of grassland and arable. Her study of plant-rich chalk grasslands found that, of the fifteen areas studied, over half had originated from arable areas abandoned within the previous fifty years. The tithe maps of the nineteenth century are particularly useful in this respect. Lydden and Temple Ewell Downs National Nature Reserve near Dover currently encompasses an area of some 75ha (180 acres) of 'ancient' chalk grassland. While many of the steeper banks show the hallmarks of well-established grassland communities, the tithe map records of 1841 indicate that some areas of current day species rich grassland, particularly those on the less severe gradients were in fact under arable crops at this time. Colour plate 22 illustrates that a considerable area of present day chalk grassland at the eastern end of the Nature Reserve around the village of Temple Ewell, was under arable cultivation. The area known as 'Round Hill' and 'The Flats' (colour plate 23) on the tithe map was predominantly under cultivation. Similarly an area simply referred to as 'Down' which abutted the steeper banks of Outlands Down was also under arable crops. Today this area of downland supports a contiguous swathe of flower rich chalk grassland communities. Only a barely detectable ridge (lynchet) on the bottom edge of this area bears testament to the former plough line that marked the edge of the cultivated ground (Fig. 79).

Historically, the more widespread nature of chalk grasslands within the landscape has always provided a relatively abundant seed source for newly establishing areas of grassland. Areas of chalk grassland that were ploughed for arable could more readily revert back to chalk grassland as plants from adjacent undisturbed grassland could easily colonise. It is the gradual fragmentation of this patchwork of chalk grasslands from the wider landscape that has caused so much concern in the post-war years, since isolated grasslands and the rich insect communities that depend upon them are naturally at a much greater risk of being lost without neighbouring populations to replenish and recruit from.

Fig. 79 A lynchet on Outlands Downs at Lydden. The lynchet bank, now ridden with rabbit holes, marks the edge of the upslope area of flatter cultivated ground and bears testament to the extent of arable land in the early nineteenth century.

The state of this ever-shifting mosaic at any particular time in history, with grassland dominating during certain periods and arable during others, has in many ways been a reflection of the economic pressures that have influenced farming and land use over the centuries. The marginal nature of the downland farming with its impoverished soils and poor yields has inevitably meant that, in times of agricultural depression, it has been one of the first areas to be hit by abandonment and neglect. The extent of neglect, from allowing land to 'tumble-down' from arable to grassland, grassland to scrub, and scrub to woodland has thus continually shifted in direct response to the degree of hardship imposed by economic conditions at the time. Conversely in times of prosperity and when demand for crops increased, the pendulum of land use swung the other way: woodland was cleared, and grassland was ploughed to produce crops. This cycle of land use change from succession to woodland on the one hand, and reversion to arable on the other, has been a constant feature of the Kent Downs landscape.

Some of the earliest evidence of these cycles of abandonment and reclamation comes from the analysis of pollens and silt deposits of a dry coombe, known as the Devil's Kneading Trough on the Wye Downs near Ashford. Evidence in the form of different mollusc shells and pollen grains found in the soil profile indicates that tree cover gave way to grassland and cultivated ground around 3000 BC. This was followed by a re-colonisation of scrub and woodland and then a second phase of clearance some 1,500 years later.

Another cycle of land use change occurs in the later medieval period when the increase in population at this time witnessed a renewed effort of woodland clearance. Crop growing became so profitable that large areas of pasture were converted into arable ground. This was the period when denehole excavation activity reached a peak to sustain the increasing demand for chalk that was used to improve the soil condition of newly won ground. An examination of woodbanks in the parish of Cudham draws particular attention to the changing use of the landscape through this period.[8] It appears that early medieval use of the landscape was primarily for the seasonal pasturing of livestock. This was then followed by the establishment of dispersed settlements which precipitated the conversion of some of the wood and pasture to arable land in the later medieval period.

The catastrophic effects of the Black Death on the population saw the cycle of land use return the other way with arable land being reverted back to pasture and more marginal land going back to woodland. Denehole digging appears to have ceased and the skill was lost for another two centuries. With less demand for corn and fewer workers on the land the keeping of sheep in large numbers became more prevalent from the latter half of the fourteenth century. Large areas of arable ground were turned back to grazing land and many areas of the Downs probably for a time became sheep walks for medieval manors.

The seventeenth century provides some of the earliest documentary evidence of the nature of these cycles. Early documents relating to the parish of Wrotham, for example, record that in 1620 the scarp slope area of the parish was predominantly under rough grazing with little woodland, yet by 1759, it is evident from written records that the grassland was more intensively grazed, with rough grazing confined to a small area.[9]

Similar cycles can be seen in the more recent historical period with the impact of the advances in farming associated with the agricultural revolution of the eighteenth and nineteenth centuries. This period probably witnessed some of the more extensive losses of chalk grassland to arable ground. The widespread uptake of crops such as sainfoin and turnips saw more land come under the plough as part of an arable rotation. Elsewhere other economic factors such as the loss of the London fuel-wood market precipitated the grubbing of woodland and conversion to arable ground. Until the beginning of the eighteenth century, London obtained much of its 'firings' from the extensive woodland of the Downs in North West Kent, but with the growing use of coal this demand was reduced. The writer and journalist Daniel Defoe, remarked in his *A Tour through England and Wales* (1724-1727), 'Since the taverns in London are come to make coal fires in their upper rooms …'tis not trifling to observe what an alteration it makes in the value of those woods in Kent, and how many more of them are stubb'd up, and the land made fit for the plow'.[10]

Further incursion undoubtedly occurred as a result of the Napoleonic Wars when demand for home-grown crops witnessed the conversion of more grassland to arable. Keymer and Leach (1990), in their study of English grasslands, identify this time as one of the key periods of grassland loss. Cornish's (1954) study of the origins of chalk grassland types in the Kent Downs gleaned information from the agricultural reports of William Marshall (*Agriculture in the Southern Counties* 1798), and John Boys (*The Agriculture of Kent* 1813) to provide evidence that the plough had, in the early nineteenth century, covered extensive areas of downland. Blackwood and Tubbs (1970) go as far to suggest that the extent of ploughing was so widespread that the remaining area of chalk grassland at this time was probably comparable to that of the current day.

This particular period of incursion however appears to have been relatively short-lived as it is likely that some of this newly won ground saw its corn producing years abruptly curtailed by the effect of the new policy of importing cheap corn from America. The marginal corn growing areas of the Downs were once again abandoned as the agricultural depression took hold through the nineteenth century and land was turned back into pasture or left as 'tumble-down' to scrub and woodland. Commenting on the agricultural depression of the county of the later nineteenth century, *The Victoria History of the County of Kent* (1908) noted that the districts most heavily hit were the stiff-clayed wheat and bean lands, 'thousands of acres of which have been laid down or tumbled down to pasture'.

The impact of the agricultural depression of the 1930s was similarly felt. Commenting on the tract of 365 acres of corn land at Waltham that at one time supported a thriving milling industry, William Coles Finch observed in the 1930s that this land was now 'just let go, not even laid down to pasture',[11] highlighting again the cycle of abandonment and reclamation that has typified the downland countryside over the centuries.

In more recent times, the mid and later half of the twentieth century have witnessed an extensive loss of chalk grassland to arable land associated with the drive for self-sufficiency during the Second World War and the desire for increased efficiency and higher yields. Losses to agricultural intensification have been compounded particularly since the1960s by a number of other factors. The gradual incursion of housing, industrial and infrastructure developments have accounted for large areas of irreversible losses. Paradoxically, the decline in livestock farming has led to the abandonment of much of the remaining chalk grassland to scrub and secondary woodland. This has been exacerbated by the drastic reduction in the rabbit population following the myxomatosis outbreaks of the 1960s which resulted in further scrub and woodland encroachment on many sites before rabbit population levels were able to recover. Rabbit grazing plays a key role in maintaining the short, close-cropped turf of chalk downland.

THE HISTORY OF BOTANICAL STUDY

The richness and diversity of our chalkland flora and fauna is perhaps one of the most enduring and cherished facets of the English countryside. The Kent Downs are no exception and the pockets of flower-rich chalk grassland that grace our scarps and slopes retain today the same enduring aesthetic appeal that have inspired generations of botanists.

Fig. 80 Yellow-wort, first recorded in the county by the sixteenth-century herbalist John Gerarde and found 'upon the chalke cliffs of Greenhithe' in 1597.

From as early as 1548, when the 'father of botany' William Turner (c.1508-1568) recorded the sea cabbage (*Brassica oleracea*), rock samphire (*Crithmum maritimum*) and yellow sea-poppy (*Glaucium flavum*) on the cliffs around Dover,[12] the well-trodden paths across the Downs from London to the coast have been a favourite haunt of many plant lovers. Within striking distance of the bustling metropolis of London it is no surprise that this rich botanical resource has been widely appreciated by city dwellers eager to practice their hobby beyond the confines of study and classroom.

The early 'botanists' were the seventeenth and eighteenth-century herbalists and apothecaries who, for the first time, began to document and record the immense variety of plants throughout the county in their pursuit of new specimens and samples for medicinal properties. Many of the first recordings of plants within the Downs were made at this time. The chalklands of the north western part of the county, in particular, appear with regularity in these early records and can claim many of the first documented records for downland plants. This early phase of plant study was very much based on the medicinal and curative properties that individual plants possessed, yet this period also marked a time when flowers and plants were becoming increasingly appreciated for their aesthetic beauty. While generations before had developed an immense body of plant lore and knowledge, the herbalists and apothecaries of the seventeenth century began to recognise the need for accurate and reliable information in the light of increasing suspicion towards the superstition that surrounded the plant lore of earlier times.

The renowned herbalist John Gerarde (1545-1612) was one of the first apothecaries to document the flora of Kent, his *Herball* of 1597 noting eighty-three 'first' records for the county and including familiar chalk downland plants such as wild basil (*Clinopodium vulgare*) and common rock-rose (*Helianthemum chamaecistus*).

Thirty-six years later these records were further augmented by Thomas Johnson who published his own revised edition of the *Herball* (1633). With an established apothecary practice at Snow Hill in London, Johnson and his botanical colleagues undertook several journeys into the north and western parts of the county amassing over 330 first records for the county. While most of his journeys were restricted to the north and west of Kent, where travel by boat afforded easy access onto the north Kent coastline and marshes, his detailed recorded excursions across arable lands between Dartford and Gravesend and, in particular, around the area known as Chalkedale near Dartford provide a fascinating insight into the diversity of flora that must have been commonplace over the lightly chalky soils of the North Downs districts. Although Johnson is unlikely to have ventured further south into the hinterland of dry valleys, his particular attention given to rare plants in this district perhaps suggest that chalk grassland was by no means a commonplace encounter in these more arable districts of the county at this time. It is at Chalkdale, a pit where 'stones had once been quarried to make quicklime'[13] that he noted, amongst many other species, fly orchid (*Ophyrs insectifera*) (Fig. 82), wild mignonette (*Reseda lutea*), kidney vetch (*Anthyllis vulneraria*) and Lady's bedstraw (*Galium verum*) (colour plate 26). Johnson's excursion to Chalkdale and the surrounding area was retraced by the Kent Field Club in 1975 and it was encouraging to note that many of the plants mentioned by Johnson were still found in the same places.[14]

Throughout the seventeenth and eighteenth centuries the dedicated work of herbalists and botanists such as John Parkinson (1567-1650), James Sherrard (1666-1737), Christopher Merret (1614-1695) and John Martyn (1699-1768), provided the first references to many of the familiar downland species and made significant contributions to the documentation of the county's flora. Towards the end of the eighteenth century the study of flora was becoming embraced by a growing body of amateur and professional botanists whose attention had turned towards the scientific study of the plants themselves rather than their curative or medicinal virtues. Learned societies were established and botanical studies and notes were published in journals such as the much acclaimed *English Botany* (1790-1814) which ran for thirty-five volumes. It was this period that marked the heyday of English field botany.

Arguably one of the most successful and celebrated botanical artists of her time, Anne Pratt (1806-1893) drew heavily on the flora of the Kent Downs for inspiration. Recognised for her talent from an early age, her blending of romantic description and accurate beautiful illustrations, appealed to a wide public audience (colour plate 28). Originally born in Stroud in 1806, she later settled at Dover where the cliff-tops and downland thereabouts provided a rich resource for her subject. A prolific writer and illustrator, she completed many works including the five volumes of *The Flowering Plants, Grasses, Sedges and Ferns of Great Britain* (1855-1866), a fascinating compendium of botanical description, illustration and plant lore.

The Victorian era marked a renewed quest for new hunting grounds for plants as the appeal of botanising and popular science took hold of an eager public.

The occasional discovery of a new unrecorded species that had hitherto escaped the attentions of earlier botanists served to fuel this growing appetite for natural history study and the Kent Downs became the focus of excursions and visits from amateurs and professionals, keen to seek out new specimens for their collections and herbariums and witness for real the captivating illustrations and drawings that filled the pages of journals, studies and books. Downland villages such as Westwell had clearly acquired a reputation throughout the nineteenth and early twentieth centuries, Sir Charles Igglesden noting it in the 1930s as 'famous for the rich botanical and entomological specimens it produces'.[15]

With its rich variety of orchid species, the flower-rich downland around Dover soon became a popular haunt for generations of Victorian and Edwardian botanists. L.W. Dillwyn's *Catalog of the More Rare Plants Found in the Environs of Dover* (1802), G.E. Smith's *Catalogue of Rare or Remarkable Phaenogamous Plants Collected in South Kent* (1829) and Frederick Apthorp Paley's *The Wild Flowers of Dover* (*c.*1850) bear testament to the generations of botanists and naturalists that have found inspiration within this corner of the Downs.

Further along the escarpment at Folkestone, the downland hills and valleys became the hunting grounds for the Folkestone Natural History Society. Throughout the county these societies provided the forum for like-minded amateurs to share knowledge, exchange specimens and undertake rambles and excursions in pursuit of their passion and hobby. Proceedings, transactions, minutes, reports, papers and studies that now lie within dusty museum archives bear witness to the widespread appeal in natural history that once captivated the nation. It is within the dedicated and painstaking studies of the many 'un-sung' local naturalists such as Henry Ullyet (*Rambles of a Naturalist around Folkestone*, 1880) and G.C. Walton (*List of Flowering Plants and Ferns found in the Neighbourhood of Folkestone*, 1894), that we owe much of our current understanding of the former distribution of downland plants and insects.

The surge of interest in plant study continued well into the twentieth century and the Downs has continued to inspire generations of botanists of more recent times. Enthralled by the flora of chalk grassland and rare elusive orchids, Jocelyn Brooke's lifelong fascination with plant study culminated in two of his most enchanting works, *The Flower in Season* (1952) and the beautifully crafted monograph and iconograph, *The Wild Orchids of Britain* (1950) both of which reflect his strong empathy for the chalk downland of Kent. Brooke's strong botanical interest became inextricably linked with his acute awareness of the ever-changing seasons, providing him with a unique ability to use the imagery of the plant world to convey the haunting atmosphere and sombre beauty of the Kent Downs. For him, 'the ecology of plant life possessed a certain element of poetry: as a quoted line of verse will suddenly evoke by association a complete poem, so a specimen of any given plant will call up not only all the flowers associated with its particular habitat, but the whole "feeling" and atmosphere of the place itself'.[16]

Plants such as the rare and poisonous stinking hellebore (*Helleborus foetidus*), one of the few true winter-flowering plants, held a special significance for Brooke

Fig. 81 Stinking hellebore.

(Fig. 81). This woodland plant, found only on the shallow soils and wooded slopes of the lowland chalk country, epitomised the mystical and potent atmosphere of the Downs in winter. It is easy to see why this plant 'august and sinister', its 'sculptured beauty' and poisonous flowers, 'like the wicked heads of adders poised to strike' gave him so much inspiration.[17] Just as in Brooke's time the plant is now only found in a few locations within the Downs, and it is encouraging to see that it still thrives in the very spot that he found it for his first time on the chalk hills near Dover where, 'beneath the silvery boles of the beeches, the big rosettes of iron-dark foliage lay'.[18]

August and sinister herb
Now springing in this unquiet
And lenten weather, your cold
And sculptured beauty once more compels
My annual and particular reverence ...

Jocelyn Brooke 'The Hellebore' in *December Spring* (1946)

The botanist J.E. Lousley, whose lifelong work culminated in the publication of *Wildflowers of Chalk and Limestone* (1950) was also greatly inspired by the North Downs of Kent, having spent many of his childhood years bicycling here from his home in south London. In more recent times renowned botanists such as Francis Rose and Peter Marren have also had strong associations with the plant-rich habitats of the Downs.

The fascination that attracted the early herbalists and botanists is the same that today lures the myriads of naturalists who travel from far and wide to appreciate the beauty of flora and fauna. For many, this appeal owes as much to the pleasure in witnessing the sheer diversity of colour and form as to the evocative scents and aromas that awaken childhood memories of wandering the springy turf of hill and vale. Richard Church's childhood memories of the Downs around Otford will be familiar to the many who have grown up within the Downs:

> Thyme was the predominant element, whose pervading scent filled the air, the cells of the body, the rooms of the memory, the deep recesses of the spirit. It seemed to come up the hill in waves, from the ruined tower. But in fact it was an exhalation from the ground at our feet, the light, chalk turf, spring-like and crisp with miniature blossoms of bread and cheese, harebell, valerian, scabious and stunted hawthorn bushes like cunning Japanese cultures on which years of skill had been lavished.[19]

In an age when the trappings of modern society have only served to dilute the once strong bond between man and the natural world it is a fitting testament to the special character of the Downs that so many continue to cherish the flora and fauna of these hills.

– THE ORCHIDS OF THE DOWNS –

Of all the flowers that grace the Kentish Downs, it is perhaps the orchid family that have acquired a unique attraction, not least for the oddity of their shape and form as for their seemingly enigmatic life cycles. Notoriously elusive and seldom commonplace in their haunts, their striking looks have bestowed upon them a reputation as the 'royalties' of the plant world.

The warm south-facing chalk hills of Kent provide an ideal environment for the many orchid species that thrive on calcareous soils. As well as being renowned for their abundant colonies of the more common orchids, these hills are able to support the principal population strongholds for a number of rarer species that have a more 'natural' range on the warmer calcareous substrates of the European continent. Hanbury's *Flora of Kent* (1899) recorded that of the forty-four British orchid species known at the time no less than thirty-three had been gathered in the county. The assortment of orchid species of the Kent Downs occur across a wide variety of chalkland habitats. Some such as the diminutive, yet strikingly elegant autumn lady's-tresses (*Spiranthes spiralis*) and the vibrantly coloured pyramidal orchid (*Anacamptis pyramidalis*) thrive in closely cropped open grassland. Others such as the slender fly orchid (*Ophrys insectifera*) and the lady orchid (*Orchis purpurea*) prefer the dappled sunlight conditions afforded within the many glades and woodland edges. Some such as the early-purple orchid (*Orchis mascula*) are more at home within the shady woodlands of the Downs.

First recorded within the county near Dartford by Thomas Johnson in 1641, the **lizard orchid** (*Himantoglossum hircinum*) is perhaps one of the more elusive members of the orchid family often occurring as solitary and sporadically flowering individuals. One of the taller orchids, sometimes growing up to 3ft (0.9m) in height, its greenish purple flowers are said to resemble small lizards. With a preference for chalky soils it favours areas of grassland where grazing pressure has been relaxed allowing a longer sward to develop. John Jacob was a renowned botanist of Dover who devoted his life to the search and study of the lizard orchid, following his first encounter with the plant in 1885. His work *Wildflowers, Grasses and Ferns of East Kent* (1936) includes a comprehensive list of each locality.

The rare **military orchid** (*Orchis militaris*) became the subject of a life-long search for the celebrated local author Jocelyn Brooke. Brooke's passion for botany grew from his early childhood experiences of hunting for orchids on the Downs, his quest for these elusive species forming the theme for his autobiographical novel, *The Military Orchid* (1948). For him the military orchid took on 'a kind of legendary quality ... its name was like a distant bugle-call, thrilling and rather sad'.[20] Yet, sadly, he was never to find the military orchid in Kent and for many years its status within the county has remained the subject of much controversy, not least for its confusion with another orchid species: its appearance is remarkably similar to that of the lady orchid and can only be readily distinguished by its smaller stature and slight variation in the flower head. In former times this distinction was often overlooked and early records of this species have inevitably been viewed with a degree of suspicion. For many years the orchid was thought to be extinct from the British Isles but in 1947 the botanist J.E. Lousley made the chance discovery of a colony in Oxfordshire. Although the orchid has remained elusive to Kent in recent years, the authentification of nineteenth-century specimens housed in surviving herbariums, does appear to prove that the military orchid has been present within the county in former times.

Brooke's passion for orchids inspired some of his most lyrical prose. The elegant **lady orchid** (*Orchis purpurea*) (colour plate 29) was one of his favourites:

> coming upon it suddenly on the fringe of some Kentish woodland, its showy spikes standing out so vividly against the dingy thickets of dog's mercury, one is struck above all by its "exotic" quality; there is something curiously alien about these tall pagodas of purple and white blossom; a suggestion of the greenhouse or the jungle, incongruous and rather startling among the homely flowers of an English spring.[21]

Arguably one of the most beautiful of our English wildflowers, this orchid is a breathtaking gem of many of the woodlands and copses of the Downs. Seldom found beyond the county borders, it has long been cherished for its unique association with the downland of Kent and it is a fitting honour that it has been adopted as the emblem of the Kent Downs Area of Outstanding Natural Beauty.

Its name derives from the shape of its flower which resembles the outline of a white crinoline dress, flushed with pink and red-dotted, and headed with a beautiful dark hood. It was variously known in Kent in former times as the 'brown-winged' and 'great brown orchid', and its resemblance to a figure dressed in wide sleeves, bonnet and apron also earned it the name of 'old woman's orchid' and 'maids of Kent' in some localities. With a stout stem it typically stands at between 1ft–2ft (30–60cm) tall. Perhaps the most astonishing record comes from that of the naturalist, Reverend Cecil Henry Fielding, the curate of Higham, who claimed a specimen 4ft 6in (1.38m) in height at Otford Mount in 1874.[22]

The colonies of this orchid appear to have been relatively stable over time with its stronghold traditionally associated with the wooded dry valleys of the East Kent Downs, occurring in around 100 sites. Francis Rose (1948) also identifies a second cluster of distribution centred on the Downs either side of the Medway valley.

The slender **fly orchid** (*Ophrys insectifera*) (Fig. 82) is another speciality of the dappled-sunlit conditions of woodland coppice and thicket-fringed banks of the chalk country. This delicate orchid is a wondrous example of the beauty of nature. Its tiny purplish-brown hued flowers, each marked with a blue tinge, are beautifully crafted to give the appearance of a fly replete with blue-sheen wings and antennae crawling up the stem. It is pollinated by a variety of digger wasp, which mistakes the flower for a female of its own species. Those who have paid homage to this enchanting orchid include The Amicci Society, a gathering of like-minded fellows of the early nineteenth century devoted to the study of natural history, who captured the splendour of this plant found on the brow of the Boxley hills in a poem entitled 'The Fly Orchis':

Sweet flower! Of all that bloom by hill or glen
Through smiling Kent, there's none I love like thee
For thour'st the truest type of true born men
Hardy, unbought, untamable and free ...

The Amicci, 'The Fly Orchis' (Lines on a fly orchis found on the brow of the Boxley Hills) (1836)

Another member of this orchid family is the **bee orchid** (*Ophrys apifera*). First recorded in the county by the herbalist John Gerarde in 1597, this plant is perhaps one of the most impressive and delightful of insect imitators. The velvety flowers, embroidered with rich brown and yellow hues are an astonishing evolutionary master piece unparalleled in our native flora, made all the more puzzling by the fact that the bee orchid is one of our several orchid species that is self-pollinating. Tightly grazed chalk downland turf provides one of the favourite haunts of this charismatic orchid. Its singular and striking appearance has long been treasured and its local abundance in former times was such that in the nineteenth century it was 'not unusual in towns contiguous to chalky hills to see them exposed for sale'.[23]

The poet and son of a clergy-man, John Langhorne (1735 – 1779) wrote the 'The Bee-Flower' in 1771 which provides one of the earliest references in literature to this plant, and is believed to have been inspired by the bee orchids on the Folkestone Downs and Beechborough Hill:

See on that flow'rets velvet breast
How close the busy vagrant lies !
His thin wrought plume, his downy breast,
The ambrosial gold that swells his thighs !

Perhaps his fragrant load may bind
His limbs;- we'll set the captive free -
I sought the living bee to find,
And found the picture of a bee.

J. Langhorne, 'Bee-Flower' in *The Fables of Flora* (1771)

Arguably less convincing insect imitators are the early and late flowering varieties of **spider orchid** (*Ophrys sphegodes* and *Ophrys fuciflora*). With a distribution largely confined to southern England, the warm south-facing hills of the East Kent Downs support the principal colonies of both early and late spider orchid within the country. Numbers at the twenty-eight recorded sites for early spider orchid have been significantly boosted in recent years by the dramatic population explosion of a colony establishing on the chalky marl soils of the newly created Samphire Hoe, near Dover. The flower of this orchid varies widely in size and form, yet the unmistakable greenish flowers are beautifully crafted with a rich brown lip to give the appearance of a spider's body. The orchid stands generally smaller in statue than that of the bee and fly orchids.

Left: Fig. 82 Fly orchid.

Below: Fig. 83 Late spider orchid.

It was not until the early nineteenth century that the Reverend Gerald Smith discovered the later flowering variety of spider orchid (Fig. 83) on the warm sun-baked slopes of the Downs near Folkestone. Today it continues to thrive in small long-established scattered colonies along the stretch of the Downs between Wye and Folkestone.

The **monkey orchid** (*Orchis simia*) is another Kent speciality, and is confined to just three sites within the British Isles, two of which lie within the dry valley grasslands of the East Kent Downs. First recorded at Faversham in 1777, it was thought to be extinct from the county until it was discovered on a chalky bank at Ospringe in 1955. From here it was introduced to Park Gate Down Nature Reserve, near Elham, where it now boasts an impressive colony of over 200 individuals. The flower's sepals and petals form a loose sharply pointed helmet and are thought to resemble the curved arms and legs of a monkey.

Still widespread in the Downs of central and west Kent, though not so common in the east, is the **man orchid** (*Aceras anthropophorum*) (colour plate 30). This delightful orchid can be sought for on grassy downland slopes but often favours the rougher vegetation associated with abandoned chalk pits, scrub edges and roadside verges. The recent discovery of a colony on a roadside nature reserve at Lydden near Dover revealed around eighty previously unrecorded specimens. Its stem of yellow-green flowers, often rust-tinged at the edges, resemble the arms, legs and head of a little man. An old superstition claimed that if the flowers were picked and brought into the house, the picker would be visited by the hangman the following day.

The uppermost dark purplish unopened flower buds that crown the **burnt-tip orchid** (*Orchis ustulata*) (colour plate 32) are the distinctive hallmarks of this lover of close-grazed slopes of the Kentish Downs. Often likened to a miniature version of the lady orchid, it was first recorded in the county in 1732 by John Martyn (1699-1768), a professor of botany at Cambridge. Its preference for warm, south-facing banks, coupled with a lengthy life cycle from rootstock to flowering and a sensitivity to shading from taller vegetation, has meant that its distribution has always been highly localised. Writing at the turn of the twentieth century, the botanist A.D. Webster aptly described the charm of this orchid: 'On some of the green sloping Kentish hills this little orchid is very abundant and during summer quite enlivens the landscape with its quaintly conspicuous flowers'.[24] It is now restricted to a handful of sparsely scattered, long-established colonies.

More plentiful and widely distributed is the **pyramidal orchid** (*Anacamptis pyramidalis*) (colour plate 31). This enchanting orchid graces many chalk grasslands with its bright rosy spike of densely clustered flowers, a delight to find scattered among the summer carpet of flowers, 'standing out like strontium flames against the neutral-tinted grasses'.[25] It can vary in colour from deep pink to almost pure white.

Pyramidal often grows in the company of the sweet smelling slender spikes of the **fragrant orchid** (*Gymnadenia conopsea*). This aromatic orchid can often be found growing in profusion forming large drifts of lilac-coloured flowers on hillsides and banks. In Kent it was formerly known as the 'gadfly orchid' and also earned the local name of 'Longtails', on account of the long spur that protrudes from the orchid flower. Both pyramidal and fragrant orchids specialise in attracting butterflies and moths to pollinate their flowers.

Open grassy downland banks provide one of the favourite haunts of the **green-winged orchid** (*Orchis morio*) although on the impoverished soils of the Downs it tends to assume a more dwarfish structure than in its other favoured habitat of lowland meadows. It owes its name to the strongly marked green veins on its sepals that converge to form a hood-shaped canopy. In some districts it was formerly known as 'cuckoos', 'king's fingers' and 'foolstones'.

While many orchids favour the sunny banks of open chalk downland a number are able to tolerate the shadier conditions of woodland. Beech woodlands, in particular, sometimes support a rich orchid flora, often well-represented with members of the helleborine family (*Cephalanthera*). The curious **bird's-nest orchid** (*Neottia nidus-avis*) can often be found living on the deep leaf litter of the woodland floor. Being unable to photosynthesize, it gathers its nourishment from decaying leaves. Both the stem and the flowers of this plant are entirely honey-coloured. Within these woodlands can also be sought **greater butterfly orchid** (*Platanthera chlorantha*), **lesser butterfly orchid** (*Plathanthera bifolia*) and **common twaybalde** (*Listera ovata*). One of our more familiar orchids of woodland haunts is the **early-purple orchid** (*Orchis mascula*), its beautiful purple flowerhead standing proudly among the spring carpet of dogs mercury and bluebells. The conspicuous rosette of glossy leaves, blotched with dark spots often appear as early as January, long before the first sign of the stalk and spike of its strongly scented purple and pink flowers which emerge in the later spring months. In Kent the orchid has acquired a variety of local names in times past including 'skeatlegs', 'kitelegs' and 'red butchers'.

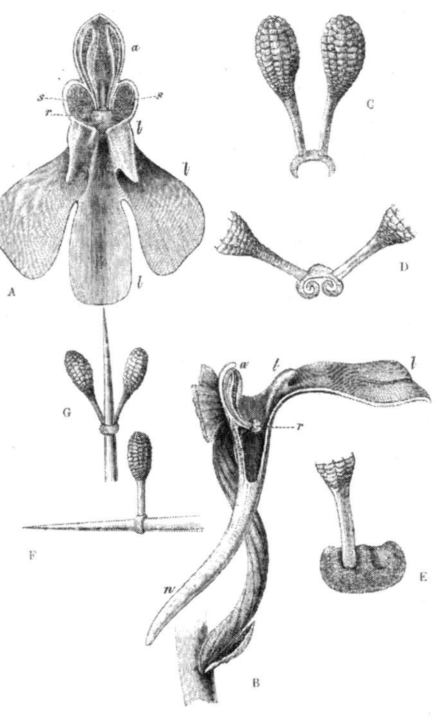

Fig. 84 'Orchis Pyramidalis' taken from a copy of a woodcut from Charles Darwin's *On the various contrivances by which British and foreign orchids are fertilised by insects* (1862). Reproduced with permission from The Complete Work of Charles Darwin Online.

Description of Fig. III.

a. anther.	*l.* labellum.
s. s. stigma.	*l'.* guiding plate on the labellum.
r. rostellum.	*n.* nectary.

A. Front view, with all sepals and petals removed, except the labellum.
B. Side view, with all sepals and petals removed, with the labellum longitudinally bisected, and with the near side of the upper part of the nectary cut away.
C. The two pollinia attached to the saddle-shaped viscid disc.
D. The disc after the first act of contraction, with no object seized.
E. The disc seen from above, and flattened by force, with one pollinium removed; showing the depression, by which the second act of contraction is effected.
F. The pollinium removed by the insertion of a needle into the nectary, after it has clasped the needle by the first act of contraction.
G. The same pollinium after the second act of contraction and depression.

THE ORCHID HUNTERS

The orchids of the Downs have always been a source of interest and fascination, occupying the attentions of botanists and herbalists over the centuries. For many, they have come to symbolise man's enduring and irresistible fascination with the rare and uncommon; an obsession that for the true 'botanophil' is played out year after year in the methodical quartering of hillsides, banks and woods, for that elusive specimen, that 'first discovery'. It is this thrill of discovery and sense of elation that Peter Marren captures so perfectly in his recollection of his childhood discovery of an early spider orchid on the cliffs above Dover, 'I roared with delight, waved my arms about and fell to my knees....a transcendent moment in which wild flowers, chalk cliffs and colours, sounds scents of nature seemed to imprint themselves in my bones'.[26]

Orchids became a particular topic of study for Charles Darwin (1809-1882). Darwin spent the last forty years of his life at Downe House, near Cudham and it was here that the flower-rich banks and woodlands provided the inspiration for his studies and experiments in biological science that became the building blocks for his 'Theory of Evolution'. Fascinated by the relationship between insect pollinators and wild orchids, Darwin devoted considerable attention to species such as the pyramidal, bee and butterfly orchids, culminating with his work *The Various Contrivances by which Orchids are Fertilised* (1862) (Fig. 84).

Downe Bank, close to the house, became a regular haunt for him and became a cherished spot for his family, which they affectionally called 'Orchis Bank'. The site is thought to have inspired his vision of a 'tangled bank' in the conclusion of *The Origin of Species* (1859), a passage which emphasises the intricate interrelations of different species. Today 'Orchis Bank' forms part of a nature reserve carefully managed by Kent Wildlife Trust and still supports many of the species first noted by Darwin. While Darwin drew on the orchid-rich localities around his home for much of his work, it is clear that many of his specimens were also sent to him from fellow botanists within the Downs. One of the many who corresponded with him was a Mr G.C. Oxenden of Broome Park who sent specimens of the lizard orchid for use in his studies.

While the heydays of nineteenth-century orchid hunting may have passed, the orchids of the Kent Downs continue to occupy a special place for many who are enticed year by year to their haunts to witness their breathtaking splendour.

– WOODLAND –

> I looked out of the window with a sense of complete incredulity ... For the last half-hour or more we had been driving through a network of narrow lanes between dense woodlands; as we went on, the lanes became narrower still ... The woods seemed never-ending – dusky, impenetrable thickets of oak and hazel, stretching as far as one could see; here and there a gap would occur, revealing a landscape of rolling hills and valleys, still densely wooded and stretching away limitlessly into the fading watery light of the spring sunset.
>
> Jocelyn Brooke, *The Dog at Clambercrown* (1955)

Woodland has always been an enduring feature of the Kent Downs landscape (colour plate 33) and today still accounts for some 14 per cent of the land use area, amounting to some 43,000 acres (18,000ha) of which 28,000 acres (12,000ha) is classed as 'ancient' (a status recognising its age as being at least 400 years old).[27]

The slightly acidic, clay-based soils of the plateau country have traditionally supported woodlands where tree species such as common (pedunculate) oak (*Quercus robur*), ash (*Fraxinus excelsior*), hornbeam (*Carpinus betulus*) and silver birch (*Betula pendula*) thrive. In many areas, sweet chestnut (*Castanea sativa*) is found in abundance, a legacy of the once thriving hop-pole industry in the Downs. The thinner chalky soils found on the steeper slopes of valleys allow a variety of other trees better adapted to the drier soil conditions to flourish. These include beech (*Fagus sylvatica*), whitebeam (*Sorbus aria*) and yew (*Taxus baccata*). Throughout these woodlands an understorey of smaller trees and shrubs such as hazel (*Corylus avellana*), field maple (*Acer campetsre*), spindle (*Euonymus europaeus*), holly (*Ilex aguifolium*) and honeysuckle (*Lonicera periclymenum*) (Fig. 85) jostle for space and light beneath the shady canopies. These woodland communities have evolved over thousands of years and their make-up reflects both adaptation to physical factors such as geology, soils, topography and climate as well as the influence of man in their management and stewardship.

Historically, woodland has always been valued for its timber and 'underwood' (the poles or stems of trees produced by periodic cutting) resource. From the everyday needs of domestic life to the exploitative demands of industry and commerce, the woodlands of the Downs embrace a rich and colourful history. For hundreds of years the tradition of coppicing (the practice of periodically cutting tree stems at ground level to encourage re-growth from the base or stool) has provided a constant supply of smaller-sized wood for a multitude of uses such as firewood, hurdles, gates and ladders.

Woodlands were also carefully managed to provide a continual harvest of timber from mature 'standard' trees for the needs of millwrights, cartwrights and wheelwrights as well as ship and house construction. The management of coppice and standard trees traditionally involved the apportionment of woodland into areas (known in Kent as 'cants'). These divided the woodland into manageable units available for harvesting. The boundaries of these cants were often marked by a prominent feature tree, which was often pollarded (cutting of the tree at 6-15ft (1.8-4.5m) above ground level), to provide a 'cantmark' or 'stub' (Fig. 86).

In medieval times the manors relied heavily on the sheep- and timber-based economy and the woods of the Downs provided an increasingly valued timber and underwood resource for house-building and woodfuel for an ever-growing population. Over time, however, it soon became apparent that the demand for corn-growing land became far more important and piecemeal clearance of woodland was undertaken to bring more land in to crop production to supply food for this increasing population.

Above: Fig. 85 Honeysuckle.

Right: Fig. 86 A Hornbeam 'stub' in Red Wood at Luddesdown.

Fig. 87 Spong Farm near Elmstead is a fine example of a jettisoned open-hall farmhouse and is believed to date to *c.* 1520. The place name is first recorded in 1334 as 'Sponge', an old Kentish dialect word referring to a long, narrow piece of land.

By the fifteenth century, woodlands experienced a renewed focus of activity with the use of standard trees for house-building timbers. The tradition of carpentry entered a 'golden age' as carpenters and craftsmen found a new outlet for their craft and skill in the emergence of timber-framed buildings and, in particular, the Wealden hall/house, the fashionable residence of the new class of wealthy yeomen and gentry.

The growth in ship-building that marked the early nineteenth century saw woodlands enter a new phase of exploitation and demand. Providing planks and beams for warships and naval vessels, the oak woodlands of the downland plateaus provided a valuable resource for the ship-building yards in the Medway and Thames estuaries. An illustration of the economic importance of these downland woods at this time is provided by John Boys who, writing at the end of the eighteenth century, noted:

> Chief of woodlands of Kent are dispersed between the great road from Rochester to Dover and the chalk-hills between Folkestone and Charing ... these woods furnish the county with firewood, tillers for husbandry uses and the dockyards with timber for ship-building.[28]

Just as the seventeenth- and eighteenth-century iron industry generated a huge woodland enterprise for the Wealden forests to the south, so the needs of the thriving nineteenth-century hop industry triggered unprecedented levels of demand from the woodlands of the Downs. Young trees of ten to fifteen years' growth were in great demand for hop-poles, several thousand being needed every three or four years for a small hop-garden (colour plate 11). As the demand for poles increased to support the ever-expanding acreage of 'gardens', growers were quick to recognise the value of the sweet chestnut tree in serving their needs. Fast growing and better able to produce straight stems when nourished on free-draining chalk soils, many woodlands witnessed a period of great change as large tracts were grubbed and re-planted with chestnut. In many areas new plantations appeared on formerly cultivated ground.

George Buckland, an agricultural writer of the mid-nineteenth century, recorded at this time, 'Woodland has of late years, in Canterbury and the Rochester district, become of great value, especially in the vicinity of the hop districts where an increasing demand for hop poles exists. Improvements have been made in recent years by grubbing up old unproductive stubs and replacing them with ash or chestnut'.[29]

Further demand came from the thriving lime-burning industry which needed a regular supply of fuel wood for the firing of kilns. As these industries declined through the twentieth century, chestnut-coppice found a new market supplying hardwood pulp for paper mills in the county. These industries have also now vanished and with the decline in demand for small-wood products such as paling and fencing, many woodlands have experienced a period of neglect. Whilst the revival of coppicing as a traditional form of woodland management is now being encouraged through financial grants, it is clear that seeking and finding new markets for woodland products is the key to ensuring that the rich resource of biodiversity, landscape and cultural heritage of the downland woods is secured for future generations.

WOODLAND FLORA

The colourful carpet of plants and flowers that furnish the woodland floors have evolved to take advantage of the seasonal changes in light and shade that is afforded beneath the woodland canopy. Many ground flora species have adapted to flower in the early spring before the over-shadowing trees are in full leaf, in order to take advantage of the sunlit woodland floor.

Among the earliest plants of the chalk woodlands to flower are stinking hellebore (*Helleborus foetidus*) (Fig. 81) and spurge-laurel (*Daphne laureola*), sometimes flowering as early as January or February. Stinking hellebore has an unpleasant smell to warn off animals from its poisonous foliage and in times past was also given the name 'setterwort'. According to the herbalist John Gerarde, this was believed to originate from the plant's use as a cure for the diseases of cattle. Country-lore tells that a piece of the root should be placed and left for several days within a slit cut into the loose skin below the throat of a cow, so curing disease and 'settering' the cattle. Today the plant is confined to just a few localities in the Downs.

One of the more curious plants of early spring is butcher's broom (*Ruscus aculeatus*) (Fig. 88), an evergreen shrub and member of the lily family. Its stiff 'leaves' are in fact flattened

Fig. 88 Butcher's broom.

leaf-like stems known as cladodes, in the centre of which appear small green flowers and, later, large scarlet berries. Its name is derived from its tough brush-like stems, which according to the apothecary John Parkinson (1567–1650) were used to 'make brooms to sweep the house' and by butchers 'to clense their stalles'.[30] Another local tradition tells of the plant being used to beat old meat and draw blood, so making the meat look fresher. An alternative name for it in times past, perhaps unsurprisingly, was 'knee holly'.

Wood anemone (*Anemone nemorosa*) (Fig. 89) heralds the emergence of some of the more widespread spring woodland flowers. Formerly known as 'windflower', a name that owes much to its readily-nodding flowerhead, it provides a spectacular carpet of white star-shaped blooms from March to May. Along woodland clearings and edges the flower is often found in the company of lesser celandine (*Ranunculus ficaria*), a plant whose golden-yellow petals are particularly sensitive to the appearance of the sun, opening fully on bright sunny days and closing with the onset of evening. The leaves are heart-shaped near the root and were once used by children in country places in Kent to rub their teeth to make them appear whiter.

By April the bluebell (*Endymion non-scriptus*) comes into flower, a conspicuous feature of many of the ancient woodlands of the Downs, transforming their floors into a spectacular sea of blue. Its appearance is often set against a carpet of the light green leaves of dog's mercury (*Mercurialis perennis*) (Fig. 90). Once locally known in some places as 'town weed' the green flowers and spear-shaped leaves of dog's mercury are believed to be poisonous.

Above: Fig. 89 Wood anemone.

Right: Fig. 90 Dog's mercury.

Ramsons, also known as wild garlic (*Allium ursinum*) (Fig. 8) is in flower at this time and is often found in dense carpets exuding its unmistakable aroma. By May, the leafy woodland canopy casts an ever-increasing shadow on the floor beneath and only those plants tolerant of the shadier conditions are able to flourish. Patches of the enchanting yellow archangel (*Galeobdolon luteum*) (colour plate 34), often intermingled with stands of fading bluebell and the rose-pink petals of red campion (*Silene dioica*) make for a colourful display. On the chalky soils less common flowers such as sanicle (*Sanicula europaea*) (colour plate 35), woodruff (*Galium odoratum*) and herb-paris (*Paris quadrifolia*) appear. The latter is a fascinating plant in that its petals, stamens, sepals and leaves all appear in fours, giving it a curiously symmetrical form.

As well as many bird species, woodlands also provide a refuge for many mammals. Dormice have a stronghold in many of the downland woods, particularly those where the understorey of hazel, honeysuckle, spindle and traveller's joy provides a dense network of pathways and an abundance of fruit and flowers from which this secretive nocturnal mammal can feed upon. The woodlands, shaves and copses are also a favourite haunt of badgers, foxes, stoats and weasels.

In former times it is evident that the downland woods were also home to pine martens, now largely extinct from England and Wales. In the early nineteenth century 'marten cats', as they were also locally known, were present in the Boxley woods and were not uncommon in the woods around Luddesdown, particularly Red Wood where, according to old accounts, they could occasionally be happened upon, lying on the top of pollarded beech stubs. These were probably some of the last known sightings of marten cats within the county before habitat loss and persecution by game-keepers eventually led to their extinction in the early to mid-1800s. The polecat is another member of this family of mammals (mustelids) which was once present within the woodlands of the Downs. Anecdotal evidence gleaned from gamekeepers of the early nineteenth century reveals that live polecats were still being caught in the woods of the Cobham area at the end of the 1700s.[31] This nocturnal mammal, slightly larger than a weasel, was also known as a 'fitch', which may account for the origin of some place names in the Downs such as the now lost hamlet of Filchborough near Sole Street.

EIGHT

The 'Back of Beyond' Forever?

The Future of the Downs

The sense of remoteness and isolation experienced within the hinterland of the Kent Downs remains a defining characteristic of this unique landscape. For hundreds of years the harsh living conditions imposed by this remoteness attracted little more than disparaging comments from the topographers, historians and commentators of the county. Edward Hasted's description of Stelling as an 'obscure' parish, Paddlesworth as 'lonely and unfrequented' and of Alkham as lying 'very much unknown' clearly portrays a region that has always remained very much on the margins of civilisation. W.H. Ireland's 1830 survey of the county portrays many parts of the Downs in a similar light, his account of the area of Bredgar 'rather an unfrequented place, lying obscure among the hills'.[1]

'Health and No Wealth'

Burdened by its 'hungry' and impoverished soils this association with remoteness has naturally gone hand in hand with the lack of wealth that has characterised downland life throughout the centuries. The waves of agricultural prosperity that swept over other parts of the county, by and large, bypassed the poverty-stricken inhabitants of the Downs. For most, life was a simple hand to mouth existence where even basic necessities such as water were often hard to come by. With little in the way of surface ponds and streams, most relied on wells for the supply of drinking water, many of which were sunk to depths of several hundred feet in the higher parts of the Downs. Water was often drawn by use of a horse which would walk round a capstan. Inevitably this dependency on well-water

Fig. 91 A disused well in a remote downland valley near Temple Ewell. Many of the domestic wells in the higher parts of the Downs were sunk to depths of over 400ft (120m) in order to reach the water table.

often led to times of great hardship, particularly when droughts occurred. In 1921 for example, a severe drought in east Kent led to the drying up of many downland wells for many months. In the small hamlet of Podlinge near Waltham, elderly inhabitants recall the lack of water being so serious 'that it was not until a few weeks before Christmas that the dewpond there began to hold enough water for the animals'.[2]

The trappings and comforts of modern society may well have now filtered through to every part of the Downs, yet it was not so long ago that many still depended on these wells for water. In areas such as Petham and Waltham they were being dug right up until the 1920s until mains water eventually arrived in 1930. Particularly affected were the isolated farms and houses on the higher parts of the Downs where water pressure was so low that even when piped water became widespread in the county, such places remained unconnected. Many of these farmsteads and settlements have only been afforded the luxury of mains water in relatively recent times. Elsewhere in the Downs, the inaccessibility of many villages meant that these districts have generally been amongst the last to enjoy the convenience of other mains services. Mains drainage in Petham did not arrive until as late as 1972.

In times past, those who chose to eke a living in these small village communities and scattered farmsteads would have had perhaps little contact with the county's busier towns and cities. The insular nature of these rural communities no doubt made for some interesting characters, as is illustrated by Ford Madox Hueffer's remarks on the curious inhabitants of Stelling Minnis at the turn of the twentieth century:

> The inhabitants of these uplands are on the one part incredibly taciturn, on the other as remarkably the opposite. One explains it by the theory that the first from dwelling so long in solitude, have lost their powers of speech; the second are thirsting for an opportunity of contact with the outer world. They make their way by 'les petits industries' … by turning fagots into bundles of firewood … they bring to market things of infinitesimally small value.[3]

Yet, while the burden of remoteness and poverty has always weighed heavy on the downland region, these high chalk hills have nevertheless been regarded, historically, as a 'healthy' place to live. The elevated situation of the Downs, with their fresh bracing airs, has always stood in marked contrast to the lower-lying wetter areas of the county which, whilst more agriculturally productive, were encumbered by the stagnant airs and ailments of marsh, mire and swamp. Hasted's dismissive remarks of the downland country are consequently often tempered by a reference to the 'healthy situation' of these districts. Describing the parish of Stowting, for example, he notes that the village 'is situated in a wild and forlorn country, for the most part on the great ridge of chalk … very comfortless and dreary country throughout which if the country cannot boast of wealth, yet it can be exceedingly healthy as all the hills and unfertile parts of this county in general are.' Similarly, of Elham, it appears that the longevity of its inhabitants was a notable feature: 'As an instance of the healthiness of this parish, there have been within these few years several inhabitants of it buried here, of the ages 95, 97 and 99 and one of 105; the age of 40 years being esteemed that of a young person in this parish'.[4] This long-established association of poverty on the one hand, and well-being on the other, has thus come to bestow upon the Downs a reputation for 'Health and no Wealth'.

Historically, whilst this inaccessibility and isolation has burdened those who have sought to live and subsist within the Downs, in many ways, it has also served to preserve its most cherished features, providing the tranquillity and hidden charm that has given inspiration to many and for which it is now treasured. In the words of H.E. Bates, 'it stands above and outside the mainstream of cultivation: strong and decorative, barren but rich, useless but remarkably lovely'.[5]

The nineteenth and twentieth centuries, in particular, have witnessed the widening appeal of this area. The new-found appreciation for the natural world and the romance of wilderness landscapes that marked the Victorian era, inspired many to explore the hidden beauty and charms of the Kent Downs. For the first time the isolation and remoteness of the downland hinterland, that had hitherto attracted little attention, was now extolled and celebrated in romantic prose and poetry. Fascinated and captivated by the breathtaking views of this 'forgotten country of a forgotten peace', some found parallels with the beauty of the wilder parts of England's upland areas. The travel writer A.G. Bradley was so enthralled by the downland valleys and hills around Dover that he likened the area to 'some rugged district in the west of England'.[6] Adam and Charles Black's nineteenth-century travel guides portrayed this seemingly incongruous scenery in a similar light, comparing the grand amphitheatre of hills rising from the Stour valley to that of scenes in the Yorkshire Dales.[7]

This appreciation for the natural beauty of the Kent Downs landscape has continued through to the present day, a recognition that culminated in the designation of the area as an Area of Outstanding Natural Beauty in 1968. Today this designation affords it a status on a par with that of National Parks in terms of landscape quality, scenic beauty and planning matters.

THE FUTURE

In an age where the trappings of modern day society and communications have found their way into much of our countryside, we are fortunate that many parts of the Kent Downs are still gifted with the unique sense of tranquillity and peace. The same unforgiving clay soils, dense woodlands and undulating country that thwarted generations of downland dwellers in times past, still exert a powerful influence in the landscape. Yet in an era of unprecedented pressure and change to the rural environment, the threat of losing this cherished quality is very real. Increasing pressures from transport infrastructure, housing and industry, in addition to the increased recreational use and changing agricultural practices have all threatened to undermine the special characteristics of the Kent Downs and continue to present difficult challenges. Thanks to positive conservation, mitigation and enhancement measures by a range of organisations, charities, individuals, landowners and farmers, these unique qualities and features remain largely intact.

The introduction of agri-environment schemes in the 1990s, in addition to the concerted effort of a host of conservation bodies such as Kent Wildlife Trust has helped to arrest the decline in wildlife habitats such as chalk grassland and has witnessed the restoration of many neglected and degraded habitats. Recent changes to the Common Agricultural Policy combined with a whole new suite of environmental options for farmers and landowners has begun to restore a more equitable balance between farming and wildlife. In the wider countryside the legacy of fifteen years of agri-environment schemes is now beginning to form large contiguous areas of environmentally sensitively managed farmland with sympathetically managed grasslands and arable habitats (Fig. 92), linked by networks of grassy field margins. On many farms wildlife is now beginning to reap the rewards of these efforts with hares, grey partridge, barn owls and lapwing returning for the first time in thirty or forty years. Farmland birds such as yellowhammer and linnet that have suffered long term declines elsewhere in the country have generally always fared well in the Kent Downs, where thickets and bushy hedgerows have remained an enduring part of the landscape. On the more open fields skylark, too, are still in respectable numbers although some will recall an age when such birds were far more abundant.

Less certain is an understanding of how the flora and fauna of the Downs will respond to the gradually increasing temperatures associated with global warming. Much research is currently underway to monitor and predict response to climate change for a wide range of species, although it is widely acknowledged that, because

Fig. 92 Field margin managed under an Environmental Stewardship Scheme to benefit annual wildflowers such as poppies.

climate is such a fundamental factor affecting wildlife, the impacts of change are likely to be extraordinarily complex, not least because different species will respond over different timescales. It is reasonable to assume that many species will change their distribution range with warmth-loving species expanding northwards. In addition some species may begin to change their habitat requirements. Already, research suggests that the silver-spotted skipper butterfly is beginning to show signs of expanding from south-facing chalk grasslands onto east-west and north-facing hillsides.[8]

Organic farming is also making resurgence and with it a revival of the traditional crop, grass leys and herbage crop rotations that were once commonplace in the Downs. At Luddesdown Organic Farm, near Rochester, herbage crops such as sainfoin, clovers, vetches and trefoils form an integral part of the organic crop rotation, valued as much for their palatability to livestock as to their value in improving soil condition and fertility. It was on and around these very same slopes and valley bottoms that the seventeenth-century agricultural commentator and writer Samuel Hartlib encountered the very same crops over 350 years ago: 'I have seen it (sainfoin) sowne in divers places in England: especially in Cobham Park in Kent … where it hath thriven extraordinarily well upon dry chalke bankes where nothing else would grow'.[9]

Sandwiched between the two motorways of the M2 and M20, and adjacent to the expanding urban areas of Ashford and the Thames Gateway, it is no surprise that the Kent Downs are under severe development pressure from the ever-expanding infrastructure of housing and transport. This, along with the cumulative damage suffered from gradual small-scale development and creeping 'suburbanisation', poses one of the most significant threats to the unique beauty of the Kent Downs. The Kent Downs Area of Outstanding Natural Beauty (AONB) organisation have done much to mitigate against this pressure in engaging with parishes and planners to produce AONB Landscape Design Guidance. This guidance provides advice to encourage sympathetic practice so that the impact of development on the landscape is kept to a minimum.

Accompanying this development pressure comes the increasing challenge posed by a growing, mobile and leisure-seeking population. The Kent Downs AONB organisation estimate that a minimum of around 22,360,000 day visits by the public are made to the Kent Downs each year.[10] Walking, cycling and horse riding have long provided an attraction for many and offer a sustainable means of accessing the hidden charms of the Downs as well as providing a useful input to the local economy. Of more concern is the increased car traffic and, in particular, the impact of such traffic on the quite rural roads of the Downs. Some local projects have started to help address this issue such as the West Kent Rural Transport Initiative which aims to bring about changes in driving behaviour.

Against this backdrop of development and population pressure lies the very real need to ensure that the villages of the Kent Downs retain their role as living and thriving rural communities. Rural poverty, social deprivation, and loss of village shops and community services have taken their toll on many villages in recent years. Significant progress has been made in some areas to help arrest the impact of these problems through finding new ways to bring in a much-needed boost to local economies. Sustainable tourism projects, grants for local businesses, diversification funds for farmers and initiatives such as farmer's markets have helped to improve the economic well-being of rural areas. At Wye, for example, the bustling fortnightly farmer's market attracts many from nearby towns and villages into the community, supporting both local stall-holders as well as other local shops and businesses. Rural development projects such as the Mid Kent Downs Leader Plus Initiative, which encompasses approximately a third of the AONB area, have also provided a much needed boost to local communities by providing grants and funds to help support local businesses and community projects.

The 'Back of Beyond' areas of the Kent Downs may have largely escaped the pressures of the last fifty years, yet it is perhaps to the words of the Victorian traveller, Charles Harper, that we should turn for the most humbling reminder of the inevitable march of progress. Remarking upon the impact of the railways at the turn of the last century on the remote character of the countryside, his description of the Elham valley, a stretch of country within which 'places … are ceasing to be remote and can no longer said to be Beyond, much less at the Back of it',[11] is perhaps an ever-constant reminder of the need to safeguard this endearing landscape for ours' and future generations.

Fig. 93 Winter sunset on the hinterland plateau country of the East Kent Downs.

GLOSSARY

Ancient woodland a term used in the United Kingdom to refer specifically to woodland dating back to at least 1600 in England and Wales, (or 1750 in Scotland). Before this, planting of new woodland was uncommon, so a wood present in 1600 was likely to have developed naturally.

Arable weeds wildflowers that have an annual life cycle and that are associated with cultivated land, often growing in competition with crops such as wheat and barley.

Bench a landform consisting of a long strip of land at constant height in an otherwise sloped area. It is typically caused by successive depositions and erosions by a river in a floodplain.

Browsing the grazing of coarser vegetation such as leaves and branches, typical of herbivores such as goats and deer.

Cant a division of land normally referring to a coppice compartment within a wood.

Coombe a short, deep, generally bowl-shaped valley or hollow on a hill, usually formed under periglacial conditions. Coombes are characteristic of chalk downland dry valley and escarpment country.

Coppicing a traditional method of woodland management in which young tree stems are cut down to a low level. In subsequent growth years, many new shoots will emerge and after a number of years the cycle begins again and the coppiced tree, or 'stool', is ready to be harvested again.

Denehole and chalkwell an underground chalk mine typified by a central shaft which opens at its base into chambers.

Dry valley a valley of chalk or limestone terrain that no longer has a surface flow of water. Dry valleys are believed to have formed when ground water levels were higher and when the frozen soil (permafrost) associated with periglacial conditions allowed surface water to flow.

Eoliths coarse chipped flints that were originally thought to have been crude stone tools made by early man. Most eoliths are now thought to have formed by natural processes.

Gavelkind an ancient Kentish custom of land inheritance whereby on the death of a landowner, the property was divided equally between all sons, or where there were no sons, between his daughters.

Holloway a sunken track, often with steep-sided banks and a canopy of over-arching trees giving the appearance of a 'tunnelled' lane.

Iron Age the stage in the development of early man when the use of iron implements as tools and weapons became prominent. In southern England, the Iron Age lasted from about the seventh century BC until the Roman conquest. This period is also called the era of 'Celtic Britain'.

Long barrow a prehistoric monument dating to the early Neolithic period. They are rectangular or trapezoidal earth mounds traditionally interpreted as collective tombs.

Lynchet a ridge in a field that has developed from the downslope movement of soil through the action of ploughing in former times.

Mesolithic the 'Middle Stone Age'. A period in human development between the Paleolithic and Neolithic periods referring in the United Kingdom to the period of around 8,500 BC to around 4,000 BC.

Minnis a Kentish word that historically referred to a 'common' or shared area of land for grazing animals. The word is believed to derive from the Anglo-Saxon word '(ge)maennes', meaning 'commonland used as pasture'.

Neolithic the 'New Stone Age'. The Neolithic era marks the period when humans took up agriculture as a way of life usually referring to the period of 4,000-2,000 BC in Britain.

Periglacial an adjective referring to places in the edges of glacial areas, normally those relating to past ice ages. 'Periglacial conditions' usually refer to the alternating freezing and thawing conditions of the soil surface in winter and summer months, often described as 'permafrost'.

Pollarding a woodland management method of encouraging the re-growth of several stems by cutting the trunk 2m or so above ground level. A tree that has been pollarded is known as a 'pollard'.

Roadside Nature Reserve a roadside verge that is recognised for its importance as a wildlife habitat. They support wildflower-rich plant communities and are sensitively managed to protect the plants and wildlife that live on them.

Scrub vegetation comprising low bushes, shrubs and saplings, often referred to in a grassland context. Scrub is a natural state of vegetation succession which if left unchecked will eventually develop into secondary woodland. Processes such as grazing and mechanical cutting help to prevent the development of scrub.

Secondary woodland the term given to woodlands that have regrown on abandoned or neglected ground that had previously been used for agriculture, grazing or development of towns, villages, industry and roads. Some secondary woodlands have been planted, but the majority have come about through the natural processes of colonisation and succession.

Shave a Kent dialect word that was usually used to describe a long narrow strip of woodland. The term 'shaw' was also used in this context but also applied to small areas of woodland and copses.

Sole old English word meaning 'miry pool'. In Kent it is believed that word specifically refers to ponds created for livestock. Many place names in their Downs containing the element 'sole' are thought to owe their origins to this farm practice.

SSSI (Site of Special Scientific Interest) a designation afforded to areas of land noted to be of exceptional wildlife or geological interest.

Tumuli a mound of earth and stones raised over a grave or graves. Tumuli are also known as barrows or burial mounds.

Wood pasture a historic habitat in which livestock graze beneath trees that are grown for timber. Such sites contain old trees sometimes mixed with younger trees and grassy glades. The associated species (lichens, fungi, invertebrates and bats) largely contribute to the ecological significance of this habitat, which is also often of historical and cultural value.

Notes

Articles and books are given by author and date. Refer to bibliography for full reference.

INTRODUCTION: THE CHALK COUNTRY

1 Hasted, E., 1797-1801.
2 Black, A. & C., 1874.
3 Bates, H.E, 1949.
4 Hasted, E., 1797-1801.
5 Harper, C.G., 1904.
6 Harper, C.G., 1904.
7 Brooke, J., *The Dog at Clambercrown*, 1955.
8 In Church, R., 1964, pp.241-3.
9 Ray, J., 1696.
10 Maidstone Journal, 2 February 1802 in Goodsall, R.H., 1974.
11 Everitt, A., 1986.
12 Church, R., 1948.
13 Hewlett, H.G., 1880, pp. 51-60.

CHAPTER ONE: CHALK AND FLINTS
THE GEOLOGY OF THE DOWNS

1 Graham Brade-Birks, S., in Buckingham, C., (ed.) 1969.
2 *Geology of the County around Canterbury and Folkestone* (HMSO 1966)
3 Ireland, W.H., 1828.
4 Phillips, W., 1822.
5 Rowe, A., 1900.

6 Sir Charles Lyell in Wooldridge, S.W., and Goldring, F., 1953, p.39.
7 Hasted, E., vol. 8, 1797-1801.
8 Observations in Dowker, G., 1886.
9 Buckingham, C., 1905, pp.11-14.
10 Brooke, J., *The Dog at Clambercrown*, 1955.
11 In Snell, F.C. & Co, 1938.
12 Seymour, C., 1776.
13 Buckingham, C., 1905.
14 Hasted, E., 1797-1801, vol. 8.
15 In Harper, C.G., 1922.
16 Maynard, D.C., in Goodsall, R.H., 1970, pp.1-19
17 Brooke. J., *The Dog at Clambercrown*, 1955.

CHAPTER TWO: LONG BARROWS AND LYNCHETS
EARLY MAN IN THE DOWNS

1 Wymer, J.J., 1982.
2 Ashbee, P., 1999.
3 Ashbee, P., 2004.
4 Fieldling, C.H., 1893.
5 Bannister, Dr N., pers.comm.
6 Wright, T., *Archaeological Journal* (1844), in Jessup, R.F., 1945.
7 Boden, D.C., 2006.
8 Margary, I.D., 1951, pp. 20-23.
9 Belloc, H., 1904.

CHAPTER THREE: STEADS AND SOLES
SETTLEMENT AND THE EVOLUTION OF THE LANDSCAPE

1 Everitt, A., 1986.
2 Everitt, A., 1986.
3 Everitt, A., 1986.
4 In Countryside Commission, 1984.
5 Baker, A.B.H., 1965, pp.152-174.
6 Thirsk, J., 1964, pp. 3-25.
7 Everitt, A., 1986.
8 Langridge, A.M., 1984, pp. 217-244.
9 In Buckingham, C., 1967.
10 Marshall, W., 1798.
11 Hueffer, F.M., 1900.
12 Marshall, W., 1798.
13 Hueffer, F.M., 1900.
14 Church, R., 1948.
15 In Goodsall, R.H., 1966, pp. 41- 45.

16 From Parish, W.D., Shaw, W.F., 1887.
17 Everitt, A., 1986.
18 Boys, J., 1798.
19 Harper, C.G., 1904.
20 N.Onslow in McDine (ed.), 1997.
21 Rackham, O., 1996.
22 Lambarde, W., 1570, repr. 1970.
23 Hasted, E., vol. 8, 1797-1801
24 Roberts, G., 1999.
25 In Goodsall, R.H., 1966, pp. 105-112.
26 Ellis, G., pers.comm.
27 For more information on field names see Field, J., *A History of English Field Names*, 1993.

CHAPTER FOUR: FIELDS, FOLDS AND FURROWS
FARMING IN THE DOWNS

1 In Lancefield, R., 1994.
2 Banister, J., 1799.
3 In Chalklin, C.W., 1965.
4 Garrad, G.H., 1954.
5 Marshall, W., 1798.
6 Marshall, W., 1798.
7 Banister, J., 1799.
8 Boys, J., 1795.
9 Marshall, W., 1798.
10 Sabin, C.W., in Page, W., 1908, vol. 1, pp. 457-470.
11 Marshall, W., 1798.
12 *The Times*, 17 September 1830
13 'Mass Meeting of Farmers at Granada Cinema, Maidstone', *The Kent Farmers Journal*, April 1940, p.132.
14 Everitt, A., 1986.
15 Marshall, W. 1798.
16 Illingworth, F., 'The Dew Pond' in Dilnot, F. (ed.), 1938.
17 In Lancefield, R., 1994.
18 Banister, J., 1799.
19 Hewitt, E.M., in Page, W., 1908, vol. 3, pp. 457-470.
20 and 21 Lodge, F.C. (ed.), 'The Account Book of a Kentish Estate' (London, 1927), p.53; Hartlib, S., His Legacies, London, 1651, p.43, in Chalklin, C.W., 1965, p.85.
22 Hewlett, H.G., 1880.
23 Thomas, E., 1928.
24 In Pearman, H., 1966.
25 Banister, J., 1799.
26 Kent Underground Research Group, 1991.
27 Johnson, T., 1629.
28 Cox, T., 1730.

CHAPTER FIVE: THE SPIRIT OF THE DOWNS
THE DOWNS IN ART AND LITERATURE

1 Laker, M., 1989.
2 Brooke, J., *The Dog at Clambercrown*, 1955.
3 Brooke, J., *The Dog at Clambercrown*, 1955.
4 Church, R., 1948.
5 Vaughan, W., Barker, E., Harrison, C., 2005.
6 Church, R., 1948.
7 Bates, H.E., 1949.
8 Brooke, J., *A Mine of Serpents*, 1949.
9 In Brooke, J., in *December Spring*, 1946.

CHAPTER SIX: CUSTOMS AND LEGENDS

1 In Hammond, J. et. al., 2004.
2 Igglesden, C., 1900, 2nd ed. vol.1.
3 Igglesden, C., 1900, 2nd ed. vol.1.
4 'Ladies Match of Running', *Kentish Gazette*, 1768.
5 Buckingham, C., 1967.
6 Winzer, P., 1995.
7 Harper, C.G., 1922.
8 In Ritchie, C., 1993.
9 In Ritchie, C., 1993.
10 Lambarde, W., 1570, repr. 1970.
11 Bovington, J., pers.comm.

CHAPTER SEVEN: SKYLARKS, SKIPPERS AND SCABIOUS
THE FLORA AND FAUNA OF THE DOWNS

1 Johnson, T., 1629.
2 Herbert Goss, F.E.S. et. al. in Page, W., 1908.
3 Harrison, J. M., 1953.
4 Holt, P., pers. comm.
5 Vera, F.W.M., 2000.
6 See, for example, Gibson, C.W.D., Brown, V.K., 1991.
7 Bannister N.R., Newsome, A., 1998.
8 Harrington, S., 2004.
9 Baker, A.R.H., 1966.
10 Defoe, D., A Tour through England and Wales, vol.1 (London, 1928 1ST edn. 1724) p.101 in Chalklin, C.W., 1965, p.106.
11 Coles Finch, W., 1933.
12 Turner, W., 1551-1568.
13 Johnson, T., 1629.

14 Brightman, F.H, in *Kent Field Club Bulletin,* January 1976, p.15 -16.
15 Igglesden, C., 1920, vol.14.
16 Brooke, J., *The Wild Orchids of Britain*, 1950.
17 Brooke, J., in *December Spring*, 1946.
18 Brooke, J., *A Mine of Serpents*, 1949.
19 Church, R., 1948.
20 Brooke, J., *The Military Orchid*, 1948.
21 Brooke, J., *The Wild Orchids of Britain*, 1950.
22 In Fielding, Revd C.H., 1896, pp. 50-54.
23 Pratt, A., 1891 (1st edn. 1873), vol.3.
24 Webster, A.D., 1898.
25 Brooke, J., *The Wild Orchids of Britain*, 1950.
26 Marren, P., 1999.
27 Kent Downs AONB Management Plan, 2004.
28 Boys, J., 1795.
29 Buckland, G., 1846.
30 Parkinson, J., 1640.
31 Notes from *Rochester Naturalist* (1884) in Howell, George O. (ed), *The Kentish Notebook*, vol.1, pp.138-139, 1894.

CHAPTER EIGHT: THE 'BACK OF BEYOND' FOREVER ?
THE FUTURE OF THE DOWNS

1 Ireland, W.H., 1828.
2 In Lancefield, R., 1994.
3 Hueffer, F.M., 1900.
4 Hasted, E., 1797-1801 (repr.1972)
5 Bates, H.E., 1949.
6 Bradley, A.G., 1921.
7 Black, A. & C., 1874.
8 Davies, Z.G., et. al., 2006.
9 Hartlib, S., 1655.
10 Kent Downs AONB Management Plan, 2004.
11 Harper, C.G., 1904.

BIBLIOGRAPHY

Ashbee, P., 'The Medway Megaliths in a European Context', *Archaeologia Cantiana*, vol. 119 (1999), pp.269-284

Ashbee, P., 'The Medway Megaliths in Perspective', *Archaeologia Cantiana*, vol. 111 (1993), pp. 57-111

Ashbee, P., 'Great Tottington's Sarsen Stones', *Archaeologia Cantiana*, vol. 124 (2004), pp.209 -226

Austin, M.D., 'With the Valley Below' in Graham Brade-Berks, S. (ed), *Kent County Journal*, vol. 4, no. 1, p.112

Baker, A.R.H., 'Field Systems in the Vale of Holmesdale', *Agricultural History Review*, vol. 14 (1966)

Baker, A.R.H., 'Some Fields and Farms in Medieval Kent', *Archaeologia Cantiana*, vol. 80 (1965), pp.152-174

Banister, J., *A Synopsis of Husbandry* (1799)

Bannister Dr N.R., 'Historic Chalk Grassland in Kent ', unpub. report prepared for The Rural Planning Group, Kent County Council (1998).

Barham, Revd, R.H., 'The Leech of Folkestone', *The Ingoldsby Legends* (Frederick Warne & Co., 1891)

Bates, H.E., *The Country Heart* (Michael Joseph: London, 1949)

Belloc, H., *The Old Road* (Archibald Constable: London, 1904)

Black, A. and C., *Black's Guide to Kent* (A. & C. Black: Edinburgh, 1874)

Blackwood, J.W., Tubbs, C.R., 'A Quantitative Survey of Chalk Grassland in England', *Biological Conservation*, vol. 3 (1970), No.1

Boden, D.C., 'A Late Iron Age/Early Roman site at Bredgar, near Sittingbourne'. *Archaeologia Cantiana*, vol. 126 (2006), pp. 345-74

Boys, J., *A General View of the Agriculture of the County of Kent* (1798)

Bradley, A.G., *England's Outpost: The Country of the Cinque Ports* (Robert Scott: London, 1921)

Braithwaite, M.E., Ellis, B., Preston, C.D., 'Change in the British Flora 1987-2004', *British Wildlife*, vol. 17. No.6 (August, 2006)

Brandon, P., *The North Downs* (Phillimore & Co. Ltd: Chichester, 2005)

Brooke, J., *A Mine of Serpents* (The Bodley Head: London, 1949)

Brooke, J., *Clouds* (unpub. c.1923)

Brooke, J., *December Spring* (The Bodley Head: London, 1946)

Brooke, J., *The Dog at Clambercrown* (The Bodley Head: London, 1955)

Brooke, J., *The Flower in Season* (The Bodley Head: London, 1952)

Brooke, J., *The Military Orchid* (The Bodley Head: London, 1948)

Brooke, J., *The Wild Orchids of Britain* (The Bodley Head: London, 1950)

Buckingham, C., *Lydden: A Parish History* (Thomas Becket Books: Lydden, 1967)

Buckingham, C., 'The Intermittent Streams of East Kent' , *East Kent Scientific and Natural History Society, Report and Transactions for the Year ending* 30 *September* 1905, Series II, vol. 5, (*Kentish Gazette* and Canterbury Press Office: Canterbury, 1905)

Buckland, G., 'On the Farming of Kent', *Journal of the Royal Agricultural Society of England*, No. 6 (1846), pp.259-60

Burton, J.F., Davis, J., *Downland Wildlife: A Naturalist's Year in the North and South Downs* (George Philip Ltd: London, 1992)

Camden, W., *Camden's Britannia, newly translated into English; with large additions and improvements* (Edmund Gibson: London, 1637)

Chalklin, C.W., *Seventeenth-Century Kent* (Longmans Green Co. Ltd: London, 1965)

Champion, T., 'The Bronze Age in Kent' in Leach, P.E. (ed.), *Archaeology in Kent to* AD 1500, (The Council for British Archaeology: London, 1982)

Church, R., *Kent* (Hale: London, 1948)

Church, R., *The Little Kingdom* (Hutchison & Co. Ltd: London, 1964)

Coles Finch, W., *Windmills and Watermills, a Historical Survey of their Rise as Portrayed by those of Kent* (C.W. Daniel, 1933)

Conrad, J., *Chance* (Methuen & Co.: London, 1914)

Conrad, J., *Romance* (George Bell and Sons: London, 1904)

Conrad, J., *The Inheritors* (McClure, Phillips & Co.: New York, 1901)

Cornish M.W., 'The Origin and Structure of the Grassland Types of the Central North Downs', *The Journal of Ecology*, vol. 42 (1954), pp.359-374

Countryside Commission, *The Kent Downs Area of Outstanding Natural Beauty: The Report of a study undertaken for the Countryside Commission by Land Use Consultants*, CCP150 (Countryside Commission: Cheltenham, 1984)

Cox, T., *A Compleat History of Kent* (London, 1730)

Curle, R., *The Last Twelve Years of Joseph Conrad* (Sampson Low: London, 1928)

Cutbush, R., *In Black and White* (Hooker Bros.: Westerham, 1950)

Darwin, C., *The Origin of Species* (John Murray: London, 1859)

Darwin, C., *The Various Contrivances by which Orchids are Fertilised* (2nd ed. John Murray: London, 1885)

Davies, Z.G., Wilson, R.J., Coles, S., Thomas, C.D., 'Changing habitats of a thermally constrained species, the silver spotted skipper butterfly, in response to climate warming', *Journal of Animal Ecology*, vol.75 (2006), pp.247-256

Davis, A., 'Song of Stone Street' in Redshaw, C.J. (ed.), *The Invicta Magazine*, vol. 1, February, 1908 (Phillips and Mowle: London, 1908)

Defoe, D., *A Tour through England and Wales*, vol.1 (London: 1928, 1st edn. 1724)

Doel, F. and G., *Folklore of Kent* (Tempus Publishing Ltd: Stroud, 2003)

Dillwyn, L.W., 'Catalog of the More Rare Plants Found in the Environs of Dover' in *Transactions of the Linnean Society*, vol. 4 (1802), pp.177-184

Dowker, G., 'The Water Supply of East Kent, in Connection with Natural Springs and Deep Wells' in *Transactions of the East Kent Natural History Society*, no. 2 (Gibbs and Sons: Canterbury, 1886)

Ede, D., Stead, P., *The Lime Burning Industry in Kent*, Results of a Sites and Monuments Record Enhancement Project 1997-8, unpub. report, Kent SMR Industrial Archaeological Series (Heritage Conservation Group, Kent County Council Planning Department, 1998)

Evans, S., *The Kent Chalk Downs Cultural Heritage Study*, unpub. report (March 2004)

Everitt, A., *Continuity and Colonization : the Evolution of Kentish Settlement* (Leicester University Press: Avon, 1986)

Felix (pseud), *Rambles around Folkestone with other special articles and notes* (Glanfield: Folkestone, c.1913)

Field, J., *A History of English Field names* (Longman: London, 1993)

Fielding, Revd C.H., 'Kentish Orchids' in *The Kent Magazine*, vol.1 (1896), pp. 50-54

Fielding, Revd C.H., *Memories of Malling and its Valley* (Henry C.H. Oliver: West Malling, 1893)

Freeman, R.A., *The Penrose Mystery* (Hodder and Stoughton Ltd: London, 1936)

Garrad, G.H., *A Survey of the Agriculture of Kent*, County Agricultural Surveys no.1 (Royal Agricultural Society of England, 1954)

Gerard, J., *Herball* (1597)

Gibson, C.W.D., Brown, V.K., 'The Nature and Rate of Development of Calcareous Grassland in Southern Britain', *Biological Conservation*, vol. 58 (1991), pp. 297-316

Gilmour, J.S.L. (ed), *Thomas Johnson, Journeys in Kent and Hampstead* (The Hunt Botanical Library: Pennsylvania, 1972)

Goodsall, R.H., 'Hunting, Shooting and Fishing' in *A Fourth Kentish Patchwork* (Stedehill Publications: Stede Hill, 1974)

Goodsall, R.H., 'Icehouses' in *A Kentish Patchwork* (Constable & Co.: London, 1966)

Goodsall, R.H., 'Mounting Blocks' in *A Kentish Patchwork* (Constable & Co.: London, 1966)

Goodsall, R.H., 'Strange Streams' in *A Third Kentish Patchwork* (Stedehill Publications: Stede Hill, 1970)

Graham Brade-Birks, S., 'Kentish Flint Work Pt.2' in Buckingham, C., (ed.) *Cantium*, vol.1, no.3 (1969)

Hammond, J. et al., *Before It's All Forgotten, Recollections of Stowting, with interviews, early documents and photography* (The Bubblegate Company: Stowting, 2004)

Hanbury, F.J., Marshall, E.S., *Flora of Kent* (F.J Hanbury: London, 1899)

Harper, C.G., *The Dover Road: Annals of an Ancient Turnpike* (Cecil Palmer: London, 1922)

Harper, C.G., *The Ingoldsby Country* (A. & C. Black: London, 1904)

Harrington, S., *A Study in Woodlands Archaeology: Cudham, North Downs* (British Archaeological Reports, British Series 368: Oxford, 2004)

Harrison, J.M., *The Birds of Kent* (H.F. & G. Witherby Ltd: London, 1953)

Hartlib, S., *His Legacie….* (London, 1651)

Hasted, E., *The History and Topographical Survey of the County of Kent* (1797-1801, repr.1972)

Hennell, T., *Change in the Farm* (Cambridge University Press: Cambridge, 1936 2nd edition, 1st published 1934)

Herbert Goss, F.E.S. et. al., 'Lepidoptera' in Page, W., *The Victoria History of the County of Kent*, vol. 1, pp.78-183 (Constable: London, 1908)

Hewitt, E.M., 'Industries' in Page, W., *The Victoria History of the County of Kent*, vol. 3, pp. 457-470 (Constable: London, 1908)

Hewlett, H.G., 'Studies in Kentish Chalk', *Cornhill Magazine*, vol. 42 (1880), pp. 51-60

Hewson, D., *Native Rights* (HarperCollins: London, 2000)

Howell, George O. (ed), *The Kentish Notebook: A Collection of Notes, Queries and Replies on Subjects connected with the County of Kent*, vol.1 (Henry Gray: London, 1894)

Hueffer, F.M., *The Cinque Ports. A Historical and Descriptive Record* (William Blackwood and Sons: Edinburgh and London, 1900)

Igglesden, Sir Charles, *A Saunter through Kent with Pen and Pencil*, (Kentish Express: Ashford, 1900 – 1946, 34 volumes)

Igglesden, Sir Charles, *Crimson Glow* (The Kentish Express: Ashford, 1925)

Iggelsden, Sir Charles, *Downs Valley Farm* (The Kentish Express: Ashford, c.1940)

Illingworth, F., 'The Dew Pond' in Dilnot, F. (ed), *Kent County Journal*, vol. 4 (1938), no. 10

Ireland, W.H., *A New and Complete History of the County of Kent: From the earliest records to the present time, including every modern improvement* (Geo.Virtue: London, 1828)

Jacob, J., *Wildflowers, Grasses and Ferns of East Kent: A Catalogue* (Dover Express and East Kent News, 1936)

Jessup, R.F., 'Holborough: A retrospect', *Archaeologia Cantiana*, vol. 58 (1945),pp. 68-75

Johnson, T., *Iter plantarum investigationis...in agrum Cantianum* (1629)

Kent Downs Area of Outstanding Natural Beauty. *A Management Plan for* 2004-2009 (2004)

Kent Field Club Bulletin (Kent Field Club, January, 1976)

Kent Underground Research Group, *Kent and East Sussex Underground* (Meresborough Books: Rainham, 1991)

Kerney, M.P. et. al., 'The late-glacial and post-glacial history of the chalk escarpment near Brook, Kent', *Philosophical Transactions of the Royal Society of London*, Series B, 248 (1964) , pp. 135-204

Keymer, R.J., Leach, S.J. (1990) 'Calcareous grassland – a limited resource in Britain' in Hillier, S.H., Watson, D.W.H., Wells, D.A. (eds.), *Calcareous Grasslands – Ecology and Management* (Bluntisham Books: Huntingdon, 1990)

Laker, M., *Kentish Memories* (Lanes Publishing: Chatham, 1989)

Lambarde, W., *A Perambulation of Kent* (1570 repr. Adams and Dart: 1970)

Lancefield, R., *Recollections of Rural Life Around Godmersham, Crundale and Waltham* (Lancefield: Hants, 1994)

Langhorne, J., *The Fables of Flora* (Printed by T. Rickaby, for E. and S. Harding: London, 1794)

Langridge, A.M., 'The Population of Chartham from 1086 to 1600', *Archaeologia Cantiana*, vol. 101 (1984), pp. 217-244

Le Gear, R.F. (ed), 'Deneholes Part 2', *Chelsea Speleological Society Records* (1979)

Lousley, J.E., *Wildflowers of Chalk and Limestone* (Collins: London, 1950)

McDine (ed.) *Bossingham and Stelling Minnis Memories* (Windmill Publishing Consultants: Stelling Minnis, 1997)

MacLeod, M., *Thomas Hennell: Countryman, Artist and Writer* (Cambridge University Press: 1989)

Margary, I.D., 'The North Downs Main Trackways', *Archaeologia Cantiana*, vol.64 (1951), pp. 20-23

Marren, P., *Britain's Rare Flowers* (Academic Press in association with Plantlife and English Nature: London, 1999)

Marshall, W., 'The Eastern Division of the Chalk Hills' in *The Rural Economy of the Southern Counties* (1798)

Massingham, H.J, *English Downland* (Batsford: London, 1936)

Mathew, W.M., 'Marling in British Agriculture: A Case of Partial Identity', *Agricultural History Review*, vol. 41 (1993), Pt.2, pp 97-100

Maylam, P., *The Hooden Horse. An East Kent Custom* (Canterbury: Cross & Jackman, 1909)

Paley, F.A., *The Wildflowers of Dover* (T. Rigden, c.1850)

Parfitt, K., 'A Round Barrow near Haynes Farm, Eythorne', *Archaeologia Cantiana*, vol.124 (2004), pp. 397-415

Parish, W.D., Shaw, W.F., *A Dictionary of the Kentish Dialect* (Trubner: London, 1887)

Parkinson, J., *Theatrum Botanicum : The Theater of Plants, or, An Herbal of a Large Extent* (1640)

Pearman, H., 'Deneholes and Kindred Phenomena', *Records of the Chelsea Speleological Society* (January 1966)

Phillips, W., 'Remarks on the Chalk Cliffs in the Neighbourhood of Dover....', *Transactions of the Geological Society*, Series 1, vol. 5 (1822), pp.16-46

Pratt, A., *The Flowering Plants, Grasses, Sedges and Ferns of Great Britain* (Frederick Warne & Co.: London, 1873)

Rackham, O., *Trees and Woodland in the British Landscape* (Phoenix: London, 1996, 2nd edn.)

Ray, J. *Synopsis Methodica Stirpium Britannicarum* (1696, 2nd edn.)

Ritchie, C., 'The Dreamer of Ewell', *Bygone Kent*, vol. 14, no.2 (1993), pp. 75-79

Roberts, G., *Woodlands of Kent* (Geerings: Ashford, 1999)

Rose F., 'Floristic Connections between S E England and N E France' in Valentine, D.H., *Taxonomy, Phytogeology and Evolution* (Academic Press: London, 1972)

Rose, F., 'Orchis purpurea, Huds.', The Journal of Ecology, vol. 36 (1948), pp. 366-377

Rowe A., 'Zones of the White Chalk of the English Coast, pt.1, Kent and Sussex' , *Proceedings of the Geological Association*, vol. 16 (1900), pp289-368

Sabin, C.W., 'Agriculture' in Page, W., *The Victoria History of the County of Kent* vol 1., pp. 457-470 (Constable: London, 1908)

Seymour, C., *A New Topographical, Historical, and Commercial Survey of the Cities, Towns and Villages of the County of Kent* (1776)

Smart, J.G.O., *Geology of the Country around Canterbury and Folkestone* (H.M.S.O., 1966)

Smith, C.J., *Ecology of the English Chalk* (Academic Press: London, 1980)

Smith, G.E., *A Catalogue of Rare or Remarkable Phaenogamous Plants, collected in South Kent, with descriptive notices and observations* (Longman, Rees, Orme, Brown and Green, 1829)

Smith, J.E. (ed.), *English Botany* (1790 – 1814)

Snell , F.C. & Co., *The Intermittent (or Nailbourne) Streams of East Kent* (Hunt: Canterbury, 1938)

Strode, W., 'On Westwell Downes' (c.1630s)

The Amicci, 'The Fly Orchis' in Howell, George O. (ed) *The Kentish Notebook*, vol. 2, p.188 (Henry Gray: London, 1920) from 'Selections from the contributions of the Amicci' (Maidstone, Printed for the Amicci, 1836)

The Amicci, 'To Kit's Coty House' in Howell, George O. (ed), *The Kentish Notebook*: A Collection of Notes, Queries and Replies on Subjects connected with the County of Kent, vol.2, p.153 (Henry Gray: London, 1894)

Thirsk, J., 'The common fields', *Past and Present*, vol.29 (1964), pp. 3-25

Thomas, E., *The Last Sheaf* (Jonathan Cape: London, 1928)

Turner, W., Herball, *The Names of Herbes* (1551-1568)

Ullyet, H., *Rambles of a Naturalist around Folkestone*, (J. English, 1880)

Vaughan, W., Barker, E., Harrison, C., *Samuel Palmer*, 1801 – 1855*: Vision and Landscape* (British Museum Press: 2005)

Vera, F.W.M., *Grazing Ecology and Forest History* (CABI: Wallingford, 2000)

Walton, G.C., *List of Flowering Plants and Ferns found in the Neighbourhood of Folkestone* (Folkestone Natural History Society, 1894)

Walton, I., *The Compleat Angler* (Penguin: Middlesex, 1985, 1st published 1653)

Watt, F., *Canterbury Pilgrims and Their Ways* (Methuen & Co., 1917)

Webster A.D., *British Orchids* (J. S.Virtue & Co. : London, 1898, 2nd edn.)

White, J., and King, G., *Jim White's Diary. A Countryman's Year on the North Downs of Kent* (Blue Cat Press: London, 1985)

White, Revd G., *The Natural History and Antiquities of Selborne* (1788 edn.)

Whittaker, W., 'On Subaerial Denudation, and on Cliffs and Escarpments of the Chalk and the Lower Tertiary beds', *Geological Magazine*, vol. 4, October 1867 and November 1867

Winzer, P.,' Witchcraft Counter-Spells in Charing', *Archaeologia Cantiana*, vol.115 (1995), pp.23-28

Wooldridge, S.W., and Goldring, F., *The Weald* (Collins: London, 1953)

Wymer, J.J., 'The Paleolithic Period in Kent' in Leach, Peter, E. (ed.), *Archaeology in Kent to AD 1500* (The Council for British Archaeology: London, 1982)

INDEX

The Kent Downs AONB

The Kent Downs Area of Outstanding Natural Beauty (AONB) was designated in July 1968. It covers an area of 878 sq.km (339 sq.m) stretching from the Surrey/ Greater London border to the Strait of Dover. AONBs are equivalent to that of National Parks in terms of their landscape quality, scenic beauty and planning status. For more information on the Kent Downs AONB and the work of the Kent Downs AONB Unit contact Kent Downs AONB Unit, West Barn, Penstock Hall, East Brabourne, Ashford, Kent TN25 5LL or visit www.kentdowns.org.uk